BACK FROM THE DEAD

12/10/2016

for: Prof. Richard Vogler

with all good wishes.

from: He Jiahong

in Brighton, UK

BACK FROM THE DEAD

Wrongful Convictions and Criminal Justice in China

He Jiahong

University of Hawai'i Press
Honolulu

21 20 19 18 17 16   6 5 4 3 2 1

Library of Congress Cataloging-in-Publication Data

Names: He, Jiahong, author.
Title: Back from the dead : wrongful convictions and criminal justice
    in China / He Jiahong.
Description: Honolulu : University of Hawai'i Press, 2016. | Includes bibliographical
    references and index.
Identifiers: LCCN 2015037688 | ISBN 9780824856618 (cloth : alk. paper)
Subjects: LCSH: Judicial error—China. | Criminal justice, Administration
    of—China.
Classification: LCC KNQ4753 .H4 2016 | DDC 345.51/0122—dc23 LC record
    available at http://lccn.loc.gov/2015037688

To my wife, Ren Xinping
And to my daughter, He Ran

Contents

Contents

Contents

FOREWORD

In the past two decades, leaders and scholars around the world have come to the realization that criminal justice systems everywhere—despite their differences—must recognize and struggle with the reality of the wrongful conviction of the innocent. While each system may operate slightly differently, each one also depends on human beings in the investigation and decision-making processes. And whenever human beings are involved in any system, there will be human error.

What we now call "the Innocence Movement" has arisen out of this context. This movement, led by legal scholars and lawyers, has freed the innocent from imprisonment and has proposed reforms necessary for the prevention of wrongful convictions. Countries in every continent have embraced this project and are now reexamining their criminal justice systems to make them more accurate.

All justice systems rely on (1) eyewitness identification of the perpetrator; (2) confession of the suspect; (3) forensic science; (4) testimony of co-defendants, who may have an incentive to lie; and (5) the good faith and honesty of investigating officers and prosecutors. In all of these areas, the Innocence Movement has demonstrated that the "old ways" of doing things are no longer acceptable, and that reform is necessary to make the outcomes as fair and accurate as possible.

China has seen many high-profile wrongful convictions come to light in recent years, as outlined in the pages of this book; however, the country has begun to implement reform to help rectify and henceforth avoid such miscarriages of justice. Scholars such as Professor He Jiahong have also convened a number of important conferences in China to bring attention to this problem and to focus on reform. The Chinese judiciary has responded not by shying away but by attempting to conquer this issue head-on—for example, by revising the Criminal Procedure Law by incorporating an exclusionary rule for improper confessions as well as a requirement that interrogations be videotaped in many instances. While every country has a long way to go to fully reform its legal system, correct bad habits, and change its collective mind-set, China is headed in the right direction.

Professor He Jiahong's *Back from the Dead: Wrongful Convictions and Criminal Justice in China* is an excellent new resource detailing several examples of wrongful convictions, as well as the country's efforts thus far to right the wrongs, identify the causes, and put measures in place to prevent and avoid wrongfully convicting the innocent or not guilty. Professor He counterbalances his empirical research with historical detail, which helps convey the message in an easy-to-read narrative that also provides for a more rounded understanding of the problems faced by reformers. This book is an important source not only for those interested in studying China's effort in this regard but also for anyone who campaigns for justice and the protection of human rights.

Back from the Dead is more than a book about legal reform and wrongful convictions in China. It provides an engaging overview of the Chinese court structure, the police investigation process, and how both prosecutors and defense attorneys work within the system. Thus, the book is an excellent starting point for any reader wishing to gain general knowledge about the criminal justice system in China.

Mark Godsey
Daniel P. and Judith L. Carmichael Professor of Law
University of Cincinnati College of Law
Director, Rosenthal Institute for Justice/Ohio Innocence Project

PREFACE

I was born in a "black family" sixty-two years ago in Beijing. I had not under-stood the meaning of this until I became a teenager.

My grandfather, a school principal in the northeast of China in the 1920s, joined the Chinese Kuomintang (KMT) army after the Japanese invasion in 1931. He rose to the rank of general in the 1940s and left the army before the founding of the People's Republic of China (PRC). My father joined the KMT army after studying economics at Fu Jen Catholic University in Beijing and served as a civilian major later. My mother was the youngest child born into what is called a "landlord family" of Manchu nationality. Though my father was of Han nationality, both families belonged to the upper class, so they married despite the difference. My sister and brother were born during the period of the civil war, when my mother followed my father's career. When the Communist Party of China (CPC) defeated the KMT in 1949, my parents became prisoners of war, forced to walk while carry-ing their two young children thousands of kilometers back to their home

They were freed in Wuhan and made their way to Beijing, where my father was able to find a job in the Forest Administration. My childhood was peace-ful. I was a good pupil and often selected as class monitor; however, my father had a cerebral hemorrhage and passed away in 1963, when I was ten years old. It was probably lucky for him; otherwise, he might have suffered again later.

The Cultural Revolution broke out when I graduated from primary school three years later. I was happy at first because classes were suspended, which meant I could play football almost every day. Some of my friends then formed the Red Guards, and they were all proud to wear the red armband associ-ated with the group. I wanted to be revolutionary, too, and asked to join them; however, my classmates turned down my application because I was from a "black family."

During that time, class origin was considered to be very important, with family backgrounds divided into basically two categories: red families and black families. The former meant revolutionary, or good, including the revolutionary army man's family, the revolution cadre's family, the worker's family, and the peasant's family. The latter meant counterrevolutionary, or bad, including the counterrevolutionary army man's family, the counter-revolutionary officer's family, the capitalist's family, and the landlord's family. The KMT was counterrevolutionary, so my family was black. I felt ashamed of my family, especially my grandfather, who at this time was forced to sweep the streets even though he was in his late seventies. The only way I could become a revolutionary would be to draw a demarcation with him. So I did.

When I nominally graduated from junior high school in 1969, I voluntarily went to a farm in Heilongjiang Province, the very northeastern part of China. The revolution required intellectual youths to be reeducated by the peasants, or so the leaders told us. The work was hard, and life was tough. We dug dunghills in temperatures that dropped to thirty-plus degrees below zero in the winter, and labored in the field for about fifteen hours a day in the summer. We had enough food, though it was simple, and ate meat once every week or two. Even so, I felt good because I believed in Communism and believed we had to suffer first to realize the great dream, not only for us Chinese but for the whole of humanity. I worked harder than other intellectual youths because of my black-family background and was praised by the farm's leaders. They selected me to learn the skill of driving a tractor. I was proud of my achievements, and happy. I dreamed of becoming a member of the Communist Party and then a political leader. I kept this to myself.

My feelings changed rapidly two years later, when Lin Biao, Mao's designated successor and a former war hero, had to flee the country and died in a plane crash in September 1971. A former general, he had been one of the role models for us revolutionary youths. I was shocked that he had been denounced as an evil traitor, and this made me have second thoughts about my beliefs. I had the obscure idea that we had been fooled by politicians, or at least some of them, and I felt lost.

I loved literature when I was a boy, and while I was on the farm I wrote some poems. I published the first of these in a local newspaper, the *Heihe Daily*, on January 1, 1971. By the time a few universities had reopened in 1973, I had begun to dream of becoming a student; however, enrollment procedures were political, and my black-family background remained an obstacle.

I was frustrated by this, yet decided to write a novel to prove my ability. I started the ambitious project in late 1975 and dedicated almost all my spare time to writing for the subsequent two years. I finished the second draft in late 1977. The novel, *When Red Clouds Spread over the Sky,* was the story of intellectual youths in a farm in the great wild north. My dream was that the novel would be published with my name on the cover. However, another turn of life was approaching.

1976 was a special year for China. Premier Zhou Enlai passed away in the winter and Chairman Mao Zedong passed away in the autumn. The Gang of Four was smashed by our new leaders, and the Cultural Revolution was finally over. With the changing of the state policy, millions of intellectual youths in the countryside were permitted to return to their home cities. In November 1977, after working on the farm in Heilongjiang Province for eight years, I returned to Beijing.

The joy of family reunion did not last long because I had to look for work. China then had a planned economy, with jobs in the cities assigned by the government. Salaries were similar across a range of professions: my mother was an accountant in a government agency, my sister a middle school teacher, and my brother a factory worker. Each of them made 40–50 yuan a month. Since there were a limited number of jobs for us returning youths, many of us had to wait for months to be employed. I was lucky to be assigned to work in a construction company at the end of the year.

I became a plumber and started to learn new skills. We worked every day, with only one day off every two weeks. I made some 40 RMB a month. In my spare time, I pursued my literary ambitions and found some teachers and editors to read and critique my novel. I was told it was not good enough to be published and that I should read more classics and write some short stories first. I was frustrated by their criticism, and it was not easy to find good literary works to read in China at that time, but I decided to take their advice and began to write short stories. I submitted these to a few journals, and despite many rejections I did not give up.

There was a clinic attached to the construction company where I worked, and one of the doctors was a young woman with a lovely nickname of Little Doctor Ren. She was the most beautiful girl in the company and had a very good job. To be a medical doctor was one of the best jobs in society then, not because of the salary but because of the power. At that time, China had a public health service for all state workers, and almost all factories and construction companies were state-owned enterprises. Although the doctors in the clinic could provide only limited treatment, they still had the power to hand out free medicine. Furthermore, they had the power to grant sick leave, which was highly coveted. Therefore, it was easy for the doctors to establish good relationships with many people, and relationships are important in Chinese society.

The doctors in the clinic provided mobile medical service to workers at various construction sites. When Little Doctor Ren went on rounds, some of the young men would pretend to be ill just to have an opportunity to talk to her. I never did that.

In the summer of 1978, I was selected to work as a temporary cadre at the company's labor union, which was like a welfare office. My role was basically to write reports about the workers, organize spare-time activities, distribute movie tickets, and visit the ill or retired workers. Later, I edited a company newspaper, which an assistant and I mimeographed and distributed.

The labor union was in the same office building as Little Doctor Ren's. We liked each other and began to chat privately. I told her about my writings and my dream. She said I was different from the other construction workers. At that time, young people were very conservative about love and sex. When we began dating, we would meet in parks after work, but the only thing I could do was hold her hands and feel the electricity passing through my arms to my heart. We fell in love but made sure to keep our courtship a secret.

Doctor Ren Xinping was born into a traditional Chinese family. Her grandfather was a Chinese traditional medicine doctor, as were her parents. She had an elder sister and two younger brothers. Her parents noticed that she had changed after she and I began seeing each other, so they "interrogated" her. She resisted for a while but finally confessed. She insisted that I was a smart and nice young man, but her parents said no! They weren't concerned by my family's political origins but by the fact that I was from a family with no power, no money, and no good relations. More important, they said, was that I was a returned intellectual youth, nothing more than a plumber without any future. I was not a good match for their lovely daughter, who, despite their rejection of me, would not surrender. After unsuccessfully trying to separate us, her parents issued a precondition for meeting me: I would have to pass the university national entrance examination, which had been restored after the Cultural Revolution without any political preconditions in place for applicants.

With the reestablishment of the examination, many of those intelligent young people who had accumulated over the past ten years tried to squeeze into the narrow gates of the universities. The examination was extremely competitive. Little Doctor Ren did not push me to take the exam. She said she would be with me wherever I would go and whatever I would do. I was moved by this and decided to take up the challenge. In the summer of 1979, after several months' intense preparation, I took the exam. Fortunately, I passed, but my score was not high, which meant I could choose from only a narrow range of subjects. To be frank, I randomly chose law as my major.

After receiving the news that I had passed, Little Doctor Ren—officially my girlfriend—and I went to a restaurant to celebrate and then walked in Tiananmen Square until late at night.

When I enrolled as a law student at People's University of China (RUC), my girlfriend's parents granted me a "visa" to see her and to meet them at their house on National Day 1979. I learned that they had waited anxiously on the great day of my examination and on the day I would be told whether I had passed or failed. When their daughter did not come home at the regular time after work, they were so worried they could not eat, and their dinner became cold on the table. We did not have telephones at home in those days, and they were afraid their daughter had run away with me, or even committed suicide. When she came home at last and told them the great news, they were extraordinarily relieved and happy. I married their daughter two years later, and they are very nice parents-in-law.

When I became a law student, I gave up my dream of becoming a writer, not only because of the intensity of study required but also due to my growing interest in law. The more I learned, the more I realized how important the subject was, especially for China. After receiving my bachelor's degree, I took and passed the examination for graduate study. There were only a small number of graduate students in China then, and both my wife's family and my family were very proud of me. After gaining my master's degree in law, I started my teaching career at RUC in 1986.

After having been closed to the outside world for dozens of years, China opened its door in the 1980s. In the 1960s and 1970s we were often told by the government that we Chinese people were living in heaven while the working-class people in the capitalist countries were living in hell. Photos of homeless people in New York City on Christmas Eve were published in our newspapers. We believed. However, when the door was opened, we were shocked to see other photos of a prosperous and thriving country, of the tall buildings and expressways in New York. Someone said, "Wow! If that's the hell, I would prefer to live there!" Going to study in the United States became a dream for many young people in China.

Since the mid-1980s, the Committee for Legal Education Exchange between the United States and the PRC, sponsored by the Ford Foundation, provided scholarships for Chinese jurists to visit and study in the United States. I was selected as a candidate and passed the examination in late 1988. However, after I received permission from both sides to go, the program was suspended because of the June 4 event at Tiananmen Square. I had to wait an anxious several months' until the Chinese government gave me the go-ahead. Finally, on January 10, 1990, my feet touched the land of America.

I was a visiting scholar at Northwestern University, where Professor Victor Rosenblum, an expert of constitutional and administrative law, hosted my visit. He and his wife were very generous, warmhearted people, who provided me with a free room in their house in Evanston, Illinois, and treated me as a member of their family. I was more than lucky.

Apart from reading in the library and attending lectures, I visited the county court, the prosecuting attorney's office, and the police department, which allowed me to go out with them as they patrolled Chicago. I was probably the first Chinese citizen to sit in an American police car and patrol the streets.

My first ride was on June 1, 1990, when Michael Blackburn, a sergeant of Cook County Police Department, arrived to pick me up. I had not met him before, but we had talked on the phone. He was tall and strong, with a sense of humor in his eyes. Michael drove us onto the highway and to the western suburbs, which he said were the so-called black ghettos. He warned me not to come to this area by myself. I recalled the disruption caused by the Black Panthers that happened in that district in 1969.

It was an interesting day. We pursued a drug dealer on the highway, stopped a young black man who had beaten up his girlfriend in the street, and handled a traffic accident at a busy intersection. When I returned to the Rosenblums, I felt content, with just a little sorrow in my heart, because I would be going back to China soon. If I had witnessed a cross fire, it would have been a greater story for me, as long as I would still have had the chance to go back home. However, two years later, I had another opportunity to patrol the streets of Chicago, and my courage would be tested.

When I returned to Northwestern in the summer of 1992, it was as a candidate for doctor of juridical science. I lived with the Rosenblum family again, and after settling in, I rang Michael Blackburn, who was then chief officer of a patrol team for Maine Township in the western Chicago suburbs.

Michael was happy to hear that I was back and agreed to give me another ride-along.

He picked me up at about 4 p.m. on September 16. When I got into the police car, Michael asked me to sign a statement declaring that I was there voluntarily and would not hold him responsible for any accident if it should happen. He smiled and said, "This is a real job. You've got to sign."

I looked at him for a substantial moment, then signed.

He asked me if I remembered the song he had taught me. He was a good singer and a part-time teacher at the Old Town School of Folk Music in Chicago. Of course I remembered: "Come on, baby. Don't you want to go back to the same old place, sweet home Chicago . . ."

We arrived at Maine Township and began patrolling. When it became dark, we went into a nightclub crowded with young people. We were standing in a shadow near the door. Michael said he wanted to see if there were minors drinking in the club. About ten minutes later, the police information center rang Michael to alert him to an emergency. We hurried back to the car. While driving at high speed, Michael kept ringing up and talking to his officers. They spoke very fast, so I could not fully understand.

We soon pulled up next to a two-story apartment building. Four or five police cars were already there. Michael sent two officers to the back of the building and led other officers, and me, to the front door. He told me to follow him closely. We walked into the building and came to a door on the first floor. An officer knocked on the door peacefully. Several minutes later, a young white woman opened the door. Her hair was unkempt, her dress was untidy, and there were fresh bruises on her face.

She asked, "What's the matter, Officer?"

"Somebody called the police," he replied, "and said there'd been terrible screaming coming from your apartment. Anything wrong?"

"No. Nothing wrong."

The woman tried to close the door but failed, because a hand was holding it open from behind. We then saw a young white man coming out. He was very big, about six feet tall and 250 pounds. He seemed rather drunk and asked, "Who's calling?"

Suddenly, his eyes fixed on me, and he rushed at me. Scared, I drew back. I was not prepared for this. Michael and another officer reacted quickly and stopped the man, who tried in vain to reach me. He shouted at me, "You fucking Japs!"

Michael said to him, "Hey! He's a friend of mine. He's not a Jap—he's Chinese!" and then pushed him back into the room.

The woman said quickly, "Nothing's wrong, Officer. Please go!"

"Are you sure?" he asked.

"Yes, please go!" The door was closed at last.

We went back downstairs, sat in the car for a while, then left. The streets were quiet, the skyline beautiful. Michael and I began singing together: "One and one is two, six and two is eight. Come on, baby, don't ya make me late. Come on, baby. Don't you want to go back to that same old place, sweet home Chicago?"

Two months later my wife and our daughter, who was born in 1983, came to Chicago. We lived happily with the Rosenblums, and I was able to devote myself to study. In September 1993, after just over a year, I finished my dissertation, "Criminal Prosecution in the PRC and the USA: A Comparative Study," and was awarded the degree of doctor of juridical science (SJD). An article about me was published in the summer issue of the *Northwestern Reporter* in 1994: "Whether or not He set a record for the fastest completion of an SJD, most of the faculty members who worked with him would agree he set an admirable academic standard. Jon R. Waltz, Edna B. and Ednyfed H. Williams Memorial Professor of Law and He's dissertation adviser, describes He's work as 'the best SJD dissertation I have ever seen.'"

After being awarded the degree, my wife, our daughter, and I went on a driving tour. We traveled to Lansing, Michigan; to Buffalo, New York; to New York City; to Atlantic City, New Jersey; to Washington D.C.; to Columbus, Ohio, and then back to sweet home Chicago. The trip became the basic story in my second novel, *Crime of Sex,* which is being translated into English and will be published by Penguin in the summer of 2014.

The year I received my degree—1993—was a special time in my life, because I was at a crossroads. I had to decide which would be my sweet home: Chicago or Beijing?

After some discussion and much contemplation, we decided to return to Beijing in late 1993. I continued teaching at RUC, my wife resumed her work at the medical clinic, and our daughter returned to her class in the primary school. I revised my dissertation and found a publisher, China Procuratorial Press. It would be the first law treatise written in English by a Chinese jurist to be published in China. I felt happy and relaxed. The old dream came back to me: writing a novel!

So, in late 1994 I decided to write a series of crime novels, similar to the stories of Sherlock Holmes. Like many other young people, I was a fan of Sir Arthur Conan Doyle. Furthermore, my major was criminal evidence and criminal investigation. I did not want the main character in my novels to be a policeman, because there were already those types of novels published in China and I wanted my novels to be different. Instead, I planned to write about a private detective.

I was one of the pioneers in the field of study on private detectives in China. In 1990 I published a book, *Private Detectives and Private Security,* to introduce those practices I had seen in the United States. In 1992, the first private detective agency was founded in Shanghai, and then others followed. However, I came to learn, with some research, that the Ministry of Public Security had issued an internal order prohibiting the establishment of private detective agencies in September 1993. The Shanghai agency was closed, along with the others. It became illegal to be a private detective in China, and I could not create such a character in my novels. But then another profession came to my mind: lawyer.

When studying in Chicago, I was influenced not only by the American legal system but also by the lawyer culture. The role of defense lawyers in both the real world and the literary world was impressive. I believed that lawyers should play more important and more active roles in promoting the rule of law in China. I knew that some American lawyers' novels were best sellers in the United States, as well as the international market. I did not have time to read novels when I was in the States, but I took some books back to China, including the novels of Scott Turow: *Presumed Innocent* and *The Burden of Proof.* Scott was an assistant U.S. attorney and then a defense attorney in Chicago. I liked the professional-sounding titles and the stories themselves. And, to be frank, presumption of innocence and proof beyond a reasonable doubt were new terms, even for some law professors in China before the 1990s.

I decided to write a lawyer's novel, but I had difficulty framing the story. The legal system in China is very different from the one known in the United States. For example, the criminal procedure in China has the inquisitorial tradition, while the one in the States has an adversarial tradition. Chinese criminal lawyers are not proactively involved in the investigation of cases. After all, the Chinese lawyering system has a relatively brief history.

After the founding of the PRC in 1949, what I call the "lawyers' system" was established slowly. There were about three thousand lawyers in China in 1957, and then the system was abolished. In 1978, when the Cultural Revolution was over, the lawyers' system began to be reconstructed. On August 26, 1980, the Standing Committee of the Fifth National People's

Congress of China enacted the Provisional Regulations on Lawyers of the PRC. By the mid-1990s, there were some thirty thousand lawyers in China.

One major difficulty for my plotting was the law of criminal defense. According to provisions in the Criminal Procedure Law (CPL) of 1979, the defendant in a criminal case should be informed of the right to a lawyer no less than seven days before the trial.[1] How to plot my story when the lawyer would have only seven days to prepare for an inquisitorial trial? Fortunately, I found inspiration from a real case. In October 1994, a group of police officers came to Beijing from Heilongjiang Province to visit our university's Forensic Science Center. They told us about a murder case that had occurred in Heilongjiang in 1989.[2] The case gave me a good idea for framing the story for Hong Jun, a private lawyer in Beijing. The story was published as my first novel, *Crime of Blood,* translated into English as *Hanging Devils.* Then I continued to write more novels about the lawyer, Hong, and have them published in Chinese. They are *Crime of Sex, Crime of X, Non-guilty Corrupt Officials,* and *Non-guilty Murder.* All five novels have been translated and published in French, and some are published in Italian and Spanish. The title of my second novel in English is *Black Holes.*

I have been teaching and researching in the field of evidence law and criminal justice in China for some thirty years. In the past ten years, the issue of wrongful convictions has been one of my main areas of legal research. This book is one of the fruits of my research.

Through highlighting and telling the story of some real cases of wrongful conviction, this book introduces the present situation in the Chinese criminal justice system and makes deep analysis of its problems and loopholes. Enlivened with a literary style, it is a treatise of critical legal study composed of three main parts, plus an introduction and a postscript.

In part 1, through telling the case story of Teng Xingshan, I analyze the causes for wrongful convictions in five chapters. These are (1) the setting of inappropriately tight deadlines for solving criminal cases, (2) the "from confession to evidence" model of criminal investigation, (3) the misinterpretation of scientific evidence, (4) the continued use of torture to extract confessions, and (5) the one-sided and prejudicial collection of evidence.

In part 2, through telling the case story of She Xianglin, I analyze the causes for wrongful convictions in five chapters. These are (1) the bowing to public opinion in contradiction to legal principles; (2) the unlawfully extended custody with tunnel vision; (3) the merely nominal checks among the police, the Procuratorate, and the Court; (4) the nominalization of courtroom trials; and (5) the reduction of punishment in a case of doubt.

In part 3, after telling the case of Zhao Zuohai, I report the new developments of the criminal justice system in China. Chapter 11 is on the exclusionary rules against illegally obtained evidence; chapter 12 is on the reform of the criminal procedure system, from investigation centeredness to trial centeredness; chapter 13 is on the reform of the people's juror system; chapter 14 is on the reform of the criminal retrial system; and chapter 15 is on changing the mind-sets for criminal justice.

This book may not be considered to be a standard academic book. Since I am not only a jurist but also a novelist, it is my style to write an academic book with the flavor of a novel. Many people complain that law books are boring and difficult to read; I would like to make my books interesting and easy to read. My dream is to write an academic legal thriller. Anyway, be aware that this author is different, and this book is different.

In recent years, I have been invited to give lectures on the issues of wrongful convictions and evidence rules or criminal justice to judges, prosecutors, lawyers, and police officers in many parts of China and around the world, in places such as Cincinnati University and New York University in the United States, the Max Planck Institute for Foreign and International Criminal Law in Germany, the Australian National University and La Trobe University in Australia, Nagoya University in Japan, and the University of Bergen in Norway.

I would like to acknowledge my very many debts to those who have assisted me in the research and preparation for this book, my family, my colleagues, and my students. I am indebted to Jonathan Benney and Jesse Field, who helped with my writing in English. Jonathan helped translate the original parts of the Teng Xingshan and She Xianglin cases into English, while Jesse helped translate the original parts of the ten misleading roads in the criminal justice system and the standards of proof in redressing a wrongful conviction. I am also greatly indebted to Kelly Falconer, a former editor of *Asia Literary Review* and the founder of Asia Literary Agency, for having provided invaluable assistance throughout the preparation of this book.

He Jiahong
Beijing, China
July 2015

Principal Cases of Wrongful Conviction in China

Teng Xingshan, in a murder case in Hunan in 1987, sentenced to death and executed in 1989, and declared innocent in 2005.

Shi Dongyu, in a murder case in Heilongjiang in 1989, sentenced to death with two-year suspension in 1992 and exonerated in 1995.

She Xianglin, in a murder case in Hubei in 1994, sentenced to fifteen years' imprisonment in 1998 and exonerated in 2005.

Tong Limin, in a rape and murder in Chongqing in 1994, sentenced to death with two-year suspension in 1999 and exonerated in 2002.

Sun Wangang, in a rape and murder case in Yunnan in 1994, sentenced to death with two-year suspension in 1997 and exonerated in 2002.

Nie Shubin, in a rape and murder case in Hebei in 1994, sentenced to death and executed in 1995, and . . . ?

Zhang Jinbo, in a rape case in Heilongjiang in 1995, sentenced to ten years' imprisonment in 1998 and exonerated in 2006.

Hugejiletu, in a rape and murder case in Inner Mongolia in 1996, sentenced to death and executed in 1996, and declared innocent in 2014.

Li Yongcai, in a murder case in Liaoning in 1998, sentenced to death with two-year suspension in 1999 and exonerated in 2001.

Du Peiwu, in a double murder case in Yunnan in 1998, sentenced to death with two-year suspension in 1999 and exonerated in 2000.

Yu Yingsheng, in a murder case in Anhui in 1998, sentenced to life in prison in 2000 and exonerated in 2013.

Zhao Xinjian, in a rape and murder case in Anhui in 1998, sentenced to death with two-year suspension in 2004 and exonerated in 2006.

Zhao Zuohai, in a murder case in Henan in 1999, sentenced to death with two-year suspension in 2003 and exonerated in 2010.

Li Huailiang, in a rape and murder case in Henan in 2001, sentenced to death with two-year suspension in 2006 and exonerated in 2013.

Li Jiuming, in a break-in and assault case in Hebei in 2002, sentenced to death with two-year suspension in 2003 and exonerated in 2004.

Zhang Hui and Zhang Gaoping, in a rape and murder case in Zhejiang in 2003, the former sentenced to death with two-year suspension and the latter fifteen years' imprisonment in 2004, and exonerated in 2013.

Nian Bin, in a poison and murder case in Fujian in 2006, sentenced to death four times and exonerated in 2014.

Introduction

Empirical Studies on Wrongful Convictions

1. The First Case of Wrongful Conviction

Late at night on April 5, 1989, on the Youyi Forest Farm of Yichun City in Heilongjiang Province, a forest-fire ranger, Guan Chuansheng, was stabbed to death with a knife. During the crime scene investigation, it was discovered that the back center of the victim's overcoat had been cut, and that a corresponding cut in the body had corner angles. Investigators concluded that the cut to the coat had been made by a bayonet and the other cuts by a single-edged cutting tool. The victim died around 12 p.m., after leaving the farm office an hour earlier, at which time the electricity of the farm had gone out.

That same night, the oldest son of a neighboring family, Shi Dongyu, who had been demobilized from the army nine days previously, was out, his whereabouts unaccounted for. Investigators listed him as a suspect, and when Dongyu returned home the next morning, he was taken in for questioning. Dongyu said that on the previous afternoon, a friend of his had shot a deer and had invited him for a drink. He returned after 8 p.m. by way of his fiancée's house to discuss the preparations for their marriage. He then went home to get some money, and then to the boiler plant after 10 p.m. to drink water, smoke, and chat. He went to the railway station after 11 p.m. and took the 2 a.m. train down the mountain to the town. On the morning he was taken in, he had been to the county government offices for his demobilization papers.

Investigators found a witness to corroborate Dongyu's statement. According to the owners of the boiler plant, Dongyu had left the plant after the electricity went off. Site investigation clarified that the plant was located on the roadside between the office and Dongyu's house, and was not far from the site of the murder. Therefore, investigators believed that Dongyu and the victim had walked along the same road at the same time. Additionally, investigators proved by experiment that it would take only twenty minutes to walk from the farm to the railway station. In a word, investigators believed Dongyu had time to commit the murder.

On the night of April 6, investigators searched Dongyu's home and found a bloodied military coat and a single-edge fruit knife with a black plastic handle. The front collar of the coat was lacerated, and three lost buttons were found in one of the pockets. The coat was stained with both O and A blood types. The victim's blood was type A. The knife was not bloodied, but the blade matched some of the cuts in the corpse.

At the beginning of his subsequent interrogation, Dongyu insisted that he hadn't killed the victim and explained that the blood on the coat was from his father and his brother when he had fought with his brother on the afternoon of April 4. But after having been questioned for more than thirty hours, Dongyu admitted to the crime.

Almost ten days later, the People's Procuratorate of Yichun City approved the arrest of Dongyu and filed for the prosecution for murder. In court, Dongyu denied his confession and insisted on his innocence to no avail: he was convicted of murder and sentenced to death with immediate execution. Dongyu appealed. On May 13, after reviewing the case, the High People's Court of Heilongjiang Province ruled that some of the facts were unclear and that, overall, there was a lack of evidence. They sent the case for retrial and listed several issues needing further investigation, such as the incomplete match of the killing tool and the cuts in the body, the existence of two types of blood on the coat, and the reason for the buttons being in the pocket.

On September 19, the Intermediate People's Court of Yichun City reopened the session to discuss the murder prosecution of Dongyu. Although the prosecutor was not able to provide more evidence, the court held that presented pieces of evidence—including the testimony of Dongyu's availability to commit the crime, the murder tool, the expertise testimony, and the crime scene search record—satisfied the two basic standards of proof required by Chinese procedural law: the facts of the case were basically clear, and the evidence was basically reliable and sufficient. On December 2, the court again convicted Dongyu and sentenced him to death with two years' probation. On January 7, 1992, the Intermediate Court transferred the case to the High Court for review. On February 26, the High Court confirmed the judgment. On August 31, Dongyu was sent to Beian Prison. However, this was not the end of the story.

In April 1994, a burglar, Ma Yunjie, was arrested in the public security bureau of Yichun City and revealed the following in his written statements: "I want to survive by giving evidence. The murder on 5 April 1989 was not committed by Shi Dongyu. The true criminal was Liang Baoyou!"

He told the police what he knew. In the early morning of April 6, 1989, he had been doing morning exercises near the railway tracks when he saw Baoyou running down the mountain with a bloodstained overcoat. He stopped him and asked what had happened. Baoyou said that nothing had happened and that the blood was from a pig he had slaughtered. Two days later, Baoyou invited him for a drink and told him that the night when the farm's electricity went out, he was waiting at the gate of the farm office to pin back Xia Baoxi's ears. At about 11 p.m., someone similar in height and shape as Baoxi walked out. Baoyou then followed him and strongly stabbed a dart into his waist. The guy turned around, grabbed the dart, and shouted. At that moment, Baoyou saw that it was not Baoxi but Chuansheng. However, because Chuansheng had recognized him, he felt he had to kill him.

The High Court of Heilongjiang, the Intermediate Court of Yichun, and the public security bureau of Yichun paid great attention to the statement and formed a special reinvestigation team of the Chuansheng murder case, quickly learning that Baoyou had been stabbed dead in a fight on October 26, 1990. Baoyou's mother told police the true story, which proved the truth of Yunjie's statement. They also found some contradictions and gaps in the case file; however, these findings were not enough to overturn the original judgment. But if DNA from the blood on Dongyu's coat was not the victim's, it would be very persuasive. The investigators made great efforts and finally obtained permission from the victim's family to open the grave of Chuansheng to collect the skull and hairs for a DNA sample.

The Forensic Medical Examination Center of the Beijing Public Security Bureau revealed that the victim's blood type was in fact AB and that Dongyu's coat was stained with type A and type O, which were the blood types of his father and his brother, respectively. Therefore, Dongyu's coat was not stained by the victim's blood, and further, it was ridiculous that the previous medical examiner had mistakenly identified the victim's blood as type A.

On April 12, 1995, the High Court of Heilongjiang Province acquitted Shi Dongyu and released him ten days later. He received 60,000 RMB in compensation and assistance.[1]

This is the first case that gave me the push toward the study of wrongful convictions in China, though the real work on the issue started ten years later.

2. The Survey of Causes for Wrongful Convictions

From August 2006 to March 2007, my team and I distributed 2,500 copies of questionnaires to legal professionals in public security bureaus, people's procuratorates, people's courts, law firms, and justice departments in nineteen regions across China, including the provinces of Heilongjiang, Liaoning, Henan, Hebei, Shandong, Sichuan, Hunan, Zhejiang, Jiangxi, Jiangsu, Anhui, Fujian, Guangdong, and Hainan; the Tibetan autonomous region; the Uygur autonomous region; Beijing; Shanghai; and Tianjin.[2] We were sent back 1,715 completed copies.

Among the 1,715 of those who responded, 1,199 were male, 467 female, and 49 unconfirmed gender; 1,659 were of the Han nationality, 1 of the Dong, 7 of the Hui, 6 of the Manchu, 1 of the Zhuang, and 41 unknown; 56 had educational backgrounds of high school or below, 356 attended junior college, 1,094 had a bachelor's degree, 120 a master's, 1 a doctorate, and 88 unknown levels of education; 854 had achieved their first major in law, and 1,195 their highest major in law.

We designed twenty questions to be included in the survey, including the following: How do you understand wrongful convictions? What situations constitute wrongful convictions? What are main causes for wrongful convictions? At which stages are wrongful convictions likely to occur? What is the relationship between wrongful evidence and wrongful convictions? What is your opinion of the wrongful-conviction accountability system? Do you have suggestions for how we could avoid wrongful convictions? How should we compensate the victims of wrongful convictions?

Now I'd like to focus on the answers to two of these questions: What are the causes for wrongful convictions, and what is the relationship between evidential mistakes and wrongful convictions? In the questionnaire, we framed a multiple-choice question, allowing for multiple answers.

(1) According to your work experience, what do you think are main causes of wrongful convictions? The choices are:

    A. unclear laws or rules
    B. fault of the parties involved

C. interference by other administrative agencies
D. public pressure
E. interference by higher agencies or superiors
F. backwardness of current investigative facilities and techniques
G. insufficient professionalism of legal officers
H. investigators who bend the law for personal interest and who extort confession by torture
I. pressure to solve 100 percent of the cases in a timely manner

To sum up the answers, 63 percent (1,074) chose "insufficient professionalism of legal officers"; 55 percent (951) chose "unclear laws or rules"; 50 percent (866) chose "interference by higher agencies or superiors"; 45 percent (771) chose "investigators who bend the law for personal interest and who extort confession by torture"; 42 percent (716) chose "backwardness of current investigative facilities and techniques"; 38 percent (653) chose "pressure to solve 100 percent of the cases in a timely manner"; 35 percent (604) chose "interference by other administrative agencies"; 24 percent (405) chose "fault of the parties involved"; while only 22 percent (373) chose "public pressure."

It was unexpected that 1,074 (63%) of those questioned—as judges, prosecutors, lawyers, and police—chose "insufficient professionalism of legal officers" and ranked it first of all the causes, but it is nonetheless representative and persuasive. Therefore, in order to prevent wrongful convictions, it is important that we begin to see improvement in the skills, abilities, and professionalism of investigators, prosecutors, and judges in obtaining, examining, and using evidence.

It is of primary necessity to improve the evidence collection abilities and procedures of investigators. Evidential problems are caused mainly by illegal collection and the lack of corresponding evidential rules. Investigators are not good at collecting evidence, especially extracting indirect evidence such as physical evidence. Second, it is necessary to improve the evidence examination and evaluation abilities of judicial officers. We should perfect the relevant rules on evidence verification and strengthen the ability to analyze the probative value of evidence. Third, it is necessary for scholars to reinforce the research of principles and rules on examination and evaluation of evidence so as to increase such skills of legal officers.

Included in the questionnaire was a question we had specially designed to analyze the relation between evidential mistakes and wrongful convictions: "How much influence do you think mistakes in evidence would have in the formation of wrongful convictions in real investigations?" The answers were to be chosen from "a great deal," "a fair deal," "a small deal," "a very small deal," and "none." What we found was that many believed evidential mistakes to have a substantial effect on the formation of wrongful convictions: 60.0 percent (1,031) chose "a great deal" and 31.4 percent (538) chose "a fair deal," for a total of 91.4 percent. However, we also had four people who chose "none" and eleven who abstained from answering.

We may conclude from this that evidential mistakes are the major or direct causes of wrongful convictions. In the survey, for the question, "Which do you think are the main causes for wrongful convictions?" 63 percent (1,031) chose "insufficient professional qualities of investigators," 45 percent (771) chose "investigators bend the law for self-interest and extort confession by torture," and 42 percent (716) chose "backwardness of current investigative facilities and techniques." These three choices all imply evidential mistakes. For another question, "How much influence do you think mistakes in evidence could have in the formation of wrongful convictions in real investigation?" 91.5 percent chose either "significant" or "fairly significant."

Certainly there are many causes for wrongful convictions, and some seem to have more impact, such as public pressure, interference by higher agencies or superiors, interference by other administrative agencies, and work pressure. But these factors usually militate through evidential mistakes. These causes manifest through, or translate into, evidential problems, including extortion of confessions and fabrication of evidence. Additionally, the backwardness of current investigative facilities and techniques and the insufficient professional qualities of investigators are causes for wrongful convictions but are also manifested by evidential mistakes. In a word, evidential mistakes are direct causes of wrongful convictions; other factors are usually indirect and express themselves via evidential mistakes.

3. The Survey of the Relationship between Seven Types of Evidence and Wrongful Convictions

From January to March 2007, seven graduate students of mine at the Renmin University of China Law School went respectively to Beijing; to the provinces of Hebei, Henan, and Shandong; and to the Tibetan autonomous region to carry out more research, combining the questionnaire with interviews and hence increasing the reliability of the survey results. They sent out 140 questionnaires and received 139 in return. Among these, 33 were judges, 66 were prosecutors, 20 were lawyers, and 20 were police officers.

Ages of those questioned varied broadly: 32 percent were between the ages of twenty and twenty-nine, fifty percent between thirty and thirty-nine, and 18 percent over forty. Of the sample, 32 percent were female. In addition to general questions, we also prepared more specific questions on each of the seven types of evidence. For brevity, we shall mainly discuss the research results of two types of evidence that affect wrongful convictions the most: witness testimony and confession of the accused.

    (1) How much influence do you think mistakes in evidence would have in the formation of wrongful convictions in judiciary practice? Choose one answer only:

        A. very big
        B. a bit big
        C. a bit small
        D. very small
        E. none

    Among those questioned, sixty-six (47.48%) chose A; fifty-five (39.57%) chose B; twelve (8.63%) chose C; and four (2.88%) chose D. No one chose E, and two did not answer.

    Legal professionals of different occupations displayed a discrepancy on this question. Although most agreed that evidential problems are important contributing factors to the formation of wrongful convictions, it was agreed on more by judges, prosecutors, and lawyers than by the police. For example, among the twenty police officers questioned, six chose A; six chose B; seven chose C; nobody chose D and E; and one did not answer. Among the twenty lawyers questioned, six chose A; eleven chose B; one chose C; one chose D; nobody chose E; and one did not answer.

    (2) Which one of the following evidence do you think most readily leads to wrongful convictions? Choose one only:

        A. physical evidence
        B. witness testimony
        C. audiovisuals
        D. confession of the accused
        E. statement of the victim
        F. expert conclusions
        G. inspection or examination record

Among those questioned, four (2.9%) chose A; forty-nine (35.3%) chose B; five (3.6%) chose C; forty-seven (33.8%) chose D; twelve (8.6%) chose E; twenty-two (15.8%) chose F; and nobody chose G. Again we noticed a discrepancy in the answers from legal professionals of different occupations. More judges, prosecutors, and lawyers deemed witness testimony and confession of the accused to be the main contributing factors causing wrongful convictions; the police showed no preference to the first six pieces of evidence. Additionally, few judges believed the statement of the victim often leads to wrongful conviction.

(3) Which one of the following situations do you think most readily leads to wrongful conviction?

    A. failure of a witness to appear in court
    B. perjury
    C. unlawful obtaining of witness testimony
    D. witnesses' mistakes in cognition
    E. judges' mistakes (when using testimony)[3]

Among those questioned, thirteen (9.4%) chose A; sixty-nine (49.6%) chose B; twenty-one (15.1%) chose C; eighteen (12.9%) chose D; and eighteen (12.9%) chose E. Judges, prosecutors, police, and lawyers held similar answers, differing in that judges and prosecutors leaned towards "perjury," whereas police leaned towards "judges' mistakes."

(4) Which of the following do you think can improve the witness rules and inhibit the formation of wrongful convictions?

    A. strengthen mutual restraint among police, prosecutors, and judges, and keep judges neutral
    B. reinforce the right to defense and increase the rate of lawyers' participation
    C. establish the witness-protection system and ensure that witnesses appear in court
    D. improve the discovery system, the cross-examination system, and supporting rules
    E. adopt the judge-controlled free-testifying model
    F. insist on the principle of evidentiary adjudication and that the court shall examine all evidence submitted by prosecutors and defenders

G. design reasonable scientific exclusionary rules of illegally
obtained evidence, and suppress its negative effect

Among those questioned, sixty-nine (50%) chose A; fifty-two (37%)
chose B; seventy-seven (55%) chose C; forty-five (32%) chose D; twenty-one
(15%) chose E; sixty-one (44%) chose F; and fifteen (11%) chose G. Judges,
prosecutors, and lawyers all attached much importance to "establish the
witness-protection system and ensure that witnesses appear in court," "insist on the principle of evidentiary adjudication and that the court shall
examine all evidence submitted by prosecutors and defenders," and "design
reasonable scientific exclusionary rules of illegally obtained evidence, and
suppress its negative effect"; however, the police didn't pay much attention
to these three, and collectively ignored the "establish the witness-protection
system" choice.

(5) Which one of the following do you think most probably prompts
false testimony of the accused?

A. extortion of a confession by torture
B. the decision to voluntarily take the rap for others for a certain
purpose
C. confusion of the accused
D. the accused wants to seek emancipation

Among those questioned, seventy-seven (55.4%) chose A; forty-three (30.9%)
chose B; seven (5.1%) chose C; and twelve (8.6%) chose D.

(6) Which one of the following do you think is the most serious
problem now regarding the confessions of the accused?

A. the confession is obtained illegally
B. investigators attach too much value to the confessions and
disregard other evidence
C. the accused intentionally conceals the facts in voluntary
confessions
D. the accused refuses to admit guilt, with a confession then
difficult to obtain

Among those questioned, forty-one (29.5%) chose A; sixty (43.2%) chose
B; fourteen (10.1%) chose C; and twenty-four (17.2%) chose D.

According to the survey, false witness testimony is a main cause of wrongful convictions, the second one behind only extortion of confession by torture and false confession of the accused, for which I will continue the discussion later. False witness testimony that could cause wrongful convictions usually slips through because there is no effective impeachment system. Therefore, in order to prevent wrongful convictions, it is necessary to establish possibility of witness impeachment and to require the appearance of witnesses at court, which is very important to the process of judgment. In legal proceedings, trial is the most crucial part, and the judge is the decider of the case. Therefore, it is necessary for the judge to have direct examination of evidence at trial; only through that can the judge form intimate knowledge relating to the truthfulness and probative value of evidence and, accordingly, find the real facts and make a fair judgment. If the judge can only indirectly examine the witness testimony on record, it impedes scientific and accurate judgment. Moreover, if witnesses appear at court, the opposing party would have the opportunity to impeach directly. So it would not only prevent preconceptions and prejudice of judicial professionals in examination and evaluation of evidence, and increase the transparency of trial, but also protect the legal rights of all parties, especially the right to have direct impeachment and a fair trial. Vagueness and contradictory provisions in Chinese procedural laws related to the appearance of witnesses at court are one cause of witness nonappearance in practice, and the main obstacles to reform of the witness system.

We also collected 137 cases of wrongful conviction uncovered from 1995 to 2008, mostly exposed by the media.[4] We conducted thorough analyses of the representative cases, including twenty well-known wrongful convictions.[5] We found that wrongful convictions are generally the result of several interconnected factors in both the investigation stage and the trial stage of criminal proceedings. These factors reflect ten misleading roads in Chinese criminal justice. I will use two well-known wrongful conviction cases to illustrate these roads in the following chapters.

Part One
The Misleading Roads Illustrated in the Teng Xingshan Case

(Back from the Dead I)

As early as 1247, Song Ci, the great legal expert of the Song Dynasty, wrote in the preface of his classic work *Collected Cases of Justice Rectified,* "As for unjust imprisonment, the majority arise out of deviations occurring at the beginning of investigation, as well as mistakes over the examination and ascertainment of evidence."[1] In other words, the occurrence of wrongful conviction is often a product of misperceptions made in the first stages of the investigation or outright mistakes in the collection and analysis of evidence. The words of the great Song Ci find new application in modern China.

Chapter One

The Setting of Inappropriately Tight Deadlines for Solving Criminal Cases

1. Time-Restricted Case Breaking

In China, the concept of setting deadlines for solving a criminal case, or "time-restricted case breaking," is not new. Generally speaking, the occurrence of a major crime prompts law enforcement officials to demand that investigators solve the case according to a time constraint. Should the case attract widespread public attention, political officials, including mayors and provincial governors, may also lean on the police to solve the case within a certain time restriction; such instructions are likely to be heralded by the media. When it comes to major crimes, all parties, from ordinary citizens to law enforcement agencies, hope for the case to be solved as quickly as possible and for the perpetrator to be duly punished.

Time-restricted case breaking reflects the reaction to these emotional conditions and serves in a certain measure to assuage the desires of the people for retribution and to deter criminal behavior through use of fear. Further, it illustrates the abilities of the relevant officials, who not only arouse the alacrity of investigators but also call up the personnel and material resources to conduct the investigation. However, time-restricted case breaking does not always result in case closure by the deadline.

Time-restricted case breaking causes subjectivity and polarization, connected as it is with punishment and reward, including promotion. Without strict orders and a deadline, investigators tend to be lazy, to shirk their responsibility, to passively resist doing their work. Dereliction of duty is rampant. Thus, there is practical value in using time-restricted case breaking to increase efficiency. Some major crimes have been successfully resolved under the demands of a time restriction, and some criminals have been punished justly; however, time-restricted case breaking also has negative consequences. If a case can be resolved in the time allotted, this is surely a cause for celebration; but if the case must extend beyond this time, those involved must continue to seek truth from facts. Yet some investigators may only be concerned with speed, not with quality; seeking quick results, they accept or perform substandard work. Some investigators stoop to using torture to extract confessions, extorting witness testimony, and even falsifying evidence. In these cases, time-restricted case breaking tempts investigators into a moral and legal quagmire.

Time-restricted case breaking reflects a value long entrenched in Chinese police work, inherited from Chinese military precepts and an excessive interest in inflating the rate of cases closed. Chinese law enforcement is greatly influenced by the military mind-set and traditions; thus, military techniques such as strike-hard operations, special attacks, and first-wave attacks are commonly employed, which do not necessarily relate to legal principles. The rate of case closure is an important measure of success in investigative work, especially for major crimes. Some regional law enforcement agencies demand not only time-restricted case breaking but also mandated death-case breaking: 100 percent of all cases involving murder or manslaughter (including acts of terrorism, poisoning, arson, robbery, rape, and kidnapping) must be successfully resolved. If this were a subjective expression of hope that all cases involving a death could be solved, there would be nothing absolutely regrettable in this slogan; however, some regional law enforcement agencies make this a concrete demand, even going so far as to force local police chiefs to issue signed promises to solve all cases or else incur punishment. These policies must be reevaluated.

In November 2004, the report of the National Meeting of the Work Team for Investigating Fatality-Related Criminal Cases upheld the methods of law enforcement in Hubei and Henan, bringing up mandated death-case breaking for particular praise.[1] While the pressure of both time-restricted case breaking and mandated death-case breaking has increased the rate of case closure in certain regions, it has also resulted in a manifest decline in the quality of investigations and so can be taken as a clear harbinger of wrongful conviction. Indeed, in some areas, it has been discovered that investigators use the mentally ill as scapegoats in murder cases.[2]

Neither time-restricted case breaking nor mandated death-case breaking is an appropriate principle on which to base criminal investigations. The basic responsibility of a criminal investigation is to bring the facts to light, collect evidence, and apprehend criminals. On the surface, this would seem to be a job for investigators alone, but in fact the questions of whether, and in what time frame, these three duties can be accomplished is not completely under the control of criminal investigators. In other words, solving crimes is not only a matter of talented and determined investigators but also the product of other factors, including the time, place, and social environment of the case; the quality and type of evidence; and the personal circumstances of those involved—especially the accused. If solving a case were only a matter of keen and determined investigators doing their jobs properly, then the principles of time-restricted case breaking and mandated death-case breaking might be reasonable. But the factors determining the results of a case are so various that to espouse any overarching demands dependent on just a single factor—as time-restricted case breaking and mandated death-case breaking both surely are—is to go against objective principles of criminal investigation.

Criminal investigation is by its nature something of a game. That is to say, it takes the form of two opposing sides, and the accuracy and effectiveness of one side depends not only on what that side does but on what the other side does as well, as in a game of chess or the shell game. Investigators and criminals are two opposed parties, or players. Both parties generally resist each other through means either open or concealed, or both. The duty of the investigator is to bring the facts of the crime to light and to arrest the criminal and, in so doing, preserve law and order while protecting the legal rights of the citizenry. The criminal, meanwhile, acts to preserve him- or herself and to accomplish criminal goals, and so must look for every means possible to avoid and oppose investigation, must put every effort into obscuring the truth and misleading investigators. During the actual investigation, the investigators must determine their steps according to the probable steps of the criminal, must think of the criminal's strategy to determine their own: "When the devil grows an inch, the priest must grow an inch, too." Under some circumstances, opposition and maneuver is carried out by both sides simultaneously. For example, after the crime has been committed, the criminal considers whether to flee to avoid arrest, and the investigator considers where to search for the criminal. During interrogation, the investigator considers how to elicit the facts, and the criminal considers how to obfuscate. In other circumstances, the opposition carries a definite time lapse. For example, the criminal considers how to prevent leaving any traces of evidence; later, the investigator considers how to unearth these traces. A criminal must consider carefully where to conceal evidence; investigators must consider where the criminal would have been likely to hide the evidence.

In the game of investigation, the effectiveness of investigators depends not only on their team but also on the team of the opposition: how clever and experienced they may be—or not be. Criminal investigation is not one-sided labor, such as construction or manufacturing, in which compensation may correspond to a very definite output. The relation between input of labor and the results this yields is not so clear in criminal investigation. Some criminal cases leave investigators with nothing to show even after many weeks or months of work.

In countries with a well-developed rule of law, investigators not only bring to light the facts of a case but also use appropriate and legally gathered evidence to prove those facts; thus, working a case means working on finding evidence, and the key to a high-quality case is high-quality evidence. Discovering and collecting evidence is the work of investigation, but the discovery of evidence is not completely a function of the will of the investigators. In theory, evidence should always be discoverable, but in practice, much of it never is. Practical experience shows that the discovery of evidence is both necessary and occasional; it is a process over which investigators do not have complete control. Some types of evidence are much desired but seldom found, and what is found is not necessarily what is desired. The ideal is to put in a half measure of effort and come up with a full solution, but the inevitable reality is that a full measure of effort is always required, even if it yields less than what was hoped for.

The officials in charge of law enforcement agencies, as well as their superiors, should demand that investigators resolve cases with all possible practical speed; however, the militaristic mind-set of time-restricted case breaking and mandated death-case breaking puts the cart before the horse. All of the wrongful convictions that have come to light in recent years testify to this. The pressure exerted by time-restricted case breaking and mandated death-case breaking clouds the eyes of investigators, sending them into a zone of misperception, where hopes are too easily taken for reality and where in the worst cases they trample the grass to save lives, which is to say they conclude too readily that the accused or primary suspect is guilty. Many a false judgment comes about in this way. The following case is a good example.

2. The Mysterious Sister Six

In the west of Hunan Province, in the Huaihua Prefecture, there is a county named Mayang, located between the northeast end of the Yunnan-Guizhou Plateau and the Xuefeng and Wuling mountain ranges. It is well known for its undulating landscape, its dense forests, and its abundant water: "Clear streams all year and pine trees as far as the eye can see," as the saying goes. There are more than two hundred streams, large and small, around Mayang, but all of them flow into the Jinjiang River, which flows between the mountains and which is called the Mayang River by the locals. To three sides of Mayang—the north, south, and west—there are mountains. In the central part of the village there is a flat plain, and to the east the terrain slopes downwards. The Jinjiang River flows into Mayang from the southwest, travels north through the plain, and then flows back southwards at the plain's northern edge, thus forming a bay. Where the river flows east out of Mayang, the bay is especially wide, and many sandbanks have thus been formed. One of these is called Malan Island. When the rains are plentiful, these sandbanks are surrounded by water on all sides and can truly be called islands; but in the dry seasons, they are linked to the riverside by land. Many plants grow on the sandbanks, and many birds nest there. Among this wilderness, there lies a mystery.

Mayang is a small, mountainous county, with a population of a few hundred thousand. More than 70 percent of the population are Hmong people, but here the Hmong economy and culture have gradually fused with those of the Han; people mostly speak Mandarin, and their customs are very similar to Chinese customs, so that the locals are sometimes called "familiar Hmong." Traditionally, the Hmong lived among the mountains, building their houses close together to form stockades, and there are still many Hmong settlements clustered along the rugged mountainsides. A local folk song describes this:

> *Everyone knows the mountains are hard,*
> *Where is more dangerous than our land?*
> *Sister tears her embroidered skirt,*
> *Brother's feet are scraped raw.*

But at the same time, the Jinjiang plain at the front of Mayang became an important transport hub. Its economy was well developed, and it was known as "the gateway to west Hunan." On the bay, there had long been a small village frequented by traveling salesmen. In the Song Dynasty it had been named Fuzhou City; it is now the seat of the Mayang county government. The river went right through the village, so the locals generally used ferries to travel from one side to the other. On the upper reaches of Malan Island, there was a fairly busy ferry port named Manshui. This port benefited from the popular Dragon King Temple in the nearby Manshui village, where the dragon-dog Panhu, said to be the ancestor of all Hmong people, was worshipped. These were typical border villages, with many crisscrossing streets filled with shops, and so it was common for migrants from Guizhou to come to the villages to do business or to look for work.

On April 27, 1987, an old man from the Mayang Town was taking a morning walk near Malan Island when he noticed that a bag made from woven plastic was floating in the river. When he fished it out of the river and opened it up, he discovered a human leg inside. He immediately informed the local police, who rushed to the scene and subsequently requested the help of the county public security bureau's investigation team.[3] In the meantime, the police discovered six other dismembered body parts by the riverbank: a head; a torso; and parts of arms, legs, and feet. From these, the forensic team deduced that the deceased was a young woman.

Normally sedate and sleepy, the county of Mayang was shocked by the news. It was not only the local citizens who were concerned; local leaders also began to pay attention. At this time, China's legal development was going through a unique period. After the central government had put into place a policy of "reform and opening up," the subsequent rapid economic development led to new legal problems, and many regions experienced a substantial increase in crime. On August 25, 1983, the Politburo of the Chinese Communist Party Central Committee released its Decree on Striking Hard against Criminal Activity, in which they requested that political and legal mechanisms at every level of China "redouble their efforts to punish criminals severely and rapidly." On September 2 of the same year, the Standing Committee of the National People's Congress issued the Decree concerning the Punishment of Criminal Elements Harming Social Order and the Decree on the Process for Rapid Trial of Criminal Elements Harming Social Order. The first of these decrees stated that those criminals deemed to cause severe harm to social order could be "punished under the most severe penalties under the Chinese Criminal Law, including the death penalty."[4] The second stated that serious crimes could be tried at high speed, with the time limit for appeals shortened from the ten days required in the Criminal Procedure Law to three days. These regulations were the prologue to the so-called Strike-Hard law-enforcement campaign. Considering all these circumstances, the higher leaders of the public security bureau attached great importance to this gruesome new case and requested that the Mayang County Police finalize its investigation within a month. Hence, the Mayang police established the Dismembered Body Case of 27 April Investigation Team. The bureau chief took command with the assistance of the local police, and with great fanfare they resolved to investigate the crime and seize the murderer.

After their initial discussion, investigation team members decided this was most likely to be a case of murder for love; it was much less likely that it was a spousal murder or a murder for money. Hence, their initial strategy worked from two angles. One was to send local police to the edges of the region to carry out investigations and interviews to discover if there were any clues connected with the case, particularly those who seemed to have been involved in difficult relationships; the other was to consult all the local police stations and village and township governments to ascertain whether there were any cases of missing people, which might make it possible to identify the deceased.

At that time, the county police force possessed only one jeep, which meant that much of the investigation had to be done using bicycles or public bus transportation. After a week, although progress had largely been very slow, a few useful pieces of information had arisen. On visiting the boatmen at the ferry port, the police found that some of the boatmen had previously seen body parts floating in the river—but when the detectives went upstream to investigate, they found no evidence of the source. One villager, who lived on the south bank of the river in Malan Village, said that one night he had heard a woman desperately calling for help from Malan Island. But since it had rained heavily that same night, all possible evidence had been eliminated. There were a few local reports of difficult relationships between couples, but the women in these cases were all still living nearby, so there was clearly no connection to the case. However, the missing-persons reports did provide two cases worthy of attention. One concerned a local girl named Zhan Jinlian; the other, a woman from the countryside, Yang Sister Six.

Zhan Jinlian was from a little village named Gao. She lived on the south bank of the river, not far from Malan Island. Her mother, Tang Fengying, had reported to the police that she had found a boyfriend who was not from the village, and that she had been missing for more than a month—during which her mother had been terrified that her daughter had been murdered. When Tang Fengying heard from one of the ferrymen that a woman's body had been found floating in the river but that it had been torn apart and was too horrifying to look at, she had run to the police station to inquire, believing the body to be her daughter's. The detectives confirmed that Zhan Jinlian was a missing person and that certain factors of description might lead to her identification as the deceased, but when they requested confirmation of the corpse's blood type from the forensic investigators, it transpired that the deceased had type A blood, whereas Zhan Jinlian's was type O; consequently, they reasoned, the body could not be Zhan Jinlian.

Yang Sister Six, on the other hand, had been working as a waitress in the City Square Hotel in the county seat. Two detectives sought out the person who had reported her missing: Liu Kuoyuan, the hotel manager. This Mr. Liu was over thirty, and seemed sensible and thoughtful. The detectives discovered from him that Yang Sister Six had come to Mayang from Songtao County in Guizhou Province. She had claimed to be the sixth of seven daughters in her family, which accounted for her name. Her family was very poor, and she had left her village to look for work at a young age. Her fifth sister had been working in the hotel at Mayang, but last October she had resigned and headed back home. The previous December, Yang Sister Six had arrived in Mayang on her own, on her sister's recommendation, but she had stayed for only a few days. But in 1987, after Chinese New Year, she had come back and started work at the hotel. Mr. Liu said he had no idea whether Yang Sister Six was her real name—at the time, villagers did not have official identity cards, and if an outsider arrived looking for work, he or she could easily make up a name.[5] Yang Sister Six's older sister had used the name Yang Xiaoyan when she worked at the hotel, but everyone called her Little Yang; after Sister Six arrived, they called her Little Yang, too, or just Sister Six. The younger Little Yang had seemed bright and was considered to be pretty. After only a short time in Mayang, she had gotten to know plenty of people and often spent her evenings out with friends. But about a month before, she had stopped coming to work, with no explanation. At the time, Mr. Liu had not dwelled on this. It was common for these country migrants to disappear without notice. But when he heard about the body in the river, he felt he needed to let the police know.

Based on Mr. Liu's description of her appearance, the detectives concluded that Little Yang was a good match for the body found in the river. But since the corpse was badly damaged, with the cheekbones broken and the face mutilated, and without any special birthmarks on the body, it was impossible to identify it properly. Additionally, since there were no clothes on any of the body parts, which were found in ordinary plastic sacks of a type you could find anywhere, there was no real means of confirming identity, apart from blood type. And as no one had been able to locate any samples of Little Yang's blood or hair, it was impossible to make a comparison.

But when they discussed the case, most members of the investigation team believed the body *was* Little Yang. So in order to move things forward, the team made a phone call to Songtao to ask for information about Yang Xiaoyan or Yang Sister Six. After a couple days, the Songtao police sent a message back: "We found no such people." Having expected that all would be revealed, the Mayang police were shocked to find that this mysterious Little Yang seemed to have no real identity at all. So the detectives began to consider another question: Was Mr. Liu, the manager, concealing something?

They began to ask questions of the people who worked and lived around the hotel, and they found out some interesting things. The people whom Little Yang associated with were very mixed: there were men and women, manual workers and businesspeople. Sometimes she would go out at night with men, possibly to do "that sort of thing." Little Yang had also said to the other waitresses that she didn't want to be a waitress and that she planned to set up a business with someone, selling medical ingredients. They also heard that Mr. Liu had actually known Little Yang before she came to Mayang and that last year, when her sister had gone home, it was Mr. Liu who had brought her back.

The local police records revealed more about Mr. Liu. It transpired that he had set up the City Square Hotel a year ago, and that he was also selling medicine on the side. It also transpired that Little Yang was known to the local police. At one point a man had gone to the police station because of a fight he had had with her. A policeman was sent to find her and to suggest that she leave Mayang. Apparently, this Little Yang was quite a hard woman to handle!

The stipulated deadline to resolve the case was approaching fast, but without any real leads, the Mayang police were feeling the pressure. They decided to persevere with the approach of investigating Little Yang's network of contacts, working out how they were all linked; this would promote the case to the public, who might provide them with information about suspicious people or events, and at the same time allow the police to mobilize their personnel and target suspects. In a short time, about half the local police were working on the case.

3. The Suspected Butcher

Several months passed, and although there were a few leads, the police had not made any substantial progress towards solving the case.

When the detectives questioned Mr. Liu a second time, he admitted that he had been to Yang Sister Six's house. He claimed that he had been going to Songtao on business, and took Little Yang's older sister back home, as it was on the way. When he was there, he met Yang Sister Six, who said she had been thinking of working in Mayang. He told her he could arrange this. After this interview, the detectives came to believe that Mr. Liu was basically reliable. He treated people kindly, his family was peaceful, and he had no motive. He and Little Yang had never been seen together on their own; hence, the detectives eliminated Mr. Liu from their list of suspects.

In October 1987, the police used the address Mr. Liu had provided to visit Little Yang's house. It turned out that she was indeed from Songtao County in Guizhou. She lived in Luping, a village in the Waxi district, and she had been born in 1968. Her real name, evidently, was Yang Xiaorong. The police visited the house, intending to confirm Yang Xiaorong's identity and to obtain samples of her hair and clothing, as well as hair samples from her sisters. Forensic investigation confirmed that Yang Xiaorong's blood type was A, the same as the body in the river. This made the investigation team even more convinced that the deceased was certainly Little Yang. However, the team had made absolutely no headway in its identification of suspects, and several associates of Little Yang had been eliminated. The investigation was grinding to a halt.

At the time, the standard of criminal investigation in China was extremely low, in terms of both theory and practice. In 1979, the Third Bureau of the Ministry of Public Security had compiled a volume titled *Penal Investigation Studies;* this was the first specialist work for training detectives in the Chinese system. In the same year, the Ministry of Justice and the Ministry of Education started to compile materials for teaching law at colleges and universities. By 1982, they had completed a volume titled *Criminal Investigation,* which became the first relatively complete source of information about the subject. But the effects of this research and training took a long time to penetrate to local areas, particularly those as small and remote as Mayang.

The members of the investigation team on the Dismembered Body Case of 27 April lacked experience and knowledge of criminal investigation, and also had very little experience in investigating such complex murder cases. But considering the pressure to solve the case, they adopted a "learn as we go" attitude: studying the theoretical documents and books on one hand, while asking for guidance from higher authorities on the other. For instance, the team used *Criminal Investigation* for inspiration. In chapter 16, section 3, the book discusses "Methods for Investigating Anonymous Murder Cases." For cases in which the body was dismembered, it states: "By examining the marks on the body, one should decide what tool was used for dismembering and, according to the method of dismemberment, speculate as to the level of technical ability possessed by the criminal."[6]

When the team discussed the case further, some members observed that it seemed as if the body had been dismembered using specialized techniques; the person involved would need to be someone who used knives regularly: a surgeon or a butcher. In Mayang, there were hardly any surgeons, but a fair few butchers, so it would be necessary to focus the investigation on identifying butchers who had had contact with Little Yang, thus providing the investigation, theretofore stalled, with new opportunities and a new way of thinking. After a short investigation along these new lines, another suspect entered the team's purview.

This man's name was Teng Xingshan. He was a Hmong man, aged thirty-nine, with a primary school education. He lived in Malan Village by the river. Teng had been a soldier, and after demobilization he had married Zhan Jinhua, a woman from a neighboring village. They had one daughter and one son. Teng had five siblings, of whom he was the second oldest, and after he was married he still lived with his father and mother. Initially, and although he was a rather coarse man and prone to drinking a lot, his relationship with his wife was good. Later on, though, his wife and his mother got on increasingly badly, and this led to arguments between him and his wife. Being an obedient son, he would sometimes beat his wife on the orders of his mother. In 1982, they agreed to divorce, with the five-year-old daughter going with the wife and the three-year-old son staying with him. Although the parents had separated, the two children remained close friends and playmates. Teng Xingshan worked as a butcher and had opened a small stall at the top of the village. Locals told the detectives that Teng was lonely and sometimes went into town to drink and enjoy himself. It was said that he had been to the City Square Hotel to "look for women," and that he had brought women home with him for the night. In their investigation, the detectives had already encountered Teng, whom they felt to be nervous, as if he had something to hide. Having considered it, the investigation team believed that Teng Xingshan had both the motive and the means to commit the crime and deserved considerable suspicion. They were happy with their conclusion and decided to take action.

Chapter Two

The "From Confession to Evidence" Model of Criminal Investigation

1. The Tradition of "No Confession, No Conviction"

The traditional Chinese criminal justice system puts great emphasis on oral testimony, particularly confession. Ancient criminal courts upheld the principle of "no confession, no conviction," and "no case without confession shall be recorded." With the Cultural Revolution came also "confession forced by torture," for which the 1979 Criminal Procedure Law was enacted to strictly prohibit such extortion. The law states:

> Determination of cases requires thorough evidence and thorough examination and review of said evidence; simple faith in confessions is not permissible. In cases in which only the defendant has given confession, and for which there is no other evidence, there are no grounds for conviction and sentencing. But if the defendant supplies no confession, yet other evidence is truthful and sufficient to prove guilt, then the defendant is eligible for conviction and sentencing.[1]

The point of this law is to weaken the function of confession as it stood and to advocate instead an investigation model based on obtaining evidence that will lead to confession.

The concept of "from evidence to confession" entails the following procedure: the investigator assigned to the case must first collect evidence to prove not only that a crime has been committed but also that the suspect or the accused has probably carried out the crime. Only then should arrest be warranted and confession obtained via lawful interrogation. In a word, first collect evidence, then make the arrest. But in practice, investigators in China have long been used to a model that works from confession to evidence. Approaching any given case, investigators use any means possible to produce a suspect, then place all their energies into extracting a confession that fits the details of the crime committed. Only after receipt of the so-called confession do they begin devising means to collect corroborating evidence, including material evidence, documents, testimony, and expert opinion. This model of investigation goes by the saying "make an arrest first and collect evidence later."

The main reason investigators in China tend so strongly to pursue cases from confession to evidence can be summed up as a stubborn love of confession. In truth, this stubborn love of confession appears not only among investigators but with procurators and judges as well. Those with a stubborn love of confession have full knowledge that confession is not a dependable device and that cases based only on confession are much more likely to result in wrongful conviction, yet refuse to operate differently. Without a confession, investigators dare not conclude their cases, procurators dare not issue indictments, and judges dare not issue sentences. The many factors leading to this method of investigation include, among investigators, a lack of industriousness, a lack of professionalism, and the continued use of outmoded investigation techniques. The Teng Xingshan case is a good illustration.

2. The Skillful Interrogation

On June 12, 1987, the detectives of the Mayang County Police seized Teng Xingshan from his butcher's stall and took him back to the police station. Based on the customary procedures at the time, the police did not formally detain criminals; rather, they used the technique of "shelter for investigation." And, according to their predesigned plans, the detectives adopted a complicated side-on tactical approach.

One detective spoke to Teng: "We've brought you in this time to check up on your relationships with women. Have you been picking up women on the side?"

Teng replied, "I am divorced, but I always play by the rules. I've never done anything like this."

"People have heard you say that you're with a woman at the moment."

"Well, I guess I was just bragging."

"There are some others who have seen women coming out of your place at midnight. Was that bragging, too?"

Teng didn't reply.

After some further questioning, Teng ultimately admitted that he had got to know a woman in the town, and that they had been associating for a while. The detective asked what the woman's name was. Teng hemmed and hawed: "Well, I don't really know. She's not from the area."

"You took her home and you slept with her, and you don't even know her name?"

Once more, Teng didn't reply.

The detective asked, "Have you been to the City Square Hotel?"

"Yes."

"And is that woman from the City Square Hotel?"

"I don't know."

The detective took out a picture of Yang Xiaorong and asked Teng if he recognized her. After a long hesitation, he replied, "Kind of."

At this, the detective's expression changed completely, and he urged Teng to confess anything about the murder. Teng looked blank.

During the subsequent interrogation, Teng's answers remained confused. Sometimes he would use the story he had originally constructed, that he had never had any contact with "outside" women; sometimes he would say the woman who spent the night with him was his former wife; sometimes he would say that he had taken home a woman from a hotel in the city but that it wasn't the woman in the hotel. But he continued to assert that he had no connection with the murder. The investigation team interrogated him one by one, using every possible trick, and after several days Teng finally admitted that he was guilty.

According to Teng's confession, he had met a girl at the City Square Hotel named Little Yang. The two of them had a "vague sort of relationship." One day, towards the end of April this year, he had brought her back to his home, and after they had had "relations," Little Yang had left. Teng noticed that the money he kept under his pillow was missing and suspected that Little Yang had stolen it, so he went after her. He followed her to the sandbank at Malan and was able to seize her. Little Yang refused to give him back the money and was struggling and yelling for her life. He had no option but to stifle her to death. After this, he went home; took a woven plastic bag, a knife, and an axe; cut up Little Yang's body into six pieces; and hurled them into the river.

But it is said that after Teng limped back to his cell after the confession, feeling himself all over with his bruised limbs, he spoke to his cellmate, Cheng Gongliang: "This is how they fixed me up, interrogating me half the time and beating me the other half, and not letting me sleep. How could anyone stand that? I had to admit that I'd killed someone." Having said this, he broke down crying. Cheng Gongliang tried to console him: "Don't worry, the government won't treat good people unfairly." Teng spoke through his tears: "You're just in here for gambling; they'll let you out after a few days, but for this crime they'll demand my head!"

After Teng had gone through the process of making this confession, the investigators took him to collect the instruments he had allegedly used in his crime. Once he was back at his family home, he protested to his family members that he had done nothing and that the government could not mal-treat him. But at the demands of the police, he retrieved a knife from his own house and an axe from his younger brother's house. The police took some photographs and then took him and his "lethal weapons" back to the police station.

Eight months after it happened, the Dismembered Body Case of 27 April had finally been cracked, and the Mayang police leadership was extremely happy, even arranging a special banquet to celebrate. They received a congratulatory phone call from the regional higher-ups and decided to present the investigation team with special honors. But the team would not be able to rest yet, as its work on this case was in fact not over.

3. The Plaster Model

China has long emphasized confession of guilt in the resolution of crimes. Judges in ancient times relied on maxims like "To judge a case, one must hear a confession" and "Without a confession, the case can never be settled." During the Cultural Revolution (1966–1976), many Chinese people experienced the pain of forced confessions, and when the Criminal Procedure Law was drawn up once more in 1979, it stated clearly that confessions extracted under torture were strictly forbidden. Furthermore, it also stated:

Sentencing, in every case, must rely on evidence and investigation; confessions should not be automatically trusted. Things that the defendant states in interrogation cannot be used to determine the outcome of the case, unless there is evidence to support them. Similarly, when the defendant had not made a statement on a particular matter, but when there is clear evidence to support it, this can be used to determine the outcome and penalties of a case.

But in practice and despite the procedural law, police often used confessions of guilt as a sign that a case had been fully resolved. So when a crime occurred, police detectives used all their efforts to identify suspects, and once they had found one, they used every trick they knew to extract a confession. Once a confession had been extracted, they would concoct strategies to boost their supplies of relevant evidence. This, then, was the pathway to certificates of confession.

Having obtained Teng Xingshan's confession of guilt in the Dismembered Body Case of 27 April, the police set about gathering related pieces of evidence. They knew that the crux of the case was the question of the identity of the deceased, and that the matching blood type did not guarantee that they knew who the body was. Consequently, they sought more persuasive evidence to demonstrate that the deceased really was Yang Xiaorong. After consultation with experts, they discovered that it was possible to identify unknown bodies through a process of cranial reconstruction and matching.[2]

The so-called cranial reconstruction technique used a three-dimensional scan of the skull of a dead body, together with an estimation of the thickness of the soft tissue, to approximate the original appearance. This could be modeled in plaster and shown to others to identify. From the 1970s onward, Chinese police had used this technique for cases in which bodies had been dismembered, had been buried for many years, had decomposed, or were otherwise difficult to recognize.

A cranial superimposition technique had also been developed. This used photographic methods to compare the skull of a dead body with photographs of a person to determine whether the skull was that of the photographed person. This particular technique had been invented by Police Research Institute 213 in Tieling, a city in Liaoning Province, using overseas research as a base for its development. In 1982, the research group—led by the institute's leader, Lan Yuwen—received a National Second Class Invention Prize for its New Technique for Identifying Crania. By 1985, Lan Yuwen and his assistants had manufactured a world first: the TLGA-1 Cranial Identification Apparatus. This machine, which used computer techniques to appraise the crania, received a Third Class Science and Technology Progress Prize in China and the Gold Medal at the Brussels Eureka World Invention Exposition Awards in 1987.

The Mayang police sent the skull and a photograph of Yang Xiaorong, via the Hunan provincial police, to the Police Research Institute 213 in Tieling for cranial reconstruction and cranial superimposition. On January 23, 1988, the institute published Appraisal Notice No. 97, in which it stated that the skull found in Mayang and the photograph of Yang Xiaorong "matched each other in appearance," with only "a few areas of dissimilarity." The institute had also made a plaster model based on its reconstruction of the skull.

Once they had received the report and the plaster model, the Mayang police took them to Songtao in Guizhou Province looking for Yang Xiaorong's older sisters. Once the sisters had seen the model, they all suggested that it closely resembled their younger sister, particularly considering the gaps in her teeth. After this, the police came to believe that they had gathered sufficient evidence to guarantee that the deceased was Yang Xiaorong.

One crucial aspect in this case was determining the process by which Teng Xingshan had divided up the body. The police had sent Teng Xingshan's knife and axe to the Forensic Evidence Appraisal Centre at Sun Yat-Sen Medical University in Guangzhou. While the appraisal did not find any blood on the knife, it found a strand of hair adhering to the axe, which was found to be from a person of blood type A, the same type as the deceased. After this, the detectives sent the axe to the Criminal Technology Unit at the Hunan Province Department of Public Security for testing. Having appraised the marks left on the axe, the technicians determined that it had been used to cut up a humerus bone. With this evidence, the investigating team believed that its work was complete.

Chapter Three

The Misinterpretation of Scientific Evidence

1. The Scientific Evidence

Since the nineteenth century, the use of scientific evidence in the field of criminal justice has developed rapidly and now occupies center stage. Since the advent of handwriting analysis, human-tissue analysis, and fingerprint analysis, new techniques for verification of identity—such as footprint analysis, bite-mark analysis, voice analysis, and lip-print analysis—have greatly expanded law enforcement's toolkit for collecting evidence that may be considered admissible. Especially significant are techniques for analysis of DNA evidence developed since the 1980s, which have launched a new era of law enforcement procedures whereby DNA represents the king of evidence. There can be little doubt that the use of scientific evidence represents a significant improvement, enabling investigators who operate in accordance with the law to ascertain the facts of cases with greater accuracy than ever before, thus lowering the probability of wrongful conviction. But not all scientific evidence is reliable, and errors still occur. For this reason, accurate interpretation of evidence is crucial. In other words, law enforcement officials should place a strong emphasis on scientific evidence, but they should not assume it to be infallible.

Once the criminal squadron of the Mayang police had completed its report on the case, it was sent to the public security bureau for pretrial examination. The Pretrial Examination Branch immediately recommended that the prosecutor's office approve the arrest of Teng Xingshan, which followed on September 2, 1988. After this, the pretrial branch prepared a case

31

report and a lawsuit submission for the court, which were then sent to the prosecutor's office.

Because this was a case of intentional homicide, with a potential sentence more serious than life imprisonment, the relevant trial provisions required that the trial be administered by an intermediate-level prosecutor's office, in this case the People's Prosecutor's Office attached to the Intermediate People's Court in Huaihua, a regional city in Hunan Province. The prosecutors, Liu Hui and Gu Jianjun, examined the case documents and then went to the guardhouse to commit Teng Xingshan for trial. Teng repeated to the prosecutors that he had not killed anyone and that his confession had been extorted. The prosecutors replied that the evidence was comprehensive and that they hoped he would repent for his crime and cooperate with the demands of the judicial authorities. On October 26, 1988, the prosecutor's office handed down its decision on the charges of intentional homicide laid against Teng Xingshan.

Judge Dong Mingqiu of the Huaihua Intermediate People's Court heard the case. Once he had read the case materials, he reported to his superiors. They believed that this case was of great potential influence and that the decision would affect the decisions of local courts, so it was important to prepare thoroughly before pronouncing the sentence. Judge Dong and two of his colleagues made up the bench of judges, with Judge Dong as the presiding judge. They read the details of the case carefully and drafted a decision in which they decided to begin the formal trial at the Mayang County People's Court on December 13.

2. Mistaking Class Identification for Individualization

Two fundamental tasks aided by scientific evidence are individualization and class identification. The former verifies whether two objects involved in a case are one and the same; the latter, whether two objects involved in the case are of the same category or class. While both techniques are exercises in comparison, each makes different and unique demands on the distinguishing features necessary for comparison. Individualization combines distinguishing features, with the result that it demands a larger number and high quality of characteristics. Class identification, on the other hand, seeks only to limit the scope or class of the object at hand, which means that number and quality of characteristics can be smaller and lower.

The second major distinction between these two tasks is that while both are used in law enforcement, their value as evidence is not equal. During criminal investigation proceedings, the core duty of the investigators is to determine the identity of the criminal, not what category of person the criminal is. Individualization determines whether a person or an object bears a direct relation to the case, and since this task cannot be accomplished through class identification, individualization holds more value.

Some investigators and prosecutorial officials consciously or unconsciously confuse class identification with individualization. This leads to error and can set the stage for a wrongful conviction. In the Teng Xingshan case, for example, the Forensic Evidence Appraisal Center at Sun Yat-Sen Medical University in Guangzhou found that blood extracted from a hair found on the axe was of type A, the same as the victim's blood type. Blood type is a form of class identification, but investigators concluded that the hair on the axe was from the deceased, mistaking class identification as individualization. Moreover, examination of the axe markings by the the Criminal Technology Unit at the Hunan Province Department of Public Security showed that they corresponded to marks delivered by a blunt instrument on the humerus of the corpse. This conclusion, derived from comparing the axe's markings to those on an experimental imitation of the axe, was also class identification only, because analysts certainly could not say for sure that the axe in question delivered the marks on the body. But both investigators and judicial officials interpreted this analysis as certification that Teng Xingshan's axe was the murder weapon.

In the case of Shi Dongyu, mentioned in the introduction, investigators determined that blood found on Shi's coat was that of the victim, based on a verification of the same blood type; this is an example of mistaking class identification for individualization. Moreover, forensic experts observed that stab wounds on the victim were sharp on one side, blunt on the other, and between 2.2 and 2.5 centimeters in width, with a wound cavity that at its deepest reached 10 centimeters. They concluded from this that the murder weapon was a single-bladed instrument of approximately 2.2 centimeters in width and no less than 10 centimeters in length. The fruit knife found in Shi's home was 2.5 centimeters wide and 12 centimeters long, so it could have been used to produce the wounds found on the body. This, too, is class identification, with both the width and the length of the blade observed to within a certain range, but without sufficient data to determine whether the object was the actual murder weapon. In other words, a knife that could have produced the wounds is not necessarily the knife that did so. Investigators and judicial officials, however, certified the knife to be the murder weapon. Again, a class identification was mistakenly taken to be an individualization, leading to a wrongful conviction.

3. Mistaking Probability for Certainty[1]

Certainty and the lack thereof are opposing concepts universal to human cognitive activity, determined as they are in large part by notions of boundaries on the categories of the object, plus how well the differences in the behavior of two objects can be determined. Verification methods also come with uncertainty, a factor determined by the quality of the object's features. Generally speaking, when the features used for verification are clear and stable, when they are readily indicative of the object, or when the differences between the object and other objects are clear, then uncertainty is reduced. Otherwise, the verification must be understood to be of high uncertainty. Two sets of fingerprint analysis, one taken in good conditions yielding clear prints, the other under poor conditions yielding unclear prints, will exhibit very different levels of uncertainty values. Uncertain verification reports generally conclude, "It is possible that . . ." or "It is probable that . . . ," which means that such conclusions may be classed as probabilistic verifications.

Even the long-anointed king of evidence, DNA analysis, cannot actually tell us directly whether blood, semen, or other biological materials found at the scene of a crime were left behind by a suspect. Rather, it merely supplies two sets of data that a qualified expert can compare analytically to calculate the probability of a match, summing up his or her conclusions with a determination. DNA analysis never reveals two sets of data with a probability of match equal to 100 percent; in the best conditions, the highest match probability is 99 percent. Of course, DNA analysis based on blood and semen samples can be certified as matching with probabilities even lower than this. A match probability of 93 percent, for example, might serve as basis for verification, while a match probability of 80 percent could serve to verify that the two data are not a match. All material analysis and sample analysis with match probabilities greater than or equal to 93 percent could be accepted as identity verification, and all such match probabilities less than or equal to 80 percent could be said to deny verification. But what about data-match probabilities between 80 percent and 93 percent? This is the gray zone; conclusions within this range qualify as uncertain. Many types of scientific analysis yield uncertain results, a fact of which law enforcement officials must be aware. Law enforcement officials often hope that expert opinion will be perfectly certain. Judges, for example, may say to the experts, "Do not speak to me of probability; just tell me whether or not the blood traces were left by the defendant" or "Are these fingerprints those of the defendant?" or "Were these words written in the handwriting of the defendant?" Such demands put the analyst in an impossible position.

When determining certainty of conclusions, it must be kept in mind that, first, uncertain verifications are not entirely inconclusive but bear some correspondence to certain verifications; the difference is a matter of degree. In other words, uncertain verification is a conclusion with a certain probability attached. Moreover, these probabilities exhibit different characteristics. Next, uncertain verifications must not be confused with class identification, because the former is still a determination of individual identity and so still qualifies as a type of individualization. Lastly, uncertainty of verification must not be confused with human error, because the former is a product of objective conditions, whereas the latter is the product of more subjective factors. Any certain verification can, under the influence of subjective factors, become an erroneous conclusion. In the Shi Dongyu case, for example, a reevaluation of the data in the case was ordered when local law enforcement discovered that the true murderer might still be at large. The victim's skull and the clothing with Shi's blood on it were sent to the Forensic Medical Examination Center of Beijing Public Security Bureau which revealed that the victim's blood type was AB, whereas the blood on the coat was of types A and O, corresponding to the types of Shi's father and younger brother, as per his earlier explanation. This proved that the coat in fact had no blood from the victim, Guan Chuansheng. The original forensic expert had mistakenly determined the blood type of the deceased to be type A.[2] Blood-type analysis carries a high degree of certainty, but in this case a determination was nevertheless made in error. This shows once again that errors can occur even with a simple and usually reliable test, which means that all scientific evidence must be questioned and examined carefully.

Understanding analytical results in terms of different categories would greatly aid in the accurate estimation of the value of such results, because it would offer a rubric by which to understand the differences in value. Certain verifications do have the highest value as evidence, given their ability to establish the facts of a case in a stand-alone manner. Less-than-certain verifications have lower value because they do not stand on their own to establish any facts in the case and can only be used as a point of reference or corroboration. But in practice, some law enforcement officials continue to treat probable conclusions as if they were certain. In the case of Teng Xing-shan, the Police Research Institute 213 in Tieling issued a report based on skull-comparison analyses with the unidentified body and a photograph of Yang Xiaorong, stating that the two matched very closely but also that some portions of the skull were not similar. This was a conclusion with probability attached, but investigators behaved as if this scientific proof were enough to verify the body as that of Yang Xiaorong; the ultimate result was the wrongful conviction.

4. Mistaking Trial-Stage Techniques for Fully Developed Techniques

New scientific techniques are constantly being developed, but awareness of these developments varies, as does agreement as to their effective use, and can seem to make an otherwise straightforward concept relating to evidence become unexpectedly complex. In *Introduction to Criminal Evidence,* Jon R. Waltz divides scientific evidence into three types: (1) evidence that has become universally accepted, such as fingerprint or DNA analysis; (2) evidence that is universally rejected, such as forensic hypnosis; and (3) evidence that is somewhere between these two conditions. This third type may potentially become universally accepted, such as the transcripts of a lie-detection test or the testimony of a qualified lie-detection expert.[3] But this third type of evidence also lacks criteria universally accepted by experts in the relevant fields, and the techniques applied may have not yet achieved sufficient reliability or accuracy, with further testing necessary. For this reason, it is known as "trial-stage evidence." But since such evidence still carries the label "scientific," it is often mistaken for plain truth, even among law enforcement officials intent on upholding the law, with the possible result that facts could be misrepresented. Let us look at another well-known wrongful conviction case:

> On April 22, 1998, two officers of the Kunming Public Security Bureau were shot. The initial investigation revealed a major suspect to be Du Peiwu, husband of one of the victims, Wang Xiaoxiang. Du, a police officer assigned to the bureau of drug-abuse control, denied any connection with the murder through several periods of interrogation. Yet investigators determined that Du had both a motive and the opportunity, even though they lacked any direct evi-

dence linking him to the scene of the crime. It was decided that Du would be required to take a lie-detection test. At the time, the Kunming Public Security Bureau lacked a lie-detection specialist, so it had to ask for the help of the specialist working at the Kunming Intermediate People's Courts.

For ideological reasons, China had long opposed the use of lie-detection technology, dismissing the field as chicanery and false science; but in the early 1980s, Chinese law-enforcement-technology experts began to research lie-detection technology and imported a lie detector (formally known as a polygraph) from the United States. The device, when properly operated, could distinguish lies with accuracy as high as 90 percent. In 1991, China began manufacturing its own polygraph, and after more than ten years of testing, as well as its increased use elsewhere in the world, many provincial and municipal law enforcement agencies began to adopt lie detection for both investigation and adjudication. By the end of the century, lie detection was being used all over the country, with only a few exceptions, including Tibet, Qinghai, and Jilin. In Shandong, use among county level and higher public security bureaus reached 50 percent.[4] However, the scientific basis for lie detection had yet to be universally agreed on by field professionals, and certain experts repeatedly raised doubts about its reliability. In addition, because there were no universal standards for lie-detection techniques or the management of lie-detection codes of conduct, the problem of incompetent lie-detection specialists loomed, with the quality and effectiveness of lie detection failing to attain a level that earned the formal approval of law enforcement. In sum, lie detection in China was still in the trial stage.

On the afternoon of April 30, 1998, investigators with the Kunming police took Du Peiwu to the Kunming Intermediate Court to undergo a lie-detection test. He was forced to answer questions interminably, including those completely unrelated to the case. The so-called specialists who performed the test issued a report saying that because there was some indication that Du Peiwu had lied when answering questions relating to the case, their conclusion was that "he probably knew the full circumstances of the case, or else participated in perpetrating the crime."[5] On hearing this, officials handling the case believed Du Peiwu to have been scientifically proven to be the murderer, and they began to take steps to force

Du to confess his alleged crime. Several days later, Du finally began to confess and narrated "the way the crime was committed," though he omitted to say that the murderer had used a Type 77 pistol, nor could he say where the items stolen from the victims had been taken or hidden.

Investigators took Du out to identify the scene of the crime and used a sniffer dog to determine the actual crime scene—all this to strengthen their case. On July 26, the public security bureau announced that it had broken the case. On July 31, the Kunming Procuratorate issued a warrant for the arrest of Du Peiwu for murder.

A little over two months later, on October 10, the same procuratorate issued an indictment to the Kunming Intermediate People's Courts.

Between December 17, 1998, and January 15, 1999, the court was in session twice, and on February 5, Du Peiwu was sentenced to death for the crime of murder. He protested, "I have not committed murder, and the public security bureau obtained my confession through torture. The facts are not clear, and the evidence is insufficient." So saying, he appealed to the Yunnan High People's Court, which authorized the use of the major evidence when approving this case for trial but also found several persistent points of doubt, so much so that nearly a year later, on November 12, 1999, the court issued a stay of execution.[6]

As with lie detection, footprint analysis does have some scientific basis, but in practice, it cannot sufficiently and with certainty distinguish the identities of two people with similar gaits. Since the 1980s, experts within the police department have conducted experiments in gait tracing as a means of identification. They also suggested a set of technical standards for inspection, measurement, and comparison. These new methods helped spread the use of footprint analysis, but results have been varied. Some technicians even went so far as to apply the technique when no shoe was available, trying to connect footprints from the scene of the crime with insole imprints of the shoes that the suspect happened to be wearing, in order to peg the suspect at the scene of the crime. The use of such methods led to both success and failure. Here is another example of wrongful conviction:

On July 12, 2002, a break-in and assault occurred in the family-housing unit of Jidong Prison, outside of Tangshan, Hebei Province.

Wang, the cadre in charge of the prison, and his wife, Song, were both stabbed and left seriously wounded, bleeding heavily. Investigators discovered two daggers at the scene as well as a length of nylon rope and a pair of brown, size 41 sandals left behind by the perpetrator. Based on the victims' statements as well as examination by the investigators, a major suspect was named as Li Jiuming, director of the Second Branch Political Division of Jidong Prison. Given the material evidence, the sandals should have been able to identify the perpetrator, which is what the investigation team hoped for.

Investigators first asked Li Jiuming whether the sandals were his, to which Li replied curtly, "No," and explained that he was a size 42. Investigators made Li try the shoes on; Li obliged and pointed out that they did not fit. Investigators then forced Li's feet into the shoes, taking photos to serve as evidence. Investigators also called in Li's wife and colleagues to help identify the sandals, but not one person could confirm that Li Jiuming had worn them or that they belonged to him. It seemed the problem could only be solved via gait analysis. Investigators located two pairs of leather sandals belonging to Li Jiuming: one, a size 42 pair of brown Jinhou brand sandals; the other, a size 42 pair of black Huanniao brand sandals. These two pairs were sent, together with the pair discovered at the crime scene, to the provincial level public security crime lab. The resulting report indicated that the gait and wear patterns of the sandals found at the scene of the crime corresponded to great degree with Li Jiuming's sandals.

Once investigators had obtained Li Jiuming's confession, and with the footprint and footwear evidence in hand, they believed that the facts of the case were more or less clear and so applied to the Tangshan Lunan District Procuratorate for a warrant for Li's arrest. On June 24, 2003, the Tangshan People's Procuratorate issued an indictment for Li Jiuming for the crimes of attempted murder and illegal possession of a personal firearm.

Four months later, on October 29, 2003, the Tangshan Municipal Intermediate People's Court opened trial proceedings. Li was found guilty on November 26 but received a stay of execution. He appealed. On August 11 of the following year, on the grounds that "the facts still have some areas lacking clarity," the court's earlier decision was reversed and a retrial ordered. In the meantime, the real murderer had been found as the result of a different case, so on November 24, 2004, Li Jiuming was declared not guilty and released.[7]

In the cases of Du Peiwu and Li Jiuming, lie detection and footprint/footwear analysis were certainly not the most important factors leading to wrongful conviction, but they nevertheless played a part. Those handling the case perhaps had no capacity to evaluate objectively the evidence these techniques supplied, and too eagerly accepted any evidence that supported their previously formed opinions. With such evidence in hand, they felt their case possessed "the certitude of science."

5. Mistaking Bi-Relational Physical Evidence for Uni-Relational Physical Evidence

All evidence must have a bearing on the facts of the case. Physical or material evidence usually bridges two facts of the case in some salient fashion, frequently one fact touching on details already known and another touching on a suspect or an object theretofore. This is the "bi-relationality" of physical evidence. In the case of the two Zhangs of Zhejiang, sentenced to death for rape and murder in 2004, investigators found traces of human tissue under the victim's fingernails. Based on the principle of bi-relationality, those in charge of the case should have first analyzed the tissue to determine whether it had any connection to what was known about the rapist-murderer, and only afterwards performed DNA analysis to establish a connection with the suspect or defendant. Previous to being certain, the main goal should have been to establish that this tissue bore some connection to the perpetrator, and only after being certain should the aim have been to establish a connection between the perpetrator and the suspect or defendant. Because investigators overlooked the first stage of this analysis and placed priority on the second stage, they put a major break in the chain of evidence and caused a misrepresentation of the facts. The case of Yu Yingsheng is another major example of this phenomenon.[8]

Around noon on December 2, 1996, the Anhui Province Bengbu Municipal Police Report Command Centre received a report from Yu Yingsheng: a robbery had occurred in his home, and his wife had been killed in the process. Police arrived at the scene and carried out an initial investigation that came up with evidence including a cleaver, a drawer that had been pried open, fingerprints, and traces of blood. The next day, during the autopsy, forensics experts discovered that the victim, surnamed Han, had been wearing both underpants and briefs. They also took three swabs from the exterior, interior, and deep interior of the victim's vagina. Further analysis revealed that the pants and both the exterior and interior of the vagina had traces of semen. Investigators identified Yingsheng, the victim's husband, as the major suspect.

Analysts at the Anhui police crime lab reported that semen samples taken from the underwear of the victim matched those taken by swabbing but did not match the DNA data of Yu Yingsheng. An extensive search for the source of the semen was then undertaken, but despite testing several hundred people, no match was found. The search was called off and the evidence declared irrelevant.

Investigators questioned Yu Yingsheng several times after the event. He was taken to the police station for interrogation on December 10, detained in connection with the crime on December 12, and sent to the detention house on December 16. Court materials documented that between December 2, 1996, and February 8, 1997, there were nine separate records of questioning, fourteen interrogation records, and forty-one accounts written by the defendant. Among all these, one point deserves extra attention: on February 1 he confessed to killing his wife and said that he fabricated an act of sexual intercourse at the scene, but after the results of the DNA analysis appeared on February 3, his oral testimony no longer touched on this topic of fabrication.

Another profound issue in this case relates to the sets of fingerprints found at the scene. The report issued by on-site investigators on December 8 mentions twenty-six prints, of which eighteen were found to be Yingsheng's, seven to be the victim's, and one to be their son's. According to this, no other person had left fingerprints at the scene. But when the case was reexamined, procurators discovered in the internal files of the public security bureau a file on "reasons the evidence against Yu Yingsheng is insufficient," which included a report on "two sets of fingerprints left on the outside of the drawer by a fourth party, which analysis found to be relatively fresh, and which required ascertainment of who had left the prints, and whether the prints were left by the perpetrator." According to what those involved in the case could remember, this analysis did not result in any consistent conclusion. Afterwards, investigators sent the two sets of fingerprints to the provincial fingerprint archive for comparison, but no match was found. For this reason, these two prints had not been entered into the official fingerprint report.[9]

In this case, the semen samples found on the victim must bear some connection to the actions of the murderer, and the two sets of fresh fingerprints found on the drawer must also yield some connection to the murderer's actions, but because investigators could not locate who had left the semen or the fingerprints, they simply denied any relation between the material evidence and the facts of the case. After Yu Yingsheng was exonerated, however, the police used DNA testing on the semen to identify the true perpetrator.[10] These methods illustrate clearly how bi-relational evidence is misinterpreted as uni-relational, with the result that material evidence of tremendous value is dismissed as irrelevant, leading to misapprehension. This also illustrates yet again the error of putting too much faith in first impressions and collecting evidence in a one-sided way.

Chapter Four
The Continued Use of Torture
to Extract Confessions

1. The Use of Torture

Extracting confessions through the use of torture is part of the universal history of law enforcement. Even in a modern civilization, torture and forced confession are still common. Certainly, in some countries where the rule of law is well developed and applied, hard-torture sessions (employing physical torture) are now rare, but even there, soft torture (employing psychological torture) is still heard of. In recent years, the revelation of so many wrongful conviction cases in China has turned the attention of many citizens towards the problem of confessions given as a result of torture; however, such practices appear stubbornly alive and well, notorious but always likely to appear again and again.

All the cases described previously in this book have involved some use of force to extract confessions, with the cases of the police officer Du Peiwu and Li Jiuming being merely the most dramatic examples. I have been asked, "With Du Peiwu being a police officer himself, how could he confess to something he had not done?" My response is that the torture he underwent during interrogation must have made him feel that life was even worse than death. To those who undergo such barbaric treatment, confession serves as a temporary reprieve. The cases of Du and Li, now that they have come to light and been redressed, give us the barest hint of these circumstances.

Du Peiwu has said that his investigators suspended his body from his outspread arms, each of his wrists in handcuffs:

They crucified me in a metal doorway. After an hour, they placed a stool under my feet and commanded me to "confess the truth." I repeatedly told my captors that what they were doing was wrong. They answered that I was just "struggling desperately with my back against the wall," then yanked the chair out from under me, leaving me to hang. This happened many times, but I refused to confess. My examiners began to beat at my toes and fingers with a high-voltage electric baton. Some of my examiners knew me personally, and said to me coldly as the interrogation progressed, "I'm sorry!"[1]

Li Jiuming writes in his petition letter:

The first time I was tortured, the Nanpu Public Security Chief Wang said to me: "You committed this crime, and we have iron-clad proof, so if you don't talk we'll flay away three layers of your skin, and you won't want to live." Chief Yang said: "Talk or we'll kill you."

They connected electrical wires to my toes and fingers and began delivering electric shocks. When I screamed they stuffed a cloth into my mouth, and said they were going to shock me below the belt. . . . Over the course of seven days and eight nights, Wang and Yang tortured me to force a confession, each time after both had been drinking. The methods they used included pouring cold water on me, pouring mustard oil on me, pouring hot pepper flakes on me, burning me with a lighter, and beating my ears. They purchased ten bottles of mustard oil and one packet of hot pepper flakes; they used the mustard oil and pepper flakes alternated with the water. They rubbed the mustard oil into my eyes and nose, then placed the bottle on the top of my head and made me balance it there, before dousing me down again with cold water. Once, they flooded my stomach with mineral water, causing me to have a bowel movement comprised entirely of water.[2]

As mentioned in chapter 3, China's Criminal Procedure Law clearly states that torture and forced confession are punishable offenses, but in practice, most such cases go unpunished due to lack of evidence. During the course of investigations into forced confession by the malfeasance inspection bureaus of the procuratorates, all kinds of obstructions—including refusal to comply, currying favor, exertion of counterpressure, and every other manner of undermining the power of the bureau can be expected. In many cases the initial efforts to prosecute bear no fruit, or else the punishments meted out are very light. In Du Peiwu's case, for instance, only two police officers were found guilty of using torture to extract confession, and one was sentenced to just one year in prison, with one year of probation; the other was sentenced to one and half years in prison, with two years of probation.[3]

Li Jiuming's torture and forced-confession trial has been classified as a most unusual case, including a large number of officers, and at very high levels.

On January 23, 2005, the Hebei Province Hejian Municipal People's Court opened proceedings for the trial of the Tangshan police officers accused of using torture to obtain confessions, with defendants including Nanpu Police Chief Wang, Deputy Chief Yang, Tangshan City Public Security Bureau Detective Division Commander Nie, Deputy Commander Zhang, Nanpu Public Security Bureau Detective Division Commander Lu, Police Instructor Huang, and Detective Song. Before the court, Nie, Zhang, Lu, Huang, and Song pleaded guilty to using torture to force confession, and made a public apology to Li Jiuming and his family. Chief Wang and Deputy Chief Yang denied the allegations. In May 2005, the Hejian Municipal Court made its judgment: Wang and Yang were found guilty of torture and producing a forced confession; each received a prison sentence of two years. The other five police officers accused were also judged guilty as charged yet avoided punishment.[4]

To summarize, use of torture to extract confession leads to wrongful convictions. Behind virtually every case of wrongful conviction lurks the specter of extorted confession.

2. Empirical Analysis of Fifty Wrongful Convictions

As mentioned in the introduction, my task force collected 137 wrongful convictions reported in China since the 1980s. We then analyzed the fifty murder convictions among them. We found that almost every wrongful conviction in these instances was due to a variety of reasons, including false witness testimony, false victim statements, false co-defendant testimony, false confessions of the accused, mistaken expert conclusions, misfeasance of investigators, misfeasance of judicial officers, ignorance of innocence evidence, deficient expert conclusion, and unclear legal provisions.[5] One particular reason—judges making mistakes in assessing and evaluating evidence—happens more or less in almost every wrongful conviction; therefore, we did not list it out as a cause to analyze.

Analysis of the Causes

Among the fifty wrongful convictions for murder, ten (20%) had as a contributing factor false witness testimony; one (2%) had false victim statements; one (2%) had false co-defendant testimony; forty-seven (94%) had false confessions; four (8%) had mistaken expert conclusions; forty-eight (96%) had misfeasance of investigators; nine (18%) had misfeasance of judicial officers; ten (20%) had ignorance of innocence evidence;[6] ten (20%) had deficient expert conclusion; and one (2%) had unclear legal provisions.[7]

Problem of Extorting Confessions by Torture

Extorting confessions by torture is common to cases of wrongful conviction. In fact, adopting the confession extorted by torture as a basis for judgment is usually one of the main causes of wrongful conviction. Among the fifty wrongful convictions for murder analyzed, four (8%) were concluded formally by the court or procuratorate on the basis of confession extorted by torture, forty-three (86%) were concluded formally by the court or procuratorate but extorted confession by torture was probable, and three (6%) did not have the confession-by-torture problem. In other words, there were false confessions made by the defendant, as well as the possibility of, if not certainty of, torture and forced confession, in forty-seven out of fifty cases (94%).

Of these forty-seven cases, investigators in three of the first category (4) were later convicted of the crime of extorting confession by torture; investigators in the remaining case were arraigned for the same crime, but the procuratorate decided not to prosecute. In the second category (43), the accused in twenty-one cases claimed that they were tortured to extract a confession during the investigation process, but they had no evidence to support the claim. The accused in seven of these cases had certain evidence to prove torture, such as bodily scars or witness testimony, but the court ruled that the evidence was insufficient. In one further case, the procuratorate found that the defendant did have light wounds on his body, consistent with confession extorted by torture; however, the court failed to affirm this finding. In the remaining fourteen cases, the defendants confessed during interrogation but later recanted. Moreover, new evidence subsequently proved those defendants who recanted to be not guilty. And since it can be reasonably assumed that the defendants would have been reluctant to fight against the police, there might actually have been some sort of torture in those cases, even if the defendants made no claim to the contrary.

In the fifty wrongful conviction cases for murder that we analyzed, forty-seven had both false confession of the accused and torture or possible torture, occupying 94 percent of the causes. Therefore, with regard to all kinds of evidence, false confession is the most predominant cause of wrongful conviction, and torture the main cause of false confession. There is a causal relationship between wrongful conviction and illegal evidence collection represented by extortion of confession by torture; hence, in order to prevent wrongful convictions, it is important that we reinforce the legal acquisition of evidence and establish reasonable and effective exclusionary rules against illegally obtained evidence.

Illegally obtained evidence means that the evidence has been collected or obtained in violation of the law. Chinese current Criminal Procedure Law does not have clear exclusionary rules, but Article 43 says: "It shall be strictly forbidden to extort confession by torture and to collect evidence by threat, enticement, deceit or other unlawful means." In addition, the Supreme People's Court and the Supreme People's Procuratorate have created supplemental rules regarding the exclusion of illegally obtained evidence in their judicial interpretations of the Criminal Procedure Law. However, those rules are too general, lack clearly specified provisions, and lack practical, effective enforcement measures.

3. Empirical Studies on the Issue of Torture

Since 2006, in conjunction with our research into wrongful convictions, my task force launched a series of empirical inquiries into the use of torture and forced confession. In September 2006, the Institute of Evidence of Renmin University of China (RUC) Law School and the Department of Anti-dereliction of Duty and Infringement on Human Rights of the Supreme People's Procuratorate jointly held a conference—Illegally Obtaining Evidence and Wrongful Conviction—in Sanya, Hainan Province. More than one hundred prosecutors, lawyers, police officers, and legal scholars participated in the event, and most of them believed, directly or indirectly, that confession as a result of torture was a major factor leading to wrongful convictions.[8]

In July and August 2008, I led two RUC Law School PhD candidates, Lu Zehua and Liang Kun, to conduct field research in the northwest of China, on the issue of the use of torture to extract confession. We looked into two major cases in particular: one of them in November 2006 in Hualong County, Qinhai Province; the other in January 2007 in the city of Guyuan, Ningxia Hui Autonomous Region. We read a selection of case files and were able to interview some of the prosecutors involved in either case.[9] We also held a seminar, The Causes of Torture and the Countermeasures, with the People's Procuratorate in Guyuan on July 30.[10] We found that several factors contributed to the phenomena of the pervasive use of torture to extract confession:

One-Sided Mentality

Influenced by a one-sided emphasis on public interest, Chinese criminal law has long stressed the needs of fighting crime while neglecting the rights of criminal suspects and defendants. The reasonableness of the motive conceals the unreasonableness of the actual procedure: the sense of acting with a good motive weakens investigators' sense of wrong when they employ torture to force confession.

Outmoded Thought Patterns

Since Chinese criminal procedure theory has for so long spurned or even explicitly denied principles for finding people innocent, some investigators are accustomed to assuming all suspects are guilty. Despite the process of investigation, the suspect must first be found guilty; otherwise, there would be no need for investigation. Moreover, some investigators are accustomed to seeing all detained suspects as bad guys, and because they assume that the bad guys will not readily admit guilt, they may feel that extraordinary measures are needed to extract a confession.

An Inhospitable Work Environment

Many investigators had never committed assault before they became police officers, and many never assault others when off duty. Assault of the kind pertaining to this discussion came to be a habit picked up gradually: during work hours and in a particular kind of environment. We were told that some young graduates fresh out of school found this environment repugnant, but according to the tradition of apprentices following masters, they soon learned to "do as the Romans do." In this kind of workplace, the use of torture may actually be encouraged due to admiration of peers, the approbation of superiors, or even the commendation of the work unit. Of course, not all police stations are the same: some are more civilized—or more barbarous—than others.

Inferior Investigative Capability

Many of the wrongful conviction cases that have recently come to light occurred in the 1980s and 1990s. Whether in terms of theory or in practice, Chinese criminal investigation was underdeveloped at the time, especially in the more remote areas of the country. According to regulations, major crimes—such as premeditated murder and rape—automatically came under the jurisdiction of the district- and county-level public security bureaus. When other major crimes occurred in even more remote areas, local investigators had little or no experience and could only learn on the job. In addition, local investigative resources were often very limited, with few methods or techniques available. Instead, questioning and interrogation were the basic methods used. Under these circumstances, forcing the suspect to confess under interrogation became the fast path to resolving cases. Compared with other methods, torture and forced confessions were low cost but yielded big results. Some investigators did not mind taking the risk of breaking the law if it meant they could pry open the mouths of suspects. Especially when investigators were under pressure to solve a case and had reached an impasse, torturing and extracting a confession from a suspect already detained became the most common choice.

Ineffective Supervision

All behavior requires some constraint, and all power needs to be kept in check, but the behavior of those exercising power is especially in need of supervision. Torture and forced confession generally occurred during the normal course of investigators' duties, and this is a sphere of criminal proceedings particularly lacking in supervision. Even though the procuratorate enjoys powers of supervision bestowed on it by the constitution as well as the Criminal Procedure Law, and even though it does in a real sense supervise investigator behavior by determining whether to issue arrest warrants or indictments, the procuratorate is influenced by the custom of working cooperatively; thus, it often treats the issue of the arrest warrant as a formality done only to maintain harmony with the investigators. When the case undergoes examination to determine whether to issue an indictment, the work of investigators being long complete means that even if the procuratorate wants some oversight, it hardly has any effect at such a late stage. In many countries, the law establishes that criminal suspects may see their lawyer at the time of interrogation, or that the lawyer may be present during an interrogation, which gives the lawyer some degree of supervision of, and check on, the power of the investigators; in China, this system of supervision has long remained undeveloped.[11] The internal affairs departments of investigative organs must then become the main agents supervising interrogation, but when the public security organs are under pressure to solve cases, such self-supervision fails to prevent torture and forced confession.

Ineffective Deterrence by Punishment for Torture

Punishment can act as a deterrent to those who might consider committing a crime, but the fear of punishment relies on the outcome of investigations. If the probability is low that a certain criminal behavior might be discovered and punished, then the corresponding punishment might be considered something akin to a scarecrow. Most deterrents work this way, but this is even more the case with torture and forced confession. China's criminal law clearly states that torture and forced confession are punishable offenses, but in practice, most such cases go unpunished due to lack of evidence. On the one hand, those who have been subject to torture and confess as a result are at most helpless and suffering from loss of freedom, so may not be in a position to give evidence. Once the incident is over, it is difficult to obtain evidence that is robust enough. On the other hand, when the courts and the procuratorate embark on their own investigations, many of the people involved are police officers. During the course of investigations into forced confession by the malfeasance of inspection bureaus of the procuratorates, all kinds of obstructions—refusal to comply, currying of favor, exertion of counterpressure, and every other manner of undermining the power of the bureau—are to be expected. In many cases, the initial efforts to prosecute bear no fruit, or else the punishments meted out are very light.

Vague Rules Regarding Illegally Obtained Evidence

As previously mentioned, the Criminal Procedure Law strongly prohibits the use of torture and forced confession, and both of the explanations of the

law by the National People's Supreme Court and the People's Supreme Procuratorate state that a confession obtained by force and under duress cannot
be used as a basis for judgment. But these rules are not clear and explicit
enough, and so fail to achieve the desired results. In many cases of wrongful conviction, the defendant will have claimed in court to have been forced
to confess, thus overturning the confession; however, the courts often refuse
to strike from evidence those pre-confessions, instead continuing to authorize such confessions along with other evidence submitted. Many factors
have led to this circumstance, one of which is that the rules for striking out
evidence obtained illegally are not clear and explicit.[12] As previously illustrated, among the judges, procurators, police, and lawyers surveyed in our
research, 55 percent believe unclear laws and regulations to be a major
factor leading to wrongful prosecution. And this includes lack of clarity not
only on corporeal rules but also on rules regarding how to strike illegal evidence. In practice, when a defendant would say that his or her pretrial confession had been made as a result of torture, the judge would ask the defendant
to prove the allegation. Because it was difficult for the defendant to do so,
the court would often, if not always, rule against the defendant. Therefore,
since the turn of the century, many legal scholars have been calling for
more clear and explicit rules regarding illegally obtained evidence.

Chapter Five

The One-Sided and Prejudicial Collection of Evidence

1. Collecting Evidence with Prejudice

The Criminal Procedure Law, Article 50, states: "Parties involved in the investigation, prosecution and trial of criminal cases must follow a program as determined by the law to gather sufficient and diverse evidence to prove whether the suspect or defendant has committed a crime or not, and the severity of said crime." According to this rule, investigators must initiate a comprehensive and objective search for evidence. Even if what they want is to collect enough evidence to prove that the suspect committed the crime, they must also collect evidence proving the suspect to be innocent—if such evidence exists. However, investigators too readily form prejudicial opinions that might be based on the circumstances of the crime scene or conclusions based on quick analysis of the case, feelings and impressions, or prior knowledge they have of a suspect. It is inevitable and even to be commended that investigators form opinions, because these can aid in drafting a plan for investigation and in ascertaining the direction of the investigation. But if investigators are constrained by their opinions into a close-minded approach, errors will certainly arise. In reality, some investigators, out of a desire to solve the case and get results, not only never seek evidence proving the innocence of the suspects but also overlook or even go so far as to conceal such evidence. Evidence supporting innocence then becomes investigators' blind spot, which they may at times look over but not consciously see, or at other times be quite conscious of but refuse to give due care and attention to. Among the 137 wrongful conviction cases reviewed by our study group, virtually all investigators exhibited this tendency to privilege first impressions and collect evidence in a one-sided fashion. Because the investigators strongly believed the apprehended suspect to be the true perpetrator, they sought only evidence of guilt, never of innocence. At times, even evidence previously discovered or else supplied by the suspect was overlooked, perhaps consciously.[1] Such evidence supplied by investigators then becomes "monotone" evidence of guilt.

In the case of Shi Dongyu, mentioned in the introduction, investigators found in the suspect's home a fruit knife with a black-plastic handle and a military coat stained with blood. Because the investigators had formed an early impression that Shi Dongyu must be the perpetrator, they were quick to believe his confession and thought his explanation for the bloodstains to be a ruse to avoid detection. Later, forensic analysis would show that the bloodstains included blood of type A and type O; the deceased, Guan Chuansheng, was initially found to be of blood type A. Investigators concluded that Shi's coat was stained with the blood of Guan Chuansheng, and failed to explain the existence of the type O blood. Further, they concluded that the fruit knife was the murder weapon and simply made no further reference to the other wound on Guan's back, which had clearly been made with an instrument of a different type or blade.

In another well-known wrongful conviction case, that of the two Zhangs in Zhejiang, the forensic examiner had collected minute amounts of human tissue underneath eight of the fingernails of the victim, surnamed Wang.[2] Investigators first asked forensic experts to compare the DNA of these tissue samples with that of the two suspects, with results showing no matches. Investigators then moved to declare this biological evidence "of no relevance to the facts of the case." Since the tissue was found while still relatively fresh, the investigators should have concluded that it did have a concrete bearing on the case—that is to say, the victim's efforts to resist her murderer had left that party's tissue under her fingernails. But because DNA analysis failed to establish a connection with the two suspects under detention, and because the police had not been able to match the DNA of any other parties involved in the case to the DNA evidence in hand, the investigator and the judges simply redesignated the DNA evidence as irrelevant. This action was most certainly a mistake. If those in charge of the case had not made such a careless error in their use of the material evidence, Zhang Hui and Zhang Gaoping would not have been wrongfully convicted, Gou Haifeng would not have had another opportunity to commit murder, and the university student surnamed Wu would not have become another victim.[3] This method of collecting evidence, dominated as it is by prejudicial subjectivity, is a major cause of wrongful conviction. Now let us go back to the Teng Xingshan case.

2. The Defense Lawyers

On December 6, the Huaihua Intermediate People's Court handed a duplicate copy of Indictment Number 33 of 1988 to Teng Xingshan. The law provided that a defendant could appoint a lawyer or a friend or relative to act in his or her defense, or could choose not to do so. But in cases in which the death penalty was a possibility, if the defendant did not appoint a defender, the court would normally appoint one. The court clerk informed Teng that the court could help him find a lawyer, but Teng seemed not to know what a lawyer did. After some explanation, he agreed that the court could appoint a defense lawyer on his behalf. As he said to the judge, he believed that the government would not maltreat him.

After the People's Republic of China was established, it completely removed the legal system set up by the Nationalists. In December 1950, the new government published *Bulletin on the Abolition of Illegal and Unscrupulous Lawyers,* which dissolved all lawyers' organizations and prevented lawyers from acting in public. The new Chinese Constitution, issued in 1954, stated that "legal defendants have the right to obtain defenders," marking the point at which the legal system gradually began to develop again. In 1957, when the Provisional Regulations for Lawyers were issued, Beijing, Tianjin, Shanghai, Shenyang, and other such cities had established law firms and legal advice bureaus, and nineteen provinces had established lawyers' associations. By this time, there were just three thousand lawyers in the whole of China; however, the anti-rightist movement of 1957 nipped the Chinese legal system in the bud. After the Cultural Revolution was over, China needed to reconstruct its legal system once again. The Criminal Procedure Law, issued in 1979, set out clear guidelines for defense lawyers, and on August 26, 1980, the Standing Committee of the National People's Congress issued an updated version of the Provisional Regulations for Lawyers. At the time of the modernizations of 1979, there were only a few hundred lawyers in China, but by 1981, there were over six thousand, and some provinces had established lawyers' associations. In 1986, the Department of Justice held China's first qualifying examinations for lawyers; and in 1987, the first general assembly of lawyers was held in Beijing, setting up a national lawyers' association.

By this time, there were over three thousand law firms and legal advice bureaus across the country, and over twenty thousand specialist lawyers and part-time lawyers.[4] However, these were largely concentrated in the east of China. Hunan Province had established a lawyers' association in 1983, but it had only around one hundred lawyers. When Teng's case took place, the Huaihua region had no lawyers' association, and there were no lawyers at all in Mayang. For people living in remote villages, "lawyer" was a totally alien concept.

By this time, Teng Xingshan had already been imprisoned in the guard-house for a year. Day after day he asked himself: How on earth had all this happened? He swore to heaven and earth that he had never killed anyone. He had never met anyone named Yang Xiaorong. Why couldn't the police believe him? He refused to believe that the police had framed him; after all, they had treated him decently, day in and day out. But how could some people be so cruel? His thoughts suddenly turned to the Dragon King Temple in the village of Manshui. The previous spring, he and some other villagers had passed by the temple. Some of them had gone in to make offerings to the god Panhu but he had not, and he had made jokes about them worshipping dogs. Was he not an offering himself, waiting to be offered to those above? When he was young, he had heard the story of Panhu from his elders. It was said that Panhu had originally been a dog, but all the Hmong people believed in him. Panhu had taken the daughter of the Yellow Emperor as his wife, upon which he turned into a god. Teng did not believe in gods, but he had fallen into this terrible plight. Perhaps this was his fate! Initially, after he had first been detained, he believed that he would not be ill treated. But he realized that his situation was not understood by the police. Later on, when his case reached the prosecutor's office, he hoped that the prosecution would believe what he said. When he first saw the prosecution's representatives, he felt they and the police were on the same side. Later on, when the judge returned, Teng felt that he was also on the side of the police. And now there was going to be a lawyer? Would a lawyer really help him? He asked his fellow inmates, who told him that a lawyer was just another government employee.[5] But Teng still believed that the government would not harm a good person, even though his faith in this notion seemed to be getting weaker and weaker.

The day before the court session was due to start, Teng Xingshan finally met his assigned lawyer: Dai Ronggang, from the legal advice bureau in Huaihua. Since there was no meeting room at the guardhouse, Mr. Dai and Teng Xingshan had to have their discussion in the courtyard outside. They did not speak for very long, as Mr. Dai had already read the case documents and had a basic understanding of the situation. Mr. Dai did not seem very interested in what Teng had to say. He asked about Teng's military service, his family, and the circumstances of his marriage. After this, he said that there was a great deal of evidence, all unfavorable to Teng, and so it would be difficult to defend him, but he guaranteed that he would try his hardest. After Mr. Dai left, Teng had a faint feeling that the lawyer was also on the same side as the police and the judge. He returned to his cell and stared at the wall in silence. If anyone spoke to him, he did not reply. He was a man and a soldier. He could not cry!

On December 13, 1988, the tribunal of the Huaihua Intermediate People's Court, temporarily located at the Mayang People's Court, began the public hearing of Teng Xingshan for the crime of murdering Yang Xiaorong. Teng's brothers had arrived at the gray-brick building very early and were sitting in the front row. After Teng had been arrested, they had gone to the police, asking to meet with him, but they were refused, so this was the first time in a year they would see their brother.[6] The court was filling up with people, and there were still people wanting to come in, so the bailiff let them stand by the doorway.

After the presiding judge declared the hearing open, two bailiffs brought in Teng Xingshan from a side door. Immediately there was uproar, with many people shouting, so the presiding judge asked the bailiffs to keep order. Once Teng had taken the defendant's seat, the judge asked him some simple questions: his full name, age, and so on. The judge then stated the full names of the judges on the bench, the court clerk, the prosecutor, and the defense lawyer. He informed Teng of his basic rights as a defendant, and then declared the court investigation open by asking the prosecutor to read out the indictment.

The prosecutor stood up and mechanically read out the indictment, which accused Teng Xingshan of the intentional homicide of Yang Xiaorong, as well as the dismemberment and disposal of the body, which behavior constituted an intentional homicide according to Article 132 of the Criminal Law of PRC. Moreover, the prosecutor added, Teng's behavior was particularly cruel and extremely harmful to society, requiring the severest punishment available by law.

With this speech complete, the presiding judge asked Teng to provide his statement of the facts, emphasizing that this was merely an assertion. Teng replied that he absolutely had not killed anyone, that he did not know anyone named Yang Xiaorong, and that his previous confession was wrong. The judge asked whether the signature on the confession was really his. Teng replied that it was, but that the police had forced him to sign. The judge then asked the prosecutor if he had any questions; the prosecutor answered in the negative. The same applied for the defense lawyer. After the judge asked the court clerk to summarize the charges and the evidence for the audience, he then declared the investigation part of the trial over and the argument part of the trial open.

The prosecutor was first invited to make his statement. He emphasized, once again, that the case was very clear and the evidence abundant. Teng Xingshan had killed and dismembered the woman and discarded her corpse— a particularly cruel and vile scheme and method, of great harm to society, which merited severe punishment.

Once the prosecutor had sat down, the defense lawyer, Mr. Dai, was asked to speak. He said that given the volume of strong evidence against Teng, he did not wish to comment on the question of guilt. However, he asked the court to consider Teng's service to the nation as a soldier, his previous record of good behavior, and the fact that the victim had stolen his money, making it a case of murder with provocation. He requested that the court consider this when they sentenced Teng.

With both sides having spoken, the presiding judge asked once again if the defendant had a final statement. Teng got to his feet and, stammering a little, repeated that he really had not killed anyone and that he believed the government would not maltreat good people. He repeated these two statements until he was cut off by the judge and made to sit down. But the audience in the court was stirred by Teng's speech and was eagerly discussing it among themselves.

With the aid of the bailiffs, the judge managed to restore order in the court. He said that considering that the facts of the case were clear and the evidence abundant, he would give his decision immediately. On this, he stood up. The two other judges and the lawyers followed suit. The bailiff gestured to Teng to stand up again, then requested that everyone else in court also stand. The presiding judge cleared his throat, then read in a loud voice Criminal Justice Decision No. 48 of the Huaihai Intermediate People's Court (1988):

> In the case of the defendant Teng Xingshan, the charge of intentional homicide was raised by the Huaihai People's Prosecutor's Office of Hunan Province.
>
> This court formed a collegial bench, and on 13 December 1988, in the Mayang County People's Court, prosecutors Liu Hui and Gu

Jianjun appeared in court to support the charges, thus facilitating the legal hearing. The findings of fact are as follows: one night towards the end of April 1987, the defendant Teng Xingshan had had a vague relationship with Yang Xiaorong, a young woman from Guizhou. After a sexual encounter at his house, he found that he had lost some money. He assumed it had been stolen, and pursued the woman to Malan Island, where he attacked and struggled with her, eventually suffocating her to death. He subsequently used a knife and a small axe to dismember the body into six parts, which he separated and threw into the Jinjiang River. On 6 December 1987, the defendant Teng Xingshan was brought to justice. The defendant Teng Xingshan is found guilty of the crime of intentional homicide and is sentenced to death and deprived of all political rights. According to the provisions of the Supreme People's Court regarding cases involving the death penalty, this judgment will take effect after ratification by the High Court of Hunan Province. Should this judgment not be accepted, it will be possible to appeal to the High Court of Hunan Province within a period of one or two days after this judgment is handed down.

With this completed, the judge announced that the hearing was closed. Teng Xingshan was left standing in his place, dumbfounded, with no idea what to do. The bailiff handcuffed him and dragged him out. The court was in an uproar, with some people yelling and many others chattering. It was even possible to discern the sound of a few people crying.

3. Overlooking Evidence of Innocence

In actual practice, the work of defense attorneys has been proven to be very important in preventing wrongful conviction, because it can help those in charge of the case gain understanding through hearing all sides. However, the collection or presentation of evidence establishing innocence by the defense often fails to gain the attention of those responsible for handling the case, even in some cases receiving no response at all. Let us go back to the Teng Xingshan case.

Zhan Jinhua, Teng Xingshan's former wife, had not attended the trial, as she did not think it was right for her to attend. In addition, she had to stay home to look after their children. The previous year, after Teng Xingshan had been arrested and the Teng household sent into chaos, she had sent her eight-year-old son to stay with her older sister. Once her son and her daughter had heard about the problems with their father, they mostly stayed at home and hardly went out to play with others, preferring to avoid the cold looks and harsh words of strangers. Jinhua repeatedly told her children that their dad was a good man and could not have done anything bad. She believed that Teng could not have killed anyone, and even less that he could have chopped the body up. He was a butcher, and could seem crude and coarse on the surface, but underneath Jinhua knew that he was kindhearted. He respected his father and mother, and that was the basis of being good. Jinhua's relationship with his mother had not been good, however, but when his mother tried to make him beat Jinhua, he would take her into a room and beat on a bed or a chair for a while, so that his mother could hear the sound of blows from outside. And even when he was absolutely forced to hit her on her body, the blows were always very light. Eventually the pressure from his relatives was so strong that they were forced to divorce, but Jinhua, knowing that there had been no other way out of the situation, did not hate Teng at all. Could someone like that really kill another person?

Jinhua had stayed at home doing housework, but she felt ill at ease. By midday, a neighbor who had gone to the trial returned and told her about the judgment. Jinhua was stunned; tears fell from her eyes ceaselessly. The neighbor stayed with her for a while, but then left. Jinhua's parents heard about the situation and went to speak with her. Once she had stopped crying, she began to reflect, and proposed that she go to Teng's parents' house. Her parents disagreed, but she said she wanted to consult them and see if there was any way to save Teng—she would do anything to help. Even though they were divorced, she still felt concern for her former husband.

So Jinhua walked into the main room of the Teng family home. She saw that Teng's parents and brothers were there, but no one spoke; there was only the sound of Teng's mother crying. When Teng's father saw Jinhua, he furrowed his brow and gruffly asked what she was doing there. Jinhua had prepared for this. She said that at a time like this, there was not much she could say: she just wanted to save Xingshan. She thought that they needed to go to someone who understood the law for help. Teng Xingshan's older brother, Teng Xingben, said that he had seen Uncle Teng Ye outside the court that day. He had heard that Uncle Teng Ye had been a lawyer out of town, and he did not know why he had come back. Teng's father explained that Teng Ye was a cousin of his, but that they had not been in contact for a few years.

Jinhua said that it could not wait and that they needed to find him today. She was willing to go into town with Teng's oldest brother to look for him, but Teng's father suggested that it was too late in the day and that they should go tomorrow.

The first thing next morning, Jinhua and Teng Xingben crossed the river and arrived at the county seat. At Teng Ye's house, they met the lawyer, who said he knew about the case. Over the past several hundred years, the Teng family had been shamed by several murder cases. He believed the court's judgment to be reasonable. The facts were clear, and there was abundant evidence, so the chances of reversing the verdict were not high. And since the court had already appointed a defense lawyer for Teng, he preferred not to get involved. Xingben replied that he had gone to the court the previous morning and that the lawyer had hardly contributed anything and seemed not to have helped Xingshan at all. At this, there was a sudden bang, as Jinhua kneeled down in front of Teng Ye. With tears in her eyes, she said, "Uncle, my family is certain that Xingshan is a victim of injustice. Please do a good deed and help him!" Teng Ye's heart softened a little. Jinhua continued: "I was married to Xinghan for many years. I can absolutely guarantee you that Xingshan has never killed anyone. He is an honest person. He knows how to kill pigs, but he could never kill a person. He would never offend the laws of nature in such a way." Teng Ye was moved by this speech and promised to help. He said he would head to Huaihua to investigate there, but he first wanted to meet the defense lawyer to discuss the circumstances of the case.

Through a mutual acquaintance, Teng Ye contacted the Huaihua regional legal advice bureau, and found out that Teng Xingshan had decided to appeal. The bureau had appointed Zhou Xianfeng and Zeng Guangfu as his appeal defense lawyers. Teng Ye found Mr. Zhou and explained his purpose in coming. Mr. Zhou replied, "This case can't be overturned. The appeal will just be a formality." Teng Ye replied, "I know it won't be easy to overturn, but I'd still like to look at the case materials, so that the appeal can be the best possible." Mr. Zhou replied, "You can have a look at the judgment and some copies of the legal materials. Perhaps you can give us some new ideas. But you'll have to be quick, as they'll certainly decide the case before the New Year."

Once Teng Ye had looked at the documents, he noticed a few doubtful points. According to Teng Xingshan's confession, he had smothered Yang Xiaorong to death with his hands. But the police autopsy report stated that the corpse's cheekbones were broken. This seemed to show that the deceased had been hit on the head with a blunt instrument. One could not break someone's cheekbones by smothering them. Furthermore, the axe and knife that Teng Xingshan had identified had no actual bloodstains. There was only a hair adhering to the axe that matched the blood type of the deceased, and this was hardly sufficient proof that the axe and knife were the lethal weapons. Also, the appraisal of the scan of the skull stated that there were some inconsistencies with the photograph of Yang Xiaorong, which led to the conclusion that it could be a case of mistaken identity.

Having discovered these inconsistencies, Teng Ye's confidence greatly increased, and he discussed his conclusions with Mr. Zhou. Mr. Zhou was interested but remained somewhat unconvinced. He said the police had already examined the axe and had a certificate establishing that it was the tool used to dissect the corpse. In addition, Police Research Institute 213 in Tieling had basically concluded that the skull was Yang Xiaorong's, besides which Yang Xiaorong's family had identified the reconstructed plastic model. As for the question of the cheekbones, it was still impossible to eliminate completely the possibility that this had happened when the body was knocked or thrown around. Teng Ye did not argue, as he knew that it would be impossible to use these issues to persuade the appeal court to overturn the decision. He decided to return to Mayang to study the situation further, hoping to find some more favorable evidence.

On New Year's Eve, Teng Ye returned to Mayang and visited some of the villagers of Malan. Everyone said that Teng Xingshan had been a good man, honest and sincere and willing to help others. Many of them suggested that they would sign a villagers' petition—if Teng Ye wrote it—swearing that Teng Xingshan had not killed anyone. During his visit, Teng Ye also found some useful clues. On the suggestion of a villager, he visited a ferryman, Wang Mingzheng, who worked at the port. The ferryman confirmed that he and some of his colleagues had noticed body parts floating in the river some time ago. Some of them suggested that this should be reported, but no one did it. Later, when the police investigated, they all mentioned this. Teng Ye believed that this testimony was important, because the police report suggested that the place where the corpse had been thrown was Malan Island, but the island was downstream from the port. Common sense suggested that the body would drift downstream, which meant that if it had been thrown into the river at Malan Island, it could not have passed by the ferry port.

Teng Ye also heard the villagers talking about how the rain had been heavy at the time of the incident, and how high the water levels had been, so that the path connecting the sandbank and the shore had been submerged, and the villagers needed a boat to reach the sandbank. But according to the sequence of events described in the police report, Teng Xingshan had followed Yang Xiaorong to the sandbank at night, first smothering her to death, then taking her home to dismember her body. If the sandbank path had been underwater at the time, Yang Xiaorong and Teng Xingshan would have needed to swim to Malan Island or taken a boat, which was obviously impossible. Having confirmed this, Teng Ye rushed to the Taoyi Hydrology Station at the Hunan Hydrology Centre and requested that the staff produce a certificate: "In the last third of April 1987, the rainfall in Mayang was heavy and the water level of the Jinjiang River was high. From Malan Village, where Teng Xingshan lived, to the location where the corpse was thrown away on Malan Island, the only possible land route was on a path which at the time had been submerged underwater."

After more than half a month of frantic action, Teng Ye believed he had uncovered sufficient evidence to exonerate Teng Xingshan. He then carefully drafted a letter of appeal, in which he stated that on the basis of the doubtful areas he had examined, he had made the following conclusions: (1) there was an 80 percent possibility that Yang Xiaorong was still alive, and a 90 percent possibility that the deceased was not Yang Xiaorong; and (2) the existing evidence did not prove that Teng Xingshan was the murderer, and conversely, it demonstrated that Teng Xingshan could not have been the murderer under the circumstances. He pointed out that the investigation was superficial, that there had been a lack of conscientious research, that the confession had been extorted, and that there had been an overall lack of regard for the law and a casual attitude towards the value of human life. He concluded by writing: "I hope the court is cool-headed and will seek the truth conscientiously, without rushing. On the other hand, if the court is careless, and repays an unjust murder with another one, those handling the case may be subject to further legal proceedings, with terrible consequences: think carefully." On the back of this appeal, many villagers had signed their names.

On January 24, 1989, Teng Ye left Mayang. He felt that time was limited, so rather than going to the legal advice bureau in Huaihua once more, he decided to take his letter of appeal to Changsha, to deliver it himself to the Hunan Province High Court. Once he had done this, as he walked out the entrance of the court, he let out a sigh of relief. It seemed that his divine mission was over. However, he was wrong.

4. The Approval Power of the Death Penalty

The death penalty is the oldest means of punishment in human history. Since ancient times, it has seemed to be a natural law that someone who kills another should pay with his or her own life. The penalty of depriving someone of the right to life has been the strictest punishment, the most effective deterrent, and the most feared. But the death penalty runs opposite to a humane and cultured society, and is inconsistent with the progressive tide of humanism. From the middle of the twentieth century, many countries worldwide have abolished the death penalty. Those who have not abolished it restrict it to the most serious circumstances.

In China, the death penalty is a controversial issue. Even within the legal community, some advocate retaining it, and others, abolishing it. Considering China's current situation and its cultural heritage, it is hard to imagine that the public would support its abolition, at least in the short term, so its retention is a relatively rational choice. But implementing the stringent restriction of the death penalty, using it infrequently and carefully, would be consistent with the trend towards respect for humaneness in the Chinese system. Hence, increasingly many scholars have been advocating a progressive or partial abolition of the death penalty. One method would be to reduce the number of offenses punishable by a sentence of death; another would be to encourage the legal system to adopt a policy of using the death penalty rarely, and as cautiously as possible. These would lessen the scope of the death penalty and see it being employed in a more civilized and humane fashion.[7]

Each country implements the death penalty differently. Beheading was the most common strategy in ancient China, but there were even crueler methods: cutting out the heart, setting the person on fire or putting the person in boiling oil, tearing the person limb from limb, cutting the person into small pieces, having horses pull the body apart, and so forth. In other countries, burning and hanging were common, but there was also drowning, crucifixion, and stoning. In line with developments in science and technology, some countries adopted newer methods: execution by firing squad, the electric chair, gassing, and so on. From the beginning of the People's Republic, Chinese courts have used the firing squad, but after the 1980s, even newer methods were being considered.

So that the death penalty is implemented fairly and accurately, Chinese law uses the "two-trial system," which provides for specialist reconsideration of cases involving the death penalty. According to the Criminal Procedure

Law, death penalties that are deferred for two years must be authorized by a higher court, and immediate death penalties must be authorized by the Supreme People's Court. Regardless of whether the defendant chooses to appeal, a sentence of death automatically enters into a process of review. In 1983, because of a policy of "striking quickly and effectively" against major crime, the Supreme People's Court delegated the approval of the death penalty in severe crimes harming social order (such as murder, rape, robbery, and bombing) to the High Courts. This strategy had the practical effect of loosening the review process to some degree. Because the provincial High Courts were the normal appeal courts for death penalty cases, they began to take on the process of review and appeal simultaneously, so that they differed only in name.[8] It was in this atmosphere that Teng Xingshan's case entered its appeal stage.

5. The Appeal of Teng Xingshan

After sentencing, Teng was placed in a one-person cell in the lockup. He lay in the dark room, sleeping for a whole night and day. He felt so tired. When he woke, he noticed a policeman standing in the doorway. He struggled to his feet and opened his eyes, not really knowing what to do. The policeman didn't reprimand him; rather, he spoke calmly, saying that Teng needed to eat. It was only then that Teng noticed the large bowl in the policeman's hand. He rushed to take the bowl and then looked distractedly at the policeman. The policeman said nothing more, turned around, locked the door, and then left. Teng walked to the doorway, tried to look out for a while, and then walked slowly back to his bed. He began to wolf down the food hungrily.

When he had finished, he sat on the bed. He felt as if his mind were returning to normal. He thought, If this is how I will live after being sentenced to death, it's not so bad. I don't have to work, no one is bothering me, and the police give me food. It's like being a Daoist immortal! But he knew that those who were sentenced to death were executed by firing squad. A single bang, and that would be that. He picked up a chopstick, pressed it to his temple, and closed his eyes. After a while, he put the chopstick back down and let out a sigh.

What would it be like to take a bullet? When he had been a soldier, there had been a training drill using live grenades. Someone had misthrown one, and Teng had nearly been killed. Later on, the commander of his company had said that when you served in the army you couldn't be afraid to die, but you shouldn't die in vain and, even more, you should never die at the hands of someone on your own side. That time, he had nearly been killed by someone on his side; this time, it seemed certain. In army training, his instructor had always said that a soldier could never be careless, because if you made even a tiny mistake, human life was at stake. His life, too, seemed to be hanging by a thread. What would the next mistake be?

He had heard the judge say the evidence proved he had done it. How could that be? Was everything that had happened decreed by fate? Who had made these mistakes? And why did they fall on him? Was it possible that he had made them? Perhaps when the police started to ask about his relationships with women, he should not have lied. Divorcing Jinhua was what his parents had wanted; the decision had been out of his hands. After the divorce, the two of them still met occasionally, and sometimes Jinhua snuck over to his house to sleep with him. When the police asked about this, he was unwilling to speak about Jinhua, so he made up a story about a woman from out of town. He had known about the woman in the river, but he had never expected that it would be used against him. Had he known that he was suspected of murder, he would never have made up such a story. Surely if he hadn't made up the story, the police wouldn't have thought him a murderer, right? And then when the police interrogated him about the murder, it would have been fine if he had been able to withstand it. If he had refused to admit anything, would the police have pointed the finger at him? He was too soft, unworthy of being called a soldier. But then again, those people had been so vicious that he really couldn't stand it, and so he was forced to admit to something. Was that his fault? What was more, he had repeatedly told the truth to the prosecutor and the judge, so why did no one believe him? Everyone always said that the government would never hurt good people, so why was he subject to injustice? *Injustice* . . . the word seemed to lie in the pit of his stomach, making it impossible to breathe. In two steps he walked to the doorway and banged on the metal door, shouting, "Injustice! This is unjust!"

Two policemen immediately ran over and told him not to yell. The one who had brought the food said, "Whether you've been treated unjustly or not, it's pointless to yell here. You have to go to court. Aren't you making an appeal? Wait for the second hearing. The lawyer's spoken to us. He'll be here tomorrow. Just wait. There's still hope."

Teng stood there for a moment, then slowly returned to his bed.

Next morning, the lawyer did come. The police put handcuffs and leg-irons on Teng, then sent him out of his cell with an escort. Although the winter sun in the courtyard was not particularly intense, its brightness on his face made him a little giddy. When he looked upward, his eyes were blinded, and he could only walk slowly. How long had it been since he had seen the sun? Its rays were warm and comfortable on his body. Already he was dreading the thought of being back in his cell. The courtyard was not very big, and in a moment he had reached a shaded area on one side.

The meeting room was small. It was separated into a north and south side by a low wall and a set of high iron railings. On the south side there were two wooden chairs, and on the north side there was a metal chair. All of these were fixed to the floor. On the metal chair there were clamps for locking the hands and feet of a prisoner. The police placed Teng in the metal chair and placed him in the clamps, although they did not actually lock them. The door on the other side was then opened, and two middle-aged men walked in, followed by a policeman.

The two lawyers introduced themselves as Mr. Zhou and Mr. Zeng from the Huaihua regional legal advice bureau. They explained that they already knew the basic details of the case and had prepared a document giving them power of attorney, as well as the appeal submission. They asked a few simple questions and had Teng sign the power of attorney document. With hope in his eyes, Teng asked, "Is there any chance of overturning the case?"

Mr. Zhou replied, "It's going to be very difficult. The main problem is your confession."

Teng replied firmly, "That was just reckless talk." He glanced at the policemen standing by the door, not daring to say that he had been beaten.

Mr. Zhou said, "We're doing our best. Have a look at the appeal submission—we've already indicated some gaps and problems with the charges and the evidence. But don't get your hopes up. We're mostly hoping that the court will commute or defer the death sentence."

"Defer? What's that?"

"It means that the death penalty would be delayed for two years. Provided that you don't commit any new crimes during that time, it won't be implemented."

"So I won't have to face the firing squad?"

Mr. Zhou nodded.

Back in the cell, when the policemen had removed his shackles, Teng felt more relaxed. He did not want to die. The proverb said that it was better to die a good man than to live as a bad man, but he had parents and children, and they all needed him. And there was Jinhua, too. Neither of them had remarried because they felt that perhaps, after a while, they could start life together again. Without the firing squad, there would be hope of that. And perhaps the judge might find him innocent! The provincial judges were experts, and they would certainly investigate the facts of his injustice. He lay on the bed, imagining a lawyer speaking in his defense in court, and planning what he would say himself. He regretted that he had not spoken properly in his own defense. It had been his first time speaking in front of so many people, and he had been very nervous. He would be more experienced the next time. He would not speak much, but he would speak very clearly. Slowly, he closed his eyes . . . and, suddenly, there was the sound of the door unlocking. He sat up at once and saw that a disciplinary policeman had walked in. The policeman said someone had come to see him.

What? He didn't believe his ears.

"Someone from home wants to see you! Hurry up!" The policeman put the handcuffs and leg-irons on again, and took him to the meeting room. He sat in the metal chair and tried to look through a crack in the door, wondering who could be coming to see him. Was it his mother or his big brother? The outside door opened, and a policeman led in Jinhua.

Teng gaped. "Why are you here?"

"I've come to see you. I need to tell you that your case can be overturned. You can go home for New Year. Everyone's waiting for you to come home and to kill a pig!"

Teng smiled and quickly said, "I'll make a whole pot of pork for you all to eat."

Teng felt so hopeful, and the days in the lockup were no longer so hard to bear. Each day he would practice his speech to the court, constantly revising and improving it. He kept counting the days to the New Year. There was still a month to go, but why was there no information from the court? He couldn't resist asking the disciplinary policeman, who said that they also had no idea about what was going on. Also, according to their past experience, the court's second hearing did not necessarily involve an actual court session; as a rule, the judge decided the case on the basis of written submissions and would come to the lockup to pronounce the sentence. Teng's enthusiasm began to dim.

6. The Execution of Teng Xingshan

On January 22, 1989, two policemen came to Teng's cell and told him that someone had come from the court. Based on their solemn expressions, Teng felt it must be bad news. With his shackles on, Teng was led to the arraignment room. After two judges from the High Court of Hunan Province had established his identity, they solemnly read the court ruling:

> On 19 January 1989, the High Court of Hunan Province issued Criminal Ruling No. 1 of 1989. This court confirms the original decision that the facts of the case are clear, and the evidence is abundant and reliable. The original decision and sentence are affirmed, and the court procedures were legitimate. As for the appeal of Teng Xingshan against the crimes of murder and dismemberment: according to the available facts, the scientific inspection and appraisal, as well as the material evidence, are inconsistent with the claim in the appeal that "I did not kill anyone, and my original confession was false." Teng Xingshan did indeed kill and dismember a person, and his method and plot were especially cruel and vile. The consequences were extremely serious, and worthy of the death penalty. According to the provisions in Article 132 and Article 53 Paragraph 1 of the Criminal Law of the People's Republic of China, as well as the discussion of the trial judges, the ruling is as follows: the appeal is turned down and the original sentence is affirmed. This is the final ruling. According to the provisions set out by the Supreme People's Court for the authorization of cases involving the death penalty, this ruling should be considered a final authorization of the death penalty for Teng Xingshan, who is also deprived of all political rights for the rest of his life.

Even before the judge had finished reading the ruling, Teng was weeping silently. Two policemen tried to stop him. Once the reading had finished, the judge asked Teng if he had any opinions about the ruling. Through his tears, Teng said, "I didn't kill anyone! This is unjust!" The judge promised to pass on his opinions to the leadership, and then made Teng sign the decision, as well as mark it with his fingerprint.

The judge then left, and Teng was once again locked in his cell. By then it seemed as if he had calmed down. When he was released from the shackles, he asked the policeman, "When am I going to die?"

The policeman replied, "The High Court will hand down the sentence today. According to the rules, it will be carried out within seven days."

"Can I still see my family?"

"The rules say that the court will inform your family."

Then the policeman left, and Teng was alone once more. He started calculating in his head. Today was the fourteenth day of the twelfth lunar month, and in seven days it would be the twenty-first. If there was a delay of, say, two days, it would be the twenty-third, and he would ascend to heaven with the Kitchen God![9] Ascend to heaven? He was going before the firing squad! Thinking of this, he collapsed on the ground, ruined.

Under such torture, Teng kept waiting for his family and for the final day to arrive. It was intolerable. Sometimes he wished the time would go faster, sometimes slower. Sometimes he imagined how he might escape. Sometimes he thought of killing himself. He thought, *I must be crazy!*

After seven days, his family had not arrived, but the death penalty had.

On the morning of January 28, Teng Xingshan was taken out to a small yard. The court official in charge verified his identity and asked if he had any final words or letters. Teng yelled, "I didn't kill anyone! I have been treated unjustly!" The judicial policeman stopped him from struggling, then implemented the execution.

The Huaihua Intermediate People's Court made a public announcement of Teng Xingshan's execution, and then informed his family that they could come to bury his corpse and collect any possessions. His family did not bury him in a cemetery. As he was executed by firing squad, his body needed to be buried far from his ancestors' graves, and so he was buried on a mountainside.

Teng Ye heard about the execution after he returned to Mayang from Changsha. When he heard the news, the hardened lawyer could not help but cry. Teng's father, too, was angry and depressed, unable to eat or sleep. Soon after the burial he became ill, and he died shortly after. Teng's mother died two years later.

This case illustrates the serious problem of one-sidedness in Chinese criminal proceedings. Evidence of innocence is refused, while evidence of guilt is admitted without question, regardless of its truth or falsity. Judicial officials one-sidedly ascertain facts using only evidence of guilt, which leads to wrongful conviction. Such is the lesson, and the admonishment, of these numerous wrongful conviction cases.

7. The Victim Returns

Eventually, news of Teng Xingshan's execution reached Yang Xiaorong's hometown. In this small village, in Songtao County in Guizhou Province, the news made some people pleased and others upset. Yang Xiaorong's family was very poor, and her parents had had seven daughters. At a very young age, Xiaorong had left home to find work, and she very rarely returned home. The year before, when they had been informed of her violent death, her parents and sisters grieved, but they quickly put it in the past. So when they heard that the murderer had been executed, they had nothing to be particularly happy about: it had all happened a while ago. The dead were dead. Only Yang Guixian, the sister who was closest to Xiaorong, let a few tears slip.

A few years went by, and when it seemed as if Xiaorong had been completely forgotten, a strange letter arrived at the Yang house. The address it was sent to was Guanzimen, Luping Village, Waxi Township, Songtao County, Guizhou, and it was addressed to iong Jiacheng, Yang Xiaorong's mother. The sender's address was given as Qianzhao Village in Zhoutang Township, part of Yutai County in Shandong Province, but no sender's name was given. Inside, there were only a few crooked characters written: "Mama, Guixian, I want to come home." It was signed "Yang Xiaorong."

At first, the Yang family was terrified by the letter. Xiaorong's mother believed her daughter's angry ghost was trying to come back, and that a great catastrophe would befall the family. She immediately kneeled on the ground and kowtowed, requesting that the gods bless and protect them. Some of Xiaorong's sisters were worried that someone was using the name of "number six" to extort something from them or to get revenge. But having reflected on it for a while, they came to believe that the writing was Xiaorong's. She had missed some years of school, and her results had never been good. She could barely write a letter, and would have asked someone for help to write the envelope. But if this were true, it would mean she was still alive. After a little more consultation, the household decided to get Guixian's husband, Zhang Changlu, to go to Shandong to look for Xiaorong.

In the autumn of 1992, Zhang Changlu took the letter and some photographs of the family to Shandong. There were a few complications along the way, but he eventually found Yang Xiaorong in the village of Qianzhao, at the house of someone named Zhao Jingyou. He asked her to identify the photos of her sisters, which she did. According to Xiaorong, in 1987 she had been caught up in a human trafficking scheme that functioned under the guise of a medicine sales business. She had been taken to the Zhao household in Shandong. For the first two years, the Zhao family did not let her have any contact with outsiders, but later, after she had given birth to a son and a daughter for the Zhao household, she had the chance to speak to people from outside. The Zhaos mostly just wanted children, and they treated her fairly well. When she said she wanted to return home, they did not oppose it particularly.

Zhang Changlu returned to Guizhou, and when he explained the situation to Xiong Jiacheng, she was very eager for her daughter to return. Guixian wrote Xiaorong a letter, to which Xiaorong replied, enclosing pictures of her two children. Eventually, the two families were able to come to an arrangement allowing Xiaorong to return home. At the beginning of 1994, the Zhao family took Xiaorong to Jishou in Hunan, after which she returned to Songtao County on her own.

Once Xiaorong had returned, her family was both pleased and sad. She spoke about all the things she had encountered during the years she was away. Her family mentioned the murder case in Mayang, but only very briefly, and Xiaorong did not ask many questions, so the family stopped bringing it up. After all, it ultimately did not concern their family. Not long after, Xiaorong was married to a local man, Liu Renshan, from Cuobajing in their village, and she began a new life.

At that time, Waxi Township had no formal household register. Originally, the township government was in charge of the census; but from 1992 onward, the township police handled it. The census was disorganized and mostly relied on villagers making their own reports. No one really needed an identity certificate in the countryside, so most families did not bother to go to the government when their family gained or lost members. Yang Xiaorong's local registration had not been canceled when she was "murdered," and so she had no need subsequently to apply for a new resident permit. If not for a chance encounter with an old friend, the matter would have probably finished right there.

In the winter of 1994, Liu Kuoyuan, the manager of the City Square Hotel in Mayang, came to Songtao County to trade in beechwood. He happened to run across Yang Guixian, who mentioned in passing that her younger sister was still alive. Mr. Liu was flabbergasted and stuttered, "You're joking, right?"

Yang Guixian replied, "Really. Sister Six is alive." She went on to explain about the letter they had received from Yang Xiaorong, and the story of her trafficking and her return home.

Hearing this, Mr. Liu said, "This could be something very big. A while ago a court ruled that a butcher named Teng Xingshan had killed her, and he was executed. If Xiaorong is alive, that means that Teng has been killed for no reason!" He asked where Xiaorong was and whether he could go and see her. Guixian explained that Sister Six had gotten married and lived in Cuobajing, and that she could take Mr. Liu there.

When Mr. Liu saw Xiaorong, he felt that she had changed a lot. When she heard about Teng Xingshan, she was also shocked. She had had no idea that her disappearance had caused someone to lose his life. She told Mr. Liu that she did not know Teng, and any "vague relationship" with him was totally out of the question. In fact, she was so indignant that she wanted to write a letter to the court in Mayang demanding that they repeal their statement that she and Teng had been in a relationship, that they admit their mistake in claiming that Teng had murdered her, as well as rehabilitating her reputation and compensating her. Finally, the three of them mourned the fate of Teng Xingshan. Mr. Liu was an energetic man, and he promised to explain the situation to Teng's family when he returned.

Mr. Liu went twice to Malan Village before he found Teng Xingshan's house and saw his oldest brother, Teng Xingben. Mr. Liu explained the whole story of how he had found Yang Xiaorong in Guizhou. Teng Xingben was not quite as excited as Mr. Liu. He was silent for a moment and then simply said that he would have to discuss the matter with his family. Mr. Liu said that he would help at any time, at which Teng Xingben was thankful.

Teng Xingben explained the story to his three brothers. Once they had discussed it, they decided that the matter ought not to be made public. First, Teng Xingshan's case had been decided by the government, and if they tried to reverse it, that would be tantamount to setting themselves against the government, which might provoke other trouble. Second, to file a lawsuit required money, as did getting a lawyer, and poor people like them had only enough money to get by, and certainly none to waste on the law. Third, Xingshan was already dead, and so the matter was in the past and not worth bringing up again. Even if the government agreed to reverse the verdict, no one could bring a dead person back, and so it would not seem very meaningful. In short, they did not want to stir things up again. While they decided not to bring up the matter with outsiders, Teng Xingben thought they should tell Zhan Jinhua, who was still raising Teng's two children.

Teng Xingben found Zhan Jinhua and explained the story from start to finish. Jinhua could not help but cry. Xingben knew that Jinhua had been bringing up two children on her own, a very difficult task. He consoled her patiently until she stopped crying. Before he left, he gave her a warning: not to tell her children about it while they were still young, so as to avoid problems. Jinhua nodded and told him that she felt the same way.

Once Xingben had left, Jinhua sat distractedly at home. She could not understand why all this had happened. The government had so many experts; how could they have made such a mistake? With so many people in Mayang, why did it have to be Xingshan who suffered such injustice? Xingshan was such a good name.[10] When they had gotten married, she had said to Xingshan that she only married him because of his name. And, just like his name, Xingshan was a good person. People always said that the good were rewarded and the bad punished. So why had Xingshan been punished? Was this the sort of thing that happened to those who killed pigs? She seemed to have heard old people saying that really good people could never take any sort of life. Was killing pigs really taking life?

Jinhua felt choked up inside. She wanted to reason with someone from the government. But when she thought about it, she still thought that Teng Xingben had a point. They were poor, ordinary people, and they should not make trouble with the government. Another consideration was her children. When Teng Xingshan had died, Jinhua had made a promise in front of his grave: whether or not he was guilty, she would raise their children with the affection of both husband and wife. Her daughter was now seventeen and her son fifteen, nearly adults. But they were both difficult children and increasingly disobedient. Probably this was because of the shadow left behind by their father's death. Xingben was right when he said that it would just create trouble for them if they knew about the injustice their father had suffered.

Jinhua walked out of the house and headed west. She left the village and headed along the curved road on the mountainside, eventually arriving at a steep cliff. Beside a pine tree, there was a small mound covered with grass, although it had been nearly flattened by the force of the rain. In front of this mound was a crude plaque made of wood. Written on this were a few words, now difficult to make out: "Teng Xingshan's grave." Jinhua kneeled in front of the grave, staring at the grass and mud. But her vision grew hazy. Tears began to plop onto the ground beneath her.

8. The Long Road to Exoneration

Teng Dayan and Teng Xiaohui had grown up under the shadow of a "murderer." When their father was arrested, Dayan was ten and Xiaohui eight. At school, many of their classmates wanted nothing to do with them. Some would even spit at them or insult them. Whenever this happened, Dayan would stand in front of Xiaohui, as if to protect her little brother. The siblings became resentful and never wanted to go to school, but their mother insisted on it. There was one occasion when a fellow student was insulting Xiaohui, who eventually could not help but do the same back. Two boys then beat him up. Dayan saw this and rushed to protect her brother, but ultimately a fight began in which several students attacked the both of them. When the teacher came to chide them, they refused to say anything. After this incident, they rushed to a quiet place, hugging each other and crying. The next morning, when they were supposed to be heading to school, they headed to their father's grave and spent the day there. Being bullied at school, together with the financial pressure on their family, meant that after Dayan and Xiaohui finished their patchy schooling, they started working in the fields around their home.

As they got older, the children started doing odd jobs when they were not doing farm work, which made home life gradually improve. At the time, there were some villagers who headed to Guangdong, where the economy was booming, for work. After the New Year of 1998, Teng Dayan and a few people from the village headed for Zhuhai. With the recommendation of someone from their area, Dayan started work in a factory making handbags. She treasured this new opportunity and worked extremely hard, even winning a prize. But one day she was told, "We're letting you go."

Dayan asked, "Why?"

The manager replied, "We've found out that you're the daughter of a murderer!"

Dayan had no reply to this and could only walk out silently.

Later on, she managed to find a new job, but after a period of time the same thing happened, and she was sacked once again. She went around Zhuhai like this for a few years, always taking on the hardest or the lowest-paying jobs. If ever she noticed a fellow villager making a success of him- or herself, she would not speak of it, but she harbored an intense dissatisfaction. If a female coworker found a boyfriend, she felt inexpressibly sad. It was not that she was less intelligent or competent than others, but opportunities in life felt extremely distant. And she knew that it was all because of her label as the daughter of a murderer.

At the start of 2004, Dayan went home to celebrate the New Year. One day, when she was talking about her experiences in Zhuhai with her mother, her anger reached the boiling point. She told her mother, "I blame you! If you hadn't left Dad, he would never have taken up with this outside woman and murdered her. It's all your fault!"

Jinhua was taken aback and started to cry, her feelings hurt. Realizing that she had gone too far, Dayan comforted her mother. Jinhua managed to pull herself together and slowly said, "About that . . . there's something I need to tell you. Yang Xiaorong isn't actually dead. Your father was unfairly blamed!"

Her eyes bulging, Dayan asked, "What do you mean?"

Jinhua explained the story from ten years ago, of Liu Kuoyuan and his visit to Guizhou.

Dayan said angrily, "Ten years! Why didn't you tell me?"

Jinhua replied, "Your uncle asked me not to tell you. I also thought that because it was a government decision, there'd be no point in explaining it to you. And we have no money, and it might be dangerous to go against the government, so it was best just to leave it. But it's been weighing on me all this time. Do you think I was happy?"

Dayan was silent. All at once, seeing the wrinkles on her mother's face and her white hair, it was as if she understood everything in Jinhua's mind. And so mother and daughter wept together.

When Xiaohui heard this commotion, he rushed in to see what had happened. Dayan explained it briefly, and once Xiaohui understood, he immediately wanted to go to court to seek a retraction. But Dayan blocked him. Having had more life experience through her work out of town, she urged her brother not to be rash and to go through the proper processes. Granted, in the past it had been impossible for poor people to file a lawsuit against the government, but it was different now. China had progressed, and it had set up a legal system that allowed everyday people to take the government to court. After some discussion, they decided to go to Mr. Liu first, to work out the exact circumstances, and then to find a lawyer in Huaihua who could exonerate their father.

When Dayan found Mr. Liu, she asked many questions about Yang Xiaorong's situation. Then, she found someone to help her write the legal appeal. In part, it read, "The available records state that the victim, Yang Xiaorong, went missing in March 1987 while working in Mayang, and infer from this that she had died. In reality, Yang Xiaorong had been kidnapped by a human trafficker and was sold to a peasant from Yutai County in Shandong, Zhao Jingyou, and his wife. In 1992, only after she had given birth to one son and one daughter, both fathered by Zhao Jingyou, she communicated with family members in Guizhou, and later on she returned to her hometown."

With this document, Teng Dayan traveled to the legal aid center in Huaihua to apply for an appeal. She explained that her father, Teng Xingshan, had made it clear many times that he had never killed anyone, and that there had been many loopholes in the evidence relating to his case. But it was always maintained that her father was a murderer, and eventually he had been executed. As his child, she needed to appeal against this injustice so that his record would be cleared. Once the legal aid center had examined the materials, it decided to accept the case, and assigned a lawyer, Zhou Kaisong, to take special responsibility for it. After Mr. Zhou had considered all the material, he submitted the appeal to the Hunan People's Prosecutor's Office on Dayan's behalf.

On July 23, 2004, the Hunan People's Prosecutor's Office received Teng Dayan's appeal. Shortly after, the responsible prosecutor visited Hunan, Guizhou, Shandong, Guangdong, Chongqing, Beijing, and Liaoning—more than ten cities and counties in all—to verify the circumstances surrounding the accusation of Teng Xingshan and to gather sufficient evidence. This included the testimony of Yang Xiaorong's mother and sisters. The investigation made clear that the woman who was claimed to be Teng Xingshan's victim, Yang Xiaorong, was the sixth daughter of Xiong Jiacheng from Guanzimen in Luping Village, Waxi Township, Songtao County, Guizhou Province, and that she had been kidnapped from her job from the City Square Hotel in Mayang, then trafficked to Zhao Jingyou of Qianzhao Village, Zhoutang Township, Yutai County, Shandong Province. In 1992, only after she had given birth to a boy and a girl, she communicated with her family in Guizhou by means of a letter. In 1994, she returned to her native home, and later married Liu Renshan. The 2000 national census register indicated that Yang Xiaorong was not living at Liu Renshan's house, but she had completed a long-term resident registration form and been issued an identity card. Later on, because she had not given him children, Yang Xiaorong and Liu Renshan divorced, and she moved to the city of Qingzhen to work. By 2002 she had married a local man, Liu Fan, and she gave birth to a daughter the next year. Thanks to the administration of the local police in Waxi Township, it was possible to alter the census register to record Yang Xiaorong's actual whereabouts. DNA evidence strongly concluded that Yang Xiaorong was Xiong Jiacheng's biological daughter, with a probability of 99.9985 percent. Hence, the conclusion of the appeal review was that the Yang Xiaorong now living in Qingzhen and the Yang Xiaorong who was referred to in the original case were the same person.

On June 13, 2005, the Hunan Province High Court handed down its Appeal Decision Number 1 of 2005, which contained both a list of recommendations and a review of the evidence relevant to the case. The list of recommendations indicated that the High Court's Criminal Ruling Number 1 of 1989, which maintained that Yang Xiaorong had been killed, dismembered, and discarded by Teng Xingshan, contained mistakes of fact, and it proposed that the court reexamine the case.

Previously, on June 9 of that same year, Dayan and Xiaohui's lawyer, Zhou Kaisong, also submitted an appeal to the court, which requested that the court hear the case again. On June 13, the court issued its Criminal Decision Number 15 of 2005, which confirmed this.

On October 25, the court produced a new judgment, which reviewed Teng's charge of intentional homicide. In its overview of the evidence and circumstances, it declared that according to Articles 206 and 189(3) of the Chinese Criminal Procedure, and after consultation by the trial panel, the decision was, first, to repeal both the High Court's Criminal Ruling Number 1 of 1989 and the Huaihua Intermediate People's Court's Ruling Number 49 of 1988, and second, to declare the former defendant, Teng Xingshan, innocent. This judgment was the final ruling.

After Teng Xingshan's case had been commuted, the main people responsible for handling the case were given an "official warning." Teng Dayan and Teng Xiaohui received compensation totaling 666,660 RMB from the government.[11]

Part Two

The Misleading Roads Illustrated in the She Xianglin Case

(Back from the Dead II)

In 1994, the eyes of the world fell on the American football star O. J. Simpson, who was alleged to have murdered his wife. At the same time, in a mountain village in China, another case of suspected murder was taking place. But these two cases took very different paths.

Chapter Six

The Bowing to Public Opinion in Contradiction to Legal Principles

1. Public Opinions in Criminal Cases

Broadly speaking, to commit a crime is to go against country and against society. For this reason, to oppose crime is to support the welfare of the people, and so answers to the call of public opinion. In cases in which a victim has been hurt directly as a result of a crime, the welfare of the victim and his or her family becomes symbolic of the greater public welfare, and so the victim and his or her family become symbols of public opinion. Legal proceedings throughout the three branches of law enforcement, from the public security bureau to the procuratorate to the courts, may be sorely tested by pressure from public opinion.

In a well-known wrongful conviction case in Yunnan in the late 1990s, a public outcry calling for severe punishment of alleged murderer Sun Wangang put much pressure on the law enforcement officers handling the case. After the event, a prosecutor responsible for issuing the indictment remarked:

> I felt at the time that there were some doubts about this case, but in the end I wanted to send it along to the Zhaotong Municipal Procuratorate, a decision which certainly depended in part on the judgment of my peers. Also, many ordinary citizens demanded harsh punishment of the murderer. Under all that pressure, I wanted the case dealt with quickly.[1]

Heinous crimes often cause an outpour of moral censure, which can lead to popular indignation. Even before the Internet age, popular indignation could broadcast itself and even accumulate via the media or simply by word of mouth. Such opinion can become powerfully influential and, if not ignored or considered objectively, lead to a perversion of the course of justice. Law enforcement officials must maintain a stiff resolve, considering the letter of the law while upholding the spirit of the law. But judicial credibility is currently low, and politicians often emphasize the social effectiveness of the judgment, regardless of whether it may be regarded as fair. In the face of vociferous public opinion or public indignation, law enforcement officials have been unable to maintain fairness and neutrality. They habitually abandon the basic principles of the law, bend to public opinion, and seek to pacify popular indignation. The cases of Zhang Jinzhu of Henan and Li Changkui of Yunnan, which shocked people all over China, illustrate to some degree how popular indignation may detrimentally influence the decisions of the courts:

> Zhang Jinzhu was a branch chief of the Zhengzhou Public Security Bureau. On the evening of August 24, 1997, while driving his Toyota Crown sedan, Zhang struck two bicyclists, a father and his eleven-year-old son, surnamed Su. The son was thrown off his bicycle, and the father, along with the two bicycles, was caught by the vehicle, between the front and rear wheels, and dragged several hundred meters down the road as Zhang sped away. He was stopped by a crowd of onlookers, who completely surrounded his car. Both victims survived the accident.
>
> The next day, the *Great River News* featured the story prominently, and with inflammatory language described how a "disgusting" traffic accident had happened the night before, how the driver of a white Crown sedan had fled the scene dragging along the injured party it had struck, how a mob of taxi drivers had chased after the vehicle, and how the car had been stopped by the crowd. This report quickly spread across the country and was picked up by the major national newspaper, the *Southern Weekly*, as well as by the popular CCTV program, *Topics in Focus*. The Zhang Jinzhu case became symbolic of the general dissatisfaction of the Chinese with their public security organizations. Local citizens used the case to stir up dissent and protests, and on December 3, when the Zhengzhou Intermediate People's Court opened proceedings, it set up a loudspeaker outside the court for a live broadcast of the proceedings. A large crowd formed to listen. On January 12, 1998, Zhang Jinzhu

was convicted and sentenced to death for the crimes of reckless driving and causing injury with intent. Zhang appealed, but the Henan High People's Court quickly moved to affirm the original decision. Zhang was executed on February 26, and just before his death, he remarked, "It was the reporters who killed me."[2]

Li Changkui was a peasant from Qiaojia County, in Yunnan. On May 16, 2009, he beat senseless and then raped a nineteen-year-old woman from his village, then murdered the woman and her three-year-old brother. He turned himself in, was penitent, and offered to compensate the family of the victims. But on July 15, 2010, the court of first instance—the Zhaotong Intermediate People's Court—sentenced him to death. Then, on March 4, 2011, the court of second instance—the Yunnan High People's Court—recognized Li's moral integrity in turning himself in and demonstrating remorse and thus ordered a stay of execution. When the court's decision was announced, the family of the victim protested, demanding "a life for a life." The news that Li was using the fact that he had turned himself in as an "avoid execution card" caused a major stir on the Internet. For a time, the entire Chinese web community seemed to buzz with voices calling loudly for Li's execution. At first the officials associated with the Yunnan High Court maintained that judgment had been made in full accordance with the law, particularly in regard to the "cautious application of the death penalty"; however, the pressure of public indignation was so great that on August 22, 2011, the court issued a second judgment against Li Changkui sentencing him to death, thereby reversing the stay of execution issued by the court of the second instance.[3]

The judiciary may listen to public opinion in the course of criminal proceedings, but for it to seek a particular judgment to satisfy the demands of society or to defer, maybe even pander, to public opinion leads to wrongful conviction. Here comes another good illustration.

2. A Decomposed Female Corpse

In the center of Hubei Province lies Jingshan County, a salt-of-the-earth place with a long history.[4] Known as the Emerald of Hubei, it is a place of forests, rivers, and lakes lying at the foot of Dahong Mountain, on the northern side of the Jianghan Plain. About two thousand years ago, the Green Wood Uprising—the second great peasant revolution—began here, and the name Green Wood (Lülin) has stayed with one particular town. In Lülin, there is a creek whose name—Mandarin Duck Creek—is synonymous with couples in love. It runs through a deep canyon, and the scenery there is expansive and lush. It is said that the winding curves of Mandarin Duck Creek are like a ten-mile-long art gallery and that its waters appear clear and jade-green against the heavy forest. To the southwest of Lülin is another famous small town, Yanmenkou. But the reason for its fame is quite different.

In the early morning of April 11, 1994, an inhabitant from the small village of Lüchong in Yanmenkou was walking home after taking his child to school. Spring had arrived, but there was still a chill in the air, and the mountain forests were shrouded in mist. The villager noticed something floating in a pond along the route. It looked like a person. He rushed back to find the village chief, and the two of them returned to the pond to take a closer look. On confirming that it was indeed a body, the villager and the chief went to the local police station to report the matter.

The officer on duty rushed to the scene and, with the help of the villagers, fished the body out of the water. The corpse had begun to decompose, and the face was very bloated. But it was clearly the body of a young woman. The officer asked the onlookers if they recognized her. None of them knew her. In fact, none of them had ever seen her before, and they were adamant that she could not be a local. The officer searched the body but found nothing to identify the woman and, consequently, reported the situation to the county police.

The forensic investigation team from the Jingshan County Public Security Bureau then hurried to the pond to examine the body. They found six wounds to the head: not bumps or bruises but blows from a blunt instrument. However, they could not ascertain whether the woman had died as a result of the blows or if she had drowned after being knocked unconscious. The dead woman was 155 centimeters tall and appeared to have had a comely figure. She had short hair and looked to have been about thirty. At some point she had given birth. From the appearance of the body and the winter clothes she had been wearing, the forensic team concluded that she had been dead for a while, perhaps two months or more.

What bewildered the investigators was that the pond where the woman was found was quite small. Although it was at the foot of a mountain, villagers passed by all the time, and sometimes even fished there. If the body had been in the pond for two months, how could no one have noticed it? It was feasible that a submerged body might float to the surface as it decomposed, but it was unlikely to have taken two months to do so. It seemed likely that this was not the scene of the murder: there was no flowing water source, so the body could not have just drifted into the pond, which meant that it must have been deposited there intentionally. But why dump a dead body after two months? Why would a murderer wait so long? If the body had been submerged, why had it stayed under water for so long, and what had made it float all of a sudden? The forensic team had no time to pursue these questions. It had been decided that this was a case of homicide, and as such, the crime squad would take over the investigation.

The investigators searched the scene of the crime and found no evidence relating to the case. After photographing the scene and making a report, they removed the body and returned with it to the Jingshan County Public Security Bureau. They had to decide whether or not to go ahead with an autopsy.

Jingshan is a peaceful county, where major criminal cases—such as intentional homicide—are rare, so the senior police treated the case seriously. They formed a special investigation team headed by Han Hua, the deputy chief of police, with Lu Cheng, the head of the crime squad, as his deputy. The other members of the team were He Liang and Pan Jun, both highly experienced policemen. After receiving the local investigators' report, the special investigation team began by looking into missing-persons reports. When they requested that Yanmenkou and nearby villages inform them of any recent disappearances, a lead appeared immediately: someone had reported a daughter missing, a woman named Zhang Aiqing. The investigators asked her relatives to come and identify the body.

When Zhang Aiqing's mother and oldest brother arrived at the public security bureau, the investigators first asked them to describe the missing woman. Mrs. Zhang said that Aiqing was twenty-nine, 155 centimeters tall, of medium build, with a round face and a slightly upturned nose. She added that Aiqing loved to keep up with fashion and had pierced ears, and that she had had surgery after a difficult birth.

When the investigators showed the body to Mrs. Zhang, she began to cry. She managed to nod, confirming that it was her daughter. But unlike Mrs. Zhang, Aiqing's brother was hesitant, and said simply that it looked a lot like Aiqing. He added that the clothes she was wearing did not seem to belong to her. Pushed to confirm absolutely that it was Aiqing, he asked if there were any other means of identifying the body. They told him there were other methods, such as cranial matching or DNA testing, but these procedures could not be carried out locally, and would have to be performed by specialists in the provincial capital or even in Beijing, which would cost a lot, maybe even 20,000 yuan (US$2,300).[5] If the family really wanted such confirmation, they would have to foot the bill themselves. Hearing this, Aiqing's brother waved his hands in surrender and said, "We have absolutely no money."

Meanwhile, Mrs. Zhang had stopped crying and said she agreed with her son about the clothes—they were not Aiqing's.

The investigators said, "We need you to identify a person, not her clothes. It's possible that she had changed clothes." Mrs. Zhang then confirmed the unidentified woman as her daughter. Aiqing's brother assented.

After the body had been formally identified, the investigators made another careful inspection. They found the physical details on the body as described by Mrs. Zhang: holes in her earlobes, and scars on the left side of her vagina, which could have been a result of surgery. The close fit between testimony and reality seemed to demonstrate Mrs. Zhang to be a reliable observer. Given the overall facts of the case, the forensic investigators came to the conclusion that the body was Zhang Aiqing. Some questions still remained, however, and the investigators suggested an autopsy be carried out so that they could submit a final forensic medical examination and expert's report. What continued to puzzle the investigators was the cause of death: did she die from blows to the head, or did she drown? And how long had she been dead? Most crucially, how had the body remained in the pond for so long without anyone discovering it?

Once the body had been identified, the direction of the special investigation became clearer—or, rather, it made the process of identifying suspects clearer. The team began to question Aiqing's mother and brother for information. Mrs. Zhang said that when she had heard that Aiqing was dead, she immediately suspected that her daughter had been murdered. After all, Aiqing had not had an easy life, and lately her problems had begun to mount. With a deep sigh, Mrs. Zhang began to describe the many misfortunes in Aiqing's life.

3. The Dangers of a Happy Marriage

Zhang Aiqing had been a bright and studious country girl. In high school she loved to read novels, particularly foreign detective stories. She always said that love stories were too slow and that you could work out the endings at a glance. She also liked to watch the news and chat with her neighbors about national affairs. She had a calm and reflective nature: when the farm work was done, she liked to sit with her next-door neighbor under a big tree outside her house, where she would repair shoes and embroider. Sometimes she would break off from this and just gaze at the white clouds above the mountain forests.

She did not go to university. At the time, in the early 1980s, it was unusual enough for a village girl to finish high school; instead, she started work at the Yanmenkou machinery factory. She had three older brothers, and she loved to ride to the market with her sisters-in-law. Even if she did not buy anything there, she was still happy. There was nothing particularly special about her appearance, but she had a graceful, delicate air. Compared to most of the other farm girls, she loved fashion: she was the first one in the village to wear flared trousers and high-heeled shoes. Once, she brought back a pair of high heels, made of plastic, from the county capital. Her mother forbade her from wearing them and hid them away. But Aiqing managed to find them, put them on immediately, and walked down the village street with her head high and her chest out.

Aiqing gradually got to know a boy from Hechang Village named She Xianglin. He was a year younger than she was and ambitious—strong, smart, and skilled in martial arts. They fell in love, and even though Xianglin's family was poor, Aiqing decided to accept his marriage proposal. She thought that being two intelligent people, they could live well and make ends meet. And, sure enough, they were not rich but they were happy.

Xianglin, however, was not satisfied with farm work and was always thinking of ways to escape the village. He left the family behind to find work as a casual laborer in the south, and then turned his hand to trading in the north. But after their daughter was born, he went to neighboring Madian Township to work as a security officer for the local neighborhood association. It seemed to be a more stable way of getting by.

Aiqing worked hard to be a good wife and mother. With Xianglin working and living in Madian, Aiqing took her daughter to live in the factory dormitory in Yanmenkou Township. She worked nights and took care of her daughter during the day, sleeping no more than four hours each day and hardly ever complaining to Xianglin. She was good with her hands and made a vest for her daughter out of old clothes, decorated with embroidered flowers and glass pearls. Everywhere she went, its artisanship was appreciated.

Xianglin was something of a male chauvinist. He did not speak much, but he liked socializing and drinking with friends. Sometimes, when he felt the situation was more formal, he would bring Aiqing along. She was a good conversationalist, at ease in company. Once, she accompanied Xianglin when he took his bosses to dinner. To the admiration of everyone present, she drank thirteen cups of wine. She said she just did not want her husband to lose face.

She was always good to him. One summer, Xianglin had such a high fever he could not stand up. They had no money for medicine, so Aiqing nursed and massaged him for five days until he recovered.

As far as anyone could tell, they had a happy marriage.

Eventually, though, the relationship ran into trouble. The problems were mostly about money. As a patrolman working both day and night shifts, Xianglin earned over 100 yuan a month, but he would spend it all within the month.[6] When Aiqing questioned him, he would say that he had spent it on inviting people to dinner and dealing with "problems." Not only did Xianglin spend his entire salary, but he also began to spend the thousands of yuan he and Aiqing had saved over the years. Aiqing questioned him about this, they argued, and Xianglin hit her. Although he appeared quiet, honest, and straightforward, he actually held back a fiery temper. Aiqing, on the other hand, was a tolerant person, and when they argued, it was always she who would concede, not wanting to hurt the marriage.

As time went on, the differences between them became more pronounced. Aiqing was realistic about life, whether it was about love or work. She just wanted to do things properly and well, from start to finish. But Xianglin was never content. It was as if every morning he awoke with a new fantasy about a different life. To have this kind of husband began to fill Aiqing with disquiet, even fear.

In 1991, Xianglin began an affair with a woman in Madian Township whom he had once helped when he was on patrol. She was single, and given that Xianglin was away from home, they would sometimes spend the night together. When Aiqing found out, she was devastated; she had worked so hard to preserve her marriage with Xianglin. Once the initial shock was over, she did not confront him. Instead, she sought out this woman and spent some time with her, chatting and playing cards so that they could have a heart-to-heart conversation. When Xianglin heard about this, he was moved, and for the first time since they were married, he talked openly with Aiqing, explaining to her how guilty he felt.

Aiqing always wanted to seem strong and save face. She hated to complain and did not like to vent her feelings. This meant that her anger and frustration were always locked inside.

In 1993, the factory met with some financial trouble, and it looked as if Aiqing would be laid off. With all the personal and financial pressure weighing down on her, Aiqing lost her spirit. Sometimes she would feel anxious for no reason; she became forgetful and often fought with Xianglin. Once, she said to her mother that she felt as if she were going to die. Her health deteriorated to the point where she became completely dependent on Xianglin.

In 1994, not long after New Year's Day, Aiqing disappeared. Her family suspected that Xianglin had murdered her, even though he claimed she had left in a rage after a quarrel. Mrs. Zhang went to Aiqing's house, and though she did not find any evidence, she noticed that all of Aiqing's warm jackets were still there. It was midwinter, so surely she would have taken a jacket with her when she left? Xianglin stated again that she had simply walked out, and said he expected her back after a few days. But Aiqing did not return, nor did she send any letters. Unwilling to wait any longer than she had already, Mrs. Zhang gathered her family together and went to the public security bureau to report her daughter missing.

4. The Suspected Husband

Once the special investigation team heard Mrs. Zhang's story, they felt Xianglin to be worthy of suspicion and decided to approach him immediately. From what they had gathered, the investigators predicted Xianglin was going to be difficult to handle.

Later that evening, two members of the special investigation team, He Liang and Pan Jun, rushed to Madian Township. With the support of the local police, they tracked down She Xianglin and took him to a local hotel. In a room there, they told him that his wife had been found dead and that someone had murdered her. When he heard this, he appeared to be very upset and demanded to see his wife's body. The investigators refused, saying it would be too far to travel. They asked him to tell them about the circumstances surrounding Aiqing's disappearance.

Xianglin spoke of his wife's mental state at the time and of their quarrel. When the investigators asked about their marriage, he first said that things had been fine; after further questioning, he admitted that they had been fighting often. When asked if there had been another woman, Xianglin flatly denied it, but then said he had "been in contact" with a young woman in Madian. He insisted that once Aiqing had found out about the other relationship, he had cut off contact with the woman.

Suddenly the investigators changed tack: "Be honest! Just tell us how you killed Aiqing!"

Xianglin became flustered but insisted that he had not killed anyone and that Aiqing had really just left the house of her own accord. Repeatedly he asked to see the body, saying that he did not believe it was really Aiqing who was dead. The investigators made no acknowledgment of the request, and kept asking him to be honest and confess. They reminded Xianglin of the well-known Communist Party saying: "Lenient on those who confess, severe on those who refuse."

There was no result that night. The next morning, the special investigation team took She Xianglin back to the Jingshan County Public Security Bureau, where the special investigation team held a meeting about the case, chaired by Lu Cheng, the head of the crime squad. First, the forensic investigators discussed the conclusions they had drawn from the autopsy. Based on the algae found in her stomach, they determined that Zhang Aiqing had been alive when she entered the water; officially, it could be classified as death by drowning. Next, He Liang discussed the process of detaining and interrogating She Xianglin. He suggested that Xianglin's description of his wife's departure was concrete and definite and sounded like the truth, although it could have been a story he had carefully practiced. Based on the limited contact they had had with him the previous night, He Liang believed that Xianglin was either an honest person or an excellent actor, or both—an assessment that Pan Jun agreed with. Xianglin seemed to have a split personality: on the one hand, his expressions of pain when he was told that his wife had died seemed disingenuous; on the other, his repeated demands to examine the body seemed sincere. If Xianglin had been telling the truth, then it was most likely that Zhang Aiqing had been murdered, and possibly raped, by another person after she had left the house. It did not seem likely that this was a crime committed out of anger or for money.

After a long discussion, the special investigation team came to a unanimous conclusion: while it was impossible to eliminate completely the possibility that Zhang Aiqing had been murdered by someone else after leaving her home, She Xianglin remained the prime suspect. In the absence of evidence pointing to any other suspects, he was still the key to solving the case. And because the victim in this case had been dead for over two months, and since her body had been submerged under water for some time, it was difficult to perform the usual crime scene examination procedures: analysis of bloodstains, foot- and handprints, and so on. With such a high-profile case in the balance, the investigators redoubled their efforts towards charging the suspect with a crime. The team decided to split into two groups: the first would handle the interrogation of She Xianglin and would be headed by He Liang and Pan Jun, together with two younger officers. As Xianglin had worked as a security officer for years, it was likely that he was familiar with police procedure. If he really had murdered his wife, it would be possible for him to concoct an elaborate alibi and stick to it. The investigators were prepared for a long and drawn-out battle. The other group, which would be headed by Lu Cheng, the head of the criminal squad, would be composed of technical criminal investigators and local policemen. They would go to Hechang Village and conduct an investigation, interview residents, search She Xianglin's house, and return to the pond to search for evidence. The search for evidence needed to be widened: if there was nothing on the banks of the pond, there might be something in the water itself or in the surrounding forest. Given the complexity of the case, Han Hua, the deputy chief of police, decided not to take the crucial step of arresting She Xianglin; instead, he would be sheltered for investigation.

Being "sheltered for investigation," or "detained pending examination," was a technique first used against habitual criminals during the Cultural Revolution. In 1975, the State Council released a notice approving this method, which allowed city-level police to set up detention locations.[7] In 1980, in order to standardize the application of shelter for investigation, the State Council released a notice on the incorporation of forced labor and shelter for investigation into "re-education through labour." The notice stated:

> Where suspects of minor crimes have not revealed their true names or addresses; where itinerant criminals have committed minor crimes; in cases of habitual criminals; or for those members of gangs who need to be restrained in order to ascertain their crimes, the people involved should be taken to a place of re-education through labour, where they can be examined by specialists.[8]

The decision to shelter for investigation was made by the local police. The criteria were broad, allowing for the subject to be sheltered for up to three months. Many public security bureaus used shelter for investigation as a substitute for actual detention in the initial stages of investigation when the identity of the suspect was known. In order for a suspect to be officially detained, the laws of criminal procedure had to be strictly adhered to. Even with police approval, the period of detention could not exceed six days, or ten days in serious cases. Furthermore, although the Ministry of Public Security had requested that all local police set up designated locations where subjects could be sheltered for investigation, many public security bureaus still placed those being sheltered in a regular police guardhouse.[9]

After the decision was made to shelter She Xianglin for investigation, the local police led the county police down to Hechang. They first went to the She family home to make inquiries. She Xianglin's daughter, aged six, hid behind her grandmother with a terrified look in her eyes. Xianglin's older brother asked to see Aiqing's body; his request was denied. When Mrs. She asked to see her son, the result was the same. Mrs. She confirmed her son's story, saying that Aiqing had simply run away from home; that she had run away twice before and had to be dragged back by her family both times. The investigators found no evidence relating to the murder in the house, and there was no evidence in the village or the forest, either. It seemed as if the case could only be resolved in court.

In order to advance the interrogation, the investigators began to focus on She Xianglin's extramarital affair. They attempted to extract statements from the people involved. Not long after the woman in question had met with Aiqing, she had left town to find work, but it turned out that she had returned to Madian late last year. A few people suggested that Xianglin had gone looking for her again. The investigators decided to use the affair to exert pressure on him and force him to admit that he had been lying. Alternating between the two groups, the investigators interrogated Xianglin for two days and two nights until his defenses finally collapsed. He admitted that he had been in love with the other woman and had murdered Zhang Aiqing, who he claimed had become mentally ill. However, even after extensive questioning, he remained evasive as to the exact circumstances of the murder.

At this time, the family members of Zhang Aiqing called for a representative to draw up a petition signed by over two hundred local citizens and demanding that the government harshly punish the alleged perpetrator, She Xianglin, according to the law. This move put enormous pressure on local government.

5. The Legal Petitions

In contemporary China, it is possible to petition higher authorities to express popular opinion and state popular demands; it is a method that has become worrisome to all levels of government. Petitions to higher authorities arise from a diverse combination of factors, the majority of them connected with adjudication. The appearance of these litigation-related petitions, or legal petitions, may lead to wrongful convictions. The case of Li Huailiang is a typical example:

On the evening of August 2, 2001, Du Yuhua, a peasant from a small village in Ye County, Henan, took her daughter to the banks of the Shahe River to gather cicada larvae (used for medicinal purposes). The daughter, Guo Xiaohong, disappeared. Du reported this to police, who found the girl's body downstream two days later. Forensic examination concluded that the girl had been choked to death and the body subsequently dropped into the river. Further, she had been raped before she was killed. Crime scene investigators collected material evidence, including traces of blood and footprints.

Through extensive investigation, the police identified the family's neighbor, Li Huailiang, as the prime suspect. Li was arrested and interrogated, initially denying any involvement; however, after repeated interrogation, he confessed to the crimes. There remained, however, some points of doubt: the blood collected at the scene of the crime was type O, whereas Li's blood was type AB; also, the footprints photographed at the crime scene corresponded to the imprints of a size 38 shoe, but Li was size 44.

Despite this conflicting evidence, in August 2003 the Ye County People's Court sentenced Li Huailiang to fifteen years' imprisonment in an effort to "hedge bets," given the paucity of evidence, and, further, to follow along with the lower-level court's decision to "prescribe light punishment in case of doubtful guilt." The defendant filed an appeal. On December 2, the Pingdingshan Intermediate People's Court issued its decision, setting aside the earlier court's decision and ordering a new trial by reason of "unclear facts and insufficient evidence." The victim's family, which had been deeply unsatisfied by the fifteen-year prison sentence, began issuing petitions at every opportunity. The Ye County People's Court duly retried the case but did not issue a decision. Afterwards, the Pingdingshan Intermediate People's Court set aside the decision of the Ye County People's Court and decided to try the case by itself as the first instance trial. Then the Pingdingshan Procuratorate issued a new prosecution to the Intermediate Court. On August 3, 2004, the Pingdingshan Intermediate Court issued a death sentence for Li

Huailiang and deprived him of all political rights for life. Li refused to accept the decision and once again issued an appeal. On January 22, 2005, the Henan High People's Court issued a second decision declaring the facts unclear and the evidence insufficient, and again put aside the decision of the lower courts and ordered another retrial. On April 11, 2006, the Pingdingshan Intermediate Court issued a stay of execution. On September 27, the Henan High Court once again issued a decision declaring the facts unclear and the evidence insufficient, and again put aside the decision of the lower courts and ordered another retrial. From this point forward, both the family of the victim and Li's family began to petition.

There is a subtle point worth further consideration regarding the legal proceedings of this case: as the court of second instance, the Pingdingshan Intermediate People's Court declared the facts unclear, the evidence insufficient, and so set out to reverse the earlier court decision in 2003, while in 2004, as the court of first instance, the same Court declared "the facts clear, the evidence full and sufficient," and subsequently sentenced Li Huailiang to death. During the intervening period, the evidence remained unaltered, so why had the court's attitude changed? A "death-sentence agreement," later widely circulated on the Internet, supplies the answer. The main contents of the document, dated May 17, 2004, and written on the official stationery of the Pingdingshan Intermediate People's Court, noted the demands made by the victim's parents that Li Huailiang be sentenced to "at least life imprisonment, if not death." There was also documentation of an agreement that if the Pingdingshan Intermediate Court acted in accordance with these demands, and even if the provincial high court sent the case back, the victim's parents would not issue further petitions. The agreement also bore the signatures of two village cadres.

On April 25, 2013, the Pingdingshan Intermediate Court retried Li Huailiang. The decision read before the court noted that the prosecution had presented five sets of evidence against Li Huailiang, and having examined among these the crime scene report, the autopsy report, and the material-evidence report, it could identify the body as Guo Xiaohong, the precise location of the crime, and the cause of death. Witness testimony from Du Yuhua, Guo Songzhang, and Li Quancheng could only show that Li Huailiang had also been digging up cicada larvae on the night of the event. Material evidence for the prosecution, including flip-flops, a pair of shorts, and a portable lamp, could only be shown to have belonged to Guo Xiaohong and bore no connection to Li Huailiang. Li had made a confession, but he had later recanted it; moreover, there were major inconsistencies in the confession, as well as points of contradiction with witness testimony and the crime scene report, with the result that Li's confession could not be used as a basis for ruling on the case. In the opinion of the court, the procuratorate's charges lacked sufficient grounds, there being many unclear facts and insufficient evidence. Finally, the court declared Li Huailiang innocent and set him free. After the decision was announced, the victim's family reacted with intense emotion, decrying the court for "harboring a murderer." According to some sources, a new investigation has been opened.[10]

In such cases, public opinion becomes a tool used by those handling the case. In the Zhao Xinjian case, the words of the judges typify this phenomenon:

> Faced with pressure from the victim's family, law enforcement officials cannot readily release the earliest suspect detained, insufficient evidence or not. And with repeated retrial, as well as harassment from family members and others, you say to yourself "What can you do?" and spend all your time putting out these fires.[11]

Adjudication must be made in adherence with legal principles, including the burden of proof, the presumption of innocence, and the collection of evidence in accordance with the law. So-called public opinion is complex and diverse and often capricious and contradictory. In criminal cases, the opinion of the defendant and his or her family will be contrary to the opinion of the victim and his or her family. Each side usually represents both sides of public opinion, never all of it. It is a mistake to confuse the aims of the victim's family with the aims of the people; to perform a similar substitution with the defendant's family would be no better. The judiciary must triangulate among three interests: those of the victim and the victim's family, those of the defendant and the defendant's family, and those of the public. The best way for the judiciary to balance these three interests is to hold fast to the provisions of the law—that is, to handle the case strictly in accordance with the law.

Chapter Seven
The Unlawfully Extended Custody with Tunnel Vision

1. The Unlawfully Extended Custody

Unlawfully extended custody and the use of torture to extort confession are two great blots on the Chinese criminal legal system. Unlawfully extended custody refers to the illegal act of detaining a suspect or the accused for a duration exceeding the period prescribed according to the Criminal Procedure Law. Unlawfully extended custody comes in both formal and substantial forms. The former refers to the extension of custody despite the expiration of the legal detention period and without formal application for further extension. The latter refers to cases in which an extension has been applied for formally, or else the detention seems to be in order, but in actuality has been unlawfully extended. Cases that are repeatedly retried or reinvestigated, for example, could be called cases of "protracted non-release."

A salient aspect of Chinese criminal procedure is high detention rates and long detention periods. In countries with a well-developed rule of law, pretrial criminal suspects are generally released on bail, with relatively few held in prison. In the United Kingdom, for example, the proportion of pretrial criminal suspects under detention is less than 10 percent. But in China, 80 percent of criminal suspects are detained, and 80 percent of those detained go on to be arrested.[1] According to Article 89 of the Chinese Criminal Procedure Law, detention should last no longer than three days, and can only be extended to seven days for unusual circumstances. Suspects who pose a flight risk, repeat offenders, and gangsters can be detained for up to thirty days, which can be extended seven additional days with judicial approval. Thus, the maximum period a criminal suspect can be detained without an arrest warrant is thirty-seven days. Before the Criminal Procedure Law was revised in 1996, public security officials used the more broadly defined measure "detention pending examination," or "sheltering for investigation," in place of criminal detention, as discussed in chapter six. This is what happened to Teng Xingshan: he was taken in for detention pending examination on December 6, 1987, and kept in detention until his arrest on September 2, 1998.

As for post-arrest detention, the Criminal Procedure Law again provides clear stipulations. Article 124 states: "The time limit for holding a criminal suspect in custody during investigation after arrest shall not exceed two months. If the case is complex and cannot be concluded within the time limit, an extension of one month may be allowed with the approval of the People's Procuratorate at the next higher level." And Article 126 stipulates the following:

> With respect to the following cases, if investigation cannot be concluded within the time limit specified in Article 124 of this law, an extension of two months may be allowed upon approval or decision by the People's Procuratorate of a province, autonomous region or municipality directly under the Central Government: (1) grave and complex cases in outlying areas where traffic is most inconvenient; (2) grave cases that involve criminal gangs; (3) grave and complex cases that involve people who commit crimes from one place to another; and (4) grave and complex cases that involve various quarters and for which it is difficult to obtain evidence.

Article 127 further states:

> If in the case of a criminal suspect who may be sentenced to fixed-term imprisonment of ten years at least, investigation of the case has still not concluded upon expiration of the extended time limit as provided in Article 126 of this Law, another extension of two months may be allowed upon approval or decision by the People's Procuratorate of a province, autonomous region or municipality directly under the Central Government.

According to these rules, the maximum time between arrest and case closure is seven months. Article 138 adds that the indictment review period is generally limited to one month but can be extended by half a month.

Article 202 stipulates that the trial in the court of first instance should generally last two months but can be extended by one month. Article 232 stipulates the trial in the court of second instance should generally last two months but can be extended by two months. According to these rules, the period a criminal suspect (the defendant) should spend in detention between arrest and the issue of a verdict should generally be approximately one year. But repeated retrial and additional investigations can spur a recalculation of the period without exceeding the sanction of the law; thus, a criminal suspect (the defendant) can be held for one and a half years—or more. But despite these rules and regulations, unlawfully extended custody remains common.

Unlawfully extended custody is an infringement of human rights. In addition, it prevents the establishment of an environment where the rule of law may be developed, and it lowers respect for the law. Unlawfully extended custody had become an extremely severe problem in China by the close of the twentieth century. According to the most authoritative statistics, between 50,000 and 80,000 people were detained unlawfully every year between 1993 and 1999 by various political organizations in China.[2] To address this, on July 23, 1999, the Central Political-Legal Work Committee announced its Notice Regarding the Handling of Cases according to Law and Resolutely Correcting the Problem of Unlawfully Extended Custody. In its wake, the Supreme People's Court, the Supreme People's Procuratorate, and the Ministry of Public Security one after the other announced their own notices regarding the correction and prevention of unlawfully extended custody.[3]

Our research found that unlawfully extended custody plays a role in wrongful conviction. In August 2006, a member of our study group conducted a series of symposia with law enforcement officials from all three departments in Harbin, Heilongjiang Province. During one conversation about the factors leading to wrongful conviction, a participant said the situation he feared most was to end up "riding the tiger and unable to get off." In other words, a suspect has been locked up for a long time, but there has not been enough evidence collected, so neither can a verdict be established nor can the suspect be released; consequently, the case is at stasis. The longer the suspect is detained, the harder it becomes to contemplate a release. In the end, the only viable solution is sentencing the suspect to fewer years.[4] When unlawfully extended custody occurs, and when further investigation has already proven ineffective, release and conviction begin to look like poor alternatives: one might give freedom to the guilty; the other might imprison the innocent. Finding themselves riding the tiger, many law enforcement officials stiffen their resolve to seek conviction, as the example of She Xianglin can well show.

2. The Four Inconsistent Confessions

Throughout the ten-day interrogation, She Xianglin never went into any detail about the circumstances of the crime. Thus, none of the investigators were able to ascertain the exact sequence of events. According to police interrogation transcripts, after admitting his guilt, Xianglin described four different scenarios and methods of murder. The fact that he felt compelled to issue four different statements illustrates the gamesmanship that went on between police and suspect:

> *Statement 1* (15 April): On the evening of 20 January 1994, I took Zhang Aiqing outside, and picked up a wooden stick outside the door on the way. I took her up the hill near the Yanmenkou Red Flag gravel factory and beat her to death with the stick, then I dumped her body in a sewer.

The investigators were not convinced that She Xianglin was being honest with this statement and thought he was using it to work out if they had found the body or not. In order to break him down, the investigators used aggressive language. One of them said, "Don't think we don't know about what you did. I'm telling you, if you've buried the body in the ground, we can dig down three feet. If you dumped it in the water, we can drain the water. We'll drain it dry!"

> *Statement 2* (17 April): On the evening of 20 January 1994, I took Zhang Aiqing outside. I saw my good friend Wei playing billiards outside the veterinarian's. I got Wei to take Aiqing to the water pump on the outskirts of the village, and to lock her up there. Three days later, I went with Wei to the pump, and we killed Aiqing with a rock. We threw her body into the well.

The investigators felt this new gambit to be more truthful. If the water pump had been the murder site, it would explain the mystery of how the body had been submerged in water for two months and not discovered by anyone. Also, if Xianglin had an accomplice, it would be useful in ascertaining the facts of the case and could help them uncover a new trail of evidence. The police followed this lead, but found the well to be watched over by a villager who slept in a room next to the pump at night and unlocked it during the day. Even if Aiqing and Wei had been the only ones who had gone to the pump room, it was impossible that no one would have seen her after three days. Consequently, the investigators believed that She Xianglin was still being dishonest, and they warned him that they could see through his clumsy lies. They felt they needed to let Xianglin believe they already had plenty of other information in order to trip him up.

That same day, good news arrived from the forensic investigators who had been searching for evidence at the pond. They had fished from the water a bag made of plastic, woven to look like snakeskin—it had four stones inside and a rope handle made of hemp attached to the top. The investigators proposed that after She Xianglin had knocked Zhang Aiqing unconscious, he had used the rope to tie her up, put the stones in the bag to weigh her down, and pushed her into the water so that she could not be found. After the body had been in the water for some time, they surmised that the rope had loosened, and the decomposing body had become more buoyant, enabling it to float to the surface. As the interrogation went on, the police continued to pressure She Xianglin: "Don't drip-feed us information. If you make things clear the first time, we can report that your attitude towards confession is good, and we'll be lenient on you. We know all about what you did—every detail. You thought you were being smart, tying up the body, dumping it in the water and using a storage bag filled with four stones to weigh it down. Did you really think we wouldn't find it?"

> *Statement 3* (19 April): During the day of 20 January 1994, I saw Wei by the veterinarian's and asked him over to my place in the evening. At 11 p.m., Wei came by, and the two of us took Zhang Aiqing to the pump room, changed her clothes, and took her to a mountain valley and beat her to death with a rock. We used a storage bag with four stones in it, tied her up, and dumped her body in the pond.

By the time Xianglin gave this confession, the investigators had discovered that Wei could not have participated in the murder. He had been seriously ill and was at the local hospital undergoing treatment. The hospital doctors issued a certificate to confirm this. The investigators came to the conclusion that Xianglin had named a random man to confuse the situation. They pointed out the gaps in Xianglin's statement and continued to add pressure, looking for a confession that he alone had killed his wife.

> *Statement 4* (21 April): When Zhang Aiqing was in a confused state, I dragged her out of bed, took her to an empty shed outside the village, and locked her up. At 2 a.m., I took our daughter to my parents' room and told them that my wife had run out and that I needed to go and look for her. After that, I took a torch, some rope, and clothes that I had prepared in advance and went back to the shed. I changed Aiqing's clothes, grabbed a storage bag I had already put in the shed, took her to a pond on the side of the mountain, and hit her on the head with a rock, which knocked her unconscious. I tied to her the bag with the four stones in it and pushed her into the water. The next afternoon, I put her discarded clothes into the stove at my house and burned them.

This time, the investigators believed Xianglin's confession to be "objective fact consistent with the case" and that it could be used to reinforce the other evidence, summarized as follows: She Xianglin was having an affair and therefore intended to eliminate his wife, who had developed a mental illness. After constructing a complicated scheme and making elaborate preparations, he put this plan into action. He had not only prepared a bag to use on the corpse but also procured replacement clothes as a red herring. After committing the crime, he had spread false information everywhere, suggesting that his wife had run away from home. After being detained, he toyed with the investigators and evaded interrogation in every possible way.

After obtaining the confession, the investigators still believed that the evidence needed to be strengthened further, so they decided to take She Xianglin to identify the exact locations where the crime had taken place. But ten consecutive days of interrogation had left Xianglin utterly exhausted. When the police first requested that he draw a diagram of the route he took, he seemed dazed and could not complete the drawing. With "assistance" he was finally able to do so. On the evening of April 21, the police took She Xianglin to identify the relevant locations. The files record the circumstances as follows:

> At 8 p.m., Group nine set out from Hechang Village with She Xianglin and the police to the shed where he had left the storage bag and locked up Zhang Aiqing.[5] The shed door faced east and had

no lock. Inside was a wooden bed. Group nine passed through town, went east along a public road for 500 meters and took a dirt road heading to Lüchong before arriving at a fork in the road and continuing to walk for one kilometer. The group then arrived at a pond, and She Xianglin pointed out a spot thirty meters from the bank where he had killed Zhang.

On April 22, Jingshan County police declared that the case of She Xianglin's deliberate murder of Zhang Aiqing had been fully investigated, and he was moved from "sheltered for investigation" to criminal detention. The next day, the investigation team requested the People's Procurator's Office in Jingshan County to approve Xianglin's arrest.[6] The approval was received from the procurator's office on April 28. Soon after, the investigation team used the relevant files to prepare "comprehensive materials" and a report on the "case-solving process." These were sent to the pretrial division of the police. After examination by the pretrial division, an opinion on prosecution was prepared. At this point, the process of police investigation ended, and the files were handed over to the procurator's office so that the trial could begin. For the smooth and successful handling of such a major case, the investigation team was praised for its work at a special meeting. The local newspaper reported that the police had arrested She Xianglin under suspicion of the murder of his wife.

Once the procurator's office received the files, it sent staff to the police station lockup to process She Xianglin for trial. When he saw the court officials, Xianglin became excited, repeatedly saying that he had not murdered anyone and that he had been forced by the police to give a false confession. The officials promised him that his case would be properly considered and seriously investigated. Once the procurator had examined the materials, he telephoned the criminal squad of the public security bureau and asked about the circumstances. A member of the criminal squad replied that investigators had acted according to the law at all times and had absolutely not extorted the confession, nor fabricated one. The squad member added that She Xianglin had definitely done it, noting that it was common at the trial stage for suspects to retract a previous confession.

By now, Mrs. She had finally obtained permission to see her son. Xianglin told her he had not killed anyone and that Zhang Aiqing had just run away from home. Mrs. She believed her son and believed that if she could find her daughter-in-law, she would be able to save her son. As she left the police station, she found herself filled with a sudden determination: she would move mountains to bring Aiqing back!

3. The First Instance Trial

The court system in China is divided into four levels: Basic People's Courts at the municipal and county levels; Intermediate People's Courts in major cities and municipalities; High People's Courts at the provincial level; and finally the Supreme People's Court in the capital. Similarly, the People's Procurator's Office functions on four levels: Basic, Intermediate, and High People's Procurator's Offices at the county, city, and provincial levels, respectively; and the Supreme People's Procurator's Office in Beijing.[7]

According to the provisions of the Criminal Procedure Law relating to the administration of trials, ordinary criminal cases should first be tried in the Basic People's Courts; cases that might result in sentences of death or life imprisonment should first be tried in the Intermediate People's Courts; cases of great importance to the province or municipality should first be tried in the High People's Court; and cases of national importance should first be tried in the Supreme People's Court. The Intermediate, High, and Supreme Courts also function as courts of appeal and can reexamine cases from lower courts. A case can only be appealed once—the so-called two-tier-trial system—and cases involving the death penalty must be reexamined by court-appointed specialists. The Criminal Procedure Law states that cases involving the death penalty on two years' probation must be approved by the High People's Court, and those cases involving the immediate application of the death penalty must be approved by the Supreme People's Court. Cases involving the death penalty must also undergo a reconsideration procedure, regardless of whether the defendant chooses to appeal. However, in 1983, in order to deal more quickly and effectively with cases involving "severe harm to social order," the Supreme People's Court authorized the High People's Court to approve the death penalty in cases of murder, rape, looting, and bombing, as well as any other cases that severely threaten public safety and social order.[8]

Because She Xianglin was suspected of the crime of intentional homicide and could be sentenced to life imprisonment or even the death penalty, the legal proceedings needed to be administered by the Intermediate People's Court in the city of Jingzhou. Accordingly, the files were sent to Jingzhou District People's Procuratorate for further examination. On September 22,

1994, the Jingzhou Procuratorate formally raised the charge of intentional homicide against She Xianglin.

Simultaneously, Zhang Aiqing's relatives were looking for people to sign a "jointly written letter"—a petition of sorts. Over two hundred local people signed the letter, stating that She Xianglin had no respect for the law or common morals, that he was prone to drunken arguments and brawls, and that he had committed adultery and murdered his sick wife. This intolerable breach of morality had created great public discontent, and the signatories demanded that the government severely punish Xianglin. This put great pressure on local officials.

The Criminal Procedure Law at the time required the court to deliver a copy of the indictment from the procurator's office to the defendant at least seven days before the trial and to inform the defendant of his right to appoint a legal representative for his defense.[9] On September 30—the day before the National Day holiday—the Jingzhou Intermediate People's Court notified She Xianglin that he could appoint a defender. Because Xianglin's family was uneducated about such things, he had no idea how to engage a lawyer, so the court appointed one on his behalf. Although the Criminal Procedure Law had no clear-cut guidelines at the time, the courts typically appointed a defense lawyer for defendants who might be subject to the death penalty.[10] Xianglin's lawyer made use of the time before the trial to inspect the court files and extract relevant information, but considering the short time frame, his preparation was relatively limited.

On Friday, October 7, 1994, the Jingzhou Intermediate People's Court began the trial of She Xianglin for intentional homicide. The courtroom was small. At the front, above the judges' stand, hung the emblem of the People's Republic of China; on the left side of the courtroom was the public procurator's place, and on the right, the defense lawyer's. Directly opposite the judges were the defendant's stand and the public gallery. There were not many people watching the proceedings, just a few friends and relatives of the victim and the defendant. The court reporter and the defense lawyer were already sitting in their respective places, waiting for the proceedings to begin.

Three judges in dark blue uniform and two procurators in green uniform walked into the courtroom. The uniforms were in a military style, with decorated collars and epaulettes, and peaked caps bearing the national emblem.[11] The three judges formed a panel, with the presiding judge sitting in the middle.[12] After declaring the judicial session open, two bailiffs led She Xianglin in from a side door and sat him on a chair in the defendant's stand.

The presiding judge began by asking the defendant's name, age, and other information, such as when he was arrested and whether he had received the indictment. After that, the presiding judge announced the names of the other judges, the court reporter, the public procurator, and the defense lawyer. He informed the defendant of his rights: to withdraw his application, to speak in his own defense, to ask questions of witnesses, to request that evidence be presented, and to make a final statement. After the presiding judge confirmed that the defendant was aware of these rights and did not wish to challenge anything, he added that if the defense asked to summon new witnesses to court, collect new material or written evidence, or reinspect and appraise existing evidence, the court would decide whether or not to grant those requests.

Once the legal proceedings had begun, the presiding judge asked the public procurator to read out the indictment. The lawyer rose to his feet and stiltedly obliged, accusing She Xianglin of deliberately murdering Zhang Aiqing, an action in offense of Article 132 of the Criminal Procedure Law, and requesting that legal proceedings be conducted to investigate his responsibility for the crime.

When the presiding judge asked the defendant to make a statement, emphasizing his responsibility to tell the truth, She Xianglin said, "I didn't kill anyone. The confession was beaten out of me by the police."

The presiding judge moved on to ask the public procurator if he had questions for the defendant; he said that he had none. The judge then asked the defense lawyer if he had questions; he also had none. The judge then asked the court reporter to read out a summary of the evidence. After this was done and after neither side expressed any objections, the judge declared that the investigation stage of the trial was over and that the court would now hear arguments.

The presiding judge asked the public procurator to make a statement. The statement was extremely simple. He first briefly repeated the parts of the indictment that indicated that the defendant had committed a crime, mentioning the related evidence. He then stated that the facts of the case were straightforward, and that there was abundant evidence. Given that public anger was high, he added, he urged the court to punish the defendant severely.

The procurator sat down, and the defense lawyer was asked to speak next. He stated that there was insufficient evidence to convict She Xianglin. Even if the court accepted the evidence of the forensic investigators and the witnesses, it was merely circumstantial, proving only that Zhang Aiqing had died and that She Xianglin had a motive to murder her. In fact, the only evidence that showed She Xianglin to have actually killed Zhang Aiqing was the defendant's confession. And since the defendant had stated that his confession had been extracted from him under torture, it should not be held up by the court. What is more, he added, the defendant had suggested four different methods by which the murder was supposedly committed, and the public procurator simply chose one of these and maintained that it was true. This was particularly unreasonable, he said. On top of all this, the charges stated that the defendant had taken Zhang Aiqing's clothes home and burned them, but there was no evidence of any kind to verify this. In closing, the defense lawyer stated that the evidence could not be considered sufficient to prove that She Xianglin had murdered Zhang Aiqing. The existing evidence could not eliminate the possibility that someone else had murdered her. The lawyer requested that the court find the defendant not guilty.

The presiding judge asked the procurator if he had any further comments. Rising to his feet again, the procurator stated that She Xianglin's confession was the key to the case. It was completely consistent with the other evidence available, including the autopsy report and the storage bag filled with stones. This bag was an especially damning piece of evidence because according to the case files, the investigators had extracted it from the pond based on Xianglin's own confession. Experience had shown, he claimed, that if investigators find corroborating evidence based on a suspect's confession, then the confession was genuinely reliable. As for the question of why no one had been able to find the ashes of the clothes at Xianglin's house, that was to be expected, because at the time the body was found, the murder would have taken place over two months before.

When it became clear that neither side had any more arguments, the presiding judge asked the defendant for a final statement. She Xianglin repeated that he had not killed anyone, noting that the police often used force to extract confessions. The judge said the court would consider the issue of whether the confession had been extorted. He then declared the trial over and set a date for the announcement of the verdict and sentence.

On October 13, six days after the trial had begun, the Jingzhou Intermediate People's Court in Hubei Province found She Xianglin guilty of the crime of intentional homicide, sentenced him to death, and permanently deprived him of his political rights.[13] When one of the judges went to the police lockup to inform Xianglin of the decision, Xianglin refused to accept it and wanted to appeal. The judge told him the Hubei Province High

People's Court would reconsider his case as a matter of course, because of the sentence of death.

4. The Second Instance Trial

Throughout this period, Mrs. She had been searching for the whereabouts of Zhang Aiqing. She searched everywhere, walking to villages of every size in her county and neighboring ones. In December 1994, in the village of Yaoling, near the city of Tianmen to the south of Jingshan, she finally heard news of Zhang Aiqing. A man told her that two months before, a mentally ill woman had arrived at the village. The woman had refused to eat or drink, and she would not talk, but sometimes she could be found sleeping in the local cemetery. The villagers took pity on her and gave her some food and clothes. One family took her to their home, where she had stayed for a couple of days. Then the woman had just left, as mysteriously as she had arrived.

After Mrs. She heard this, she immediately sought out Mr. Ni, the party secretary of that village.[14] Once Mr. Ni had heard the story, he wrote a certificate of sincerity, on which he affixed the official seal of the Communist Party Branch Committee, Yaoling Village, Hezhen County, Tianmen City. The certificate was dated December 30, 1994, and its contents were as follows:

> In the middle of October some people from Group Eight in our village—Ni Xinhao, Ni Boqing, Li Qingzhi and others—discovered a mentally ill woman. She was about thirty, had a Jingshan accent and was about 150 centimetres tall, with an oily, pockmarked face. She said her surname was Zhang, that she had a six-year-old daughter at home and that she had become lost while trying to visit some relatives. She seemed to have the energy level of an old woman. She stayed at Ni Xinhao's house for two days, but after that we do not know where she went. I hereby confirm these facts and request that they be investigated.

Thanking Mr. Ni again and again, Mrs. She left the village.

When she returned to Jingshan, Mrs. She took the certificate of sincerity to the police. After a policeman had examined it, he said only, "This is too late."

"Why?" Mrs. She asked.

"They've decided it already."

"Can't it be appealed to the provincial court?"

"I'm not sure," the policeman replied. "I'll give it to the bosses. Come back later."

When the senior police saw the certificate of sincerity, they felt it was unreliable. Zhang Aiqing had been murdered, and it was impossible for anyone to have seen her half a year later. Mrs. She had clearly found someone to write a fake letter because she wanted to save her son. Granted, some of the villagers had probably seen some crazy woman, but it could not have been Zhang Aiqing; they must have written down a description that Mrs. She gave them. Besides, it would be a lot of extra trouble to go through an appeal with new evidence. The senior police produced a document outlining their position, titled "Process of Re-examination and Verification of Materials."

But She Xianglin's family was unaware of this. They believed that the certificate of sincerity would save him, and might even help the government find the real murderer.

On October 10, 1995, the Hubei Province High People's Court handed down its reconsideration in the case of She Xianglin's intentional homicide. It found that the facts were unclear, and the evidence insufficient. It repealed the original decision and sent the case back for reinvestigation.[15] The judge singled out some concrete problems and dubious areas leading to the previous decision: for example, the constant contradictions in the defendant's statements, as well as his repeated confessions and subsequent retractions; his four different statements about the course of events surrounding the murder of his wife; the unfairness of using only one of these statements as a basis for the decision; relying on the defendant's confession to maintain that the murder weapon was a stone without any other basis for this belief; the question of Zhang Aiqing's missing clothes; and the reliance on pieces of indirect testimony that did not form a coherent chain of evidence. For all these reasons, the court decided that the possibility that the deceased had run away from home and been murdered by someone else must be considered. Although the relatives of the deceased had provided a petition with over 220 signatures demanding that the murderer be executed with all speed, cases for which the sentence might be death required "ironclad evidence."

Once the Jingzhou Intermediate People's Court received the reconsideration ruling, it returned the case to the procurator's office, which then sent it back to the police requesting further evidence. The police, however, believed that the case was water under the bridge and that there was no longer any means of gathering new evidence. Also, since the defendant had completely retracted his confession, there was no means of verifying any of the oral testimony. Hence, they produced an "explanation of the situation," which discussed their process of investigation, emphasizing that "the entire process had been lawful, and that the confession had not been extracted under torture." The document was endorsed with the seal of the Jingshan County Public Security Bureau. When the procurator's office received this and consulted with the Intermediate Court, they believed the documents to be insufficient to satisfy the demands of the High Court, and sent them back to be modified. The police stuck to the belief that the evidence was enough to convict She Xianglin and refused to investigate further. The case, therefore, was shelved.

Additionally, the local government was facing pressure from two different sources. Zhang Aiqing's family continued to petition and demand for the severe punishment of She Xianglin. At the same time, She Xianglin's family, with its certificate of sincerity, was petitioning and lobbying for his release. Suddenly, the case that the government had lauded as a model of policing had turned into a hot potato they could not drop. Not only were they grappling with whether or not the facts of the case were accurate, but they were also dealing with the reputation of the police and their own future prospects. With their backs to the wall, the Jingshan police had no choice but to go on the offensive. Knowing that the certificate of sincerity was their biggest threat, they devised a plan of attack.

Mrs. She was seized by the police on the grounds of "constant petitioning" and taken to the police lockup, where she was imprisoned for nine months.[16] Originally a sturdy village woman, when Mrs. She was released she was half deaf and blind, and died a few months later. She Xianglin's older brother was imprisoned on the same grounds for more than forty days and was released with a warning to never go above the police again. In addition, the police tracked down some of the villagers from Yaoling Village who had supported the certificate of sincerity and forced them to change their testimony to state that no such woman had been in their village. The villagers resisted, and as a result, two of them were imprisoned in the Jingshan County Public Security Bureau for more than three months, while others were compelled to flee the area. What had begun as a seemingly straightforward lawsuit had become a matter of life and death.

Chapter Eight

The Nominal Checks among the Police, the Procuratorate, and the Court

1. The Investigation-Centered Criminal Procedure Model

The criminal justice proceedings in China follow an assembly-line model. Article 7 of the Criminal Procedure Law states: "In conducting criminal proceedings, the People's Courts, the People's Procuratorates and the Public Security Bureaus shall divide responsibilities, coordinate their efforts and check each other to ensure the correct and effective enforcement of law."

Under this system, the public security bureaus are in charge of investigation, the procuratorates authorize approval for arrests and institute public prosecutions, and the courts are responsible for adjudication.[1] The work of the three branches is divided and arranged in sequence, with the common goal of maintaining close control over the quality of case procedure, guaranteeing that the criminal justice system produces "social products" that are up to standard, thus fulfilling their duty to fight crime and protect the public. The first "production stage"—the police investigation—is seen as the most important, but such a model has the propensity to overlook the importance of the prosecution and the trial, which become mere issues of inspection and review at the later stages.

Under the investigation-centered assembly-line model, the procuratorates and the courts basically deal with the documents and records in the case files, which have been sent up by the police investigators. The documents and records form the main bulk of evidence and the basis on which procuratorates decide whether to issue an indictment and on which the courts ultimately pass judgment. Both the procuratorates and the courts review and evaluate these documents and records, which include interrogation transcripts as well as records of examinations, searches, and identifications. In practice, the procuratorate frequently uses a revised version of what is called the "proposal letter for prosecution," submitted by police investigators, as the formal indictment, while the court uses a revised version of that formal indictment as the judgment. It then becomes common for the written decision of the courts to agree in large part with the documentation of the investigators.

Throughout its exceptionally long history, Chinese criminal proceedings have typically followed the investigation-centered model. The review and inspection leading to the indictment and the judgment then become mere appendages; thus, there is nothing unusual about having both the procuratorate and the court accept the decision of the public security bureau.

Opinions vary widely on the subtle relations among the public security bureau, the people's procuratorate, and the people's court.[2] A metaphor goes that the public security bureau slaughters the pig, the procuratorate dehairs it, and finally the court sells its flesh. The assembly line of production includes three stages: slaughtering (detecting), dehairing (prosecuting), and selling (judging). Obviously, the first stage of the production line is most important, because whether the pig (case) dies or not depends on the public security bureau's knife. Although the metaphor is not gracious or subtle, it reflects to some extent the characteristics of the relations among the people's court, the people's procuratorate, and the public security bureau. In the procedural mode—investigating by the public security bureau, prosecuting by the procuratorate, and judging by the court—the three departments divide the work and cooperate with one another, with the aim of guaranteeing that the criminal cases are handled properly and ensuring the satisfactory "social product" produced by the criminal judicial system.[3] As the first stage of criminal procedure, the investigation becomes the central stage in finding the facts of the case; while the trial is relatively easy to lose its function in finding the facts, since it has turned into a course merely checking the product of the upper reaches.

There is another metaphor used: that of the public security bureau cooking, the procuratorate selling, and the court eating. Also embodying the assembly-line model, this comparison is meaningful and thought provoking in consideration of the relations among production, vending, and consumption. In the vendor's market, vending (prosecution) is decided by production (investigation), and the consumption (judgment) depends on the buying (prosecution). Investigation, therefore, is at the center of criminal procedure. Yet in the buyer's market, the vending is decided by consumption, and the production depends on the vending. Thus, it becomes a judgment-centered proceeding. However, the criminal procedure in China has not entered the stage of the buyer's market, and so the investigation-centered model prevails. The function of the Communist Party's political-legal work committees is an endorsement for this model.

The political-legal work committees at each party level are leaders of the three branches of criminal justice, with their main responsibilities being to support and supervise each branch in exercising its functions and powers; to coordinate relationships among the three; and to oversee cases that are controversial, important, or in doubt. In practice, local political leaders place too much emphasis on the importance of "coordinating efforts." And if a case is noteworthy or difficult, the committee urges the three branches to "handle the case cooperatively," which often means holding meetings attended by the heads of the three branches to discuss the case. The three branches are to manage cases with attention to the principles of "coordination in battle" and "unity of command," which more often than not means that when the public security bureau has finished its investigation, the procuratorate can do no more than issue the indictment, and the court can do no more than issue a guilty verdict. When the political and legal-work committee becomes involved, it often does no more than coordinate matters in such a way that the procuratorate and the court align with the findings and decision of the public security bureau. The situation is just as some scholars have already pointed out:

> Because the joint-handling system lacks any mechanism of checks and balances, and because those employing the system lack any concept of due process, the system is easily thrown off-kilter. The joint meetings are not simple discussions of the facts and the law, but instead take as their main theme the compromises the departments will make on the case to arrive at consensus. Once the joint meeting becomes nothing more than a process of decision-making based on compromises while ignoring what should be the ultimate aim— adherence to the rule of the law—then law enforcement has lost its most important raison d'etre: justice.[4]

The joint-handling case system emphasizes cooperation and unified command: after the public security bureau completes its investigation and the procuratorate its prosecution, the court would have no choice but to convict the defendant at the trial. It is said that to minimize the amount of paperwork, some judges require prosecutors to submit the indictment electronically so that they can amend the document themselves as necessary, even if this means changing just a few words. It does beg the question of the point of the criminal trial in China.

2. A Decision of the Committee

At the beginning of the 1990s, China began a process of merging cities and prefectures. One working paper, published in 1993 by the State Council, suggested: "Regional institutional reform should be combined with the simultaneous adjustment of administrative subdivisions. State agencies at all levels need to be dramatically simplified. In principle, where prefecture-level cities and existing prefectures co-exist, they should be administratively merged."[5] On December 2, 1996, after the State Council approved the merger of Jingzhou Prefecture with Jingzhou City, Jingshan County, which was administered by Jingzhou City, was incorporated into the administration of neighboring Jingmen City.

In October 1997, the Political-Legal Work Committee of Jingmen City convened a meeting attended by representatives from the Jingmen City courts, the procurator's office, and the police, as well as from the Jingshan County Politics and Law Committee.[6] At the meeting, while the police representatives continued to emphasize their belief that She Xianglin had murdered Zhang Aiqing, the court representatives reemphasized the problems that the Hubei Province High People's Court had raised about the lack of clarity in the case. After some discussion, the Jingmen City Committee decided to apply the modified principle: "If the proof is unclear, the sentence should be lighter." They intended to downgrade the case from the intermediate court to the basic court before proceeding with a three-step plan. First, the Jingshan County People's Procurator's Office would raise charges in the Jingshan County Basic People's Court. Second, the county court would attempt to "cap the case at first instance"—that is, it would sentence the defendant to the severest term available in cases of doubtful guilt, in this case, fifteen years' imprisonment. Then, the intermediate court would affirm this sentence, thereby ensuring that the legal process would be kept local and not return to the provincial high court, which might require further police investigation.

On June 15, 1998, the Jingshan County Basic People's Court sentenced She Xianglin to fifteen years' imprisonment and deprived him of his political rights for five years. On September 22, 1998, the Jingmen City Intermediate People's Court rejected She Xianglin's application for appeal and affirmed the original decision, stating in its ruling that the murder charges had been substantiated by the forensic evidence, photographs of the autopsy, reports of the murder locations, the oral testimony of witnesses, and the defendant's "diagram of his route," which had been verified by the police. The ruling took immediate effect, and She Xianglin was taken to Hubei Shayang Prison to serve his sentence.

In prison, She Xianglin complained and appealed unceasingly. He wrote thick volumes of appeal documents and kept several diaries, which revealed some thought-provoking details about the interrogations he had undergone:

(1) At one point I said I had used a stone to murder her. That was because the previous time I had said I used a wooden stick, which the investigators pressured me to produce. But I hadn't killed anyone, so how could I do that? I said it was a stone instead, so that if they asked again, I could just hand over any old stone. That way I might not have to suffer so much.

(2) The storage bag was something the investigators told me about. They had found a storage bag in the pond that looked as if it were made of snakeskin and they made me mention it in my confession.

(3) The investigators made me draw a diagram of Guanqiao Reservoir but I had never been there, and since I had never killed anyone, how could I draw what happened? On the afternoon of 21 April 1994, when the investigators realised that I was unable to tell them the location of the body, they pulled me to a desk and drew a diagram for me and made me copy it.

(4) On the way to the scene of the crime, we arrived at an intersection on the side of a mountain. I began to turn down one road, but then the investigators pulled me in another direction, saying, "No, over this way."

(5) When we got to the pond, they asked me where I had killed her. I pointed to a random place. They took a photo and demanded I show them the stone I was supposed to have used as the murder weapon. As it happened, there weren't any stones nearby so they took me to another location and asked me where I had dumped the body. There was a lot of rubbish scattered

nearby and so I said that I had dumped the body there. They took a photo.

(6) After ten days of beatings, I was numb and tired. My whole body was bruised, and I couldn't walk or stand. I only wanted one thing, which was to rest. I would comply without hesitation to their demands so long as they would let me rest.

She Xianglin had no idea whether his notes were being read by anyone, but it seemed as if they were disappearing into the void. When his family came to visit, he urged them to appeal to higher authorities, but their efforts yielded no results. She Xianglin's only hope was that the real murderer would come forward. He had no idea where that person was, but he felt certain the murderer knew he was being wrongfully imprisoned. He would call out in his sleep and awaken to a different nightmare. As time went on, he began to lose hope.

3. The Pretrial Decision

The criminal trials of the first instance are commonly held by a collegial panel of three judges or people's jurors. The pretrial decision of the political and legal-work committee of the party makes the collegial panel a figurehead. In China, the political and legal-work committees at all levels exercise direct leadership over the people's court, the people's procuratorate, and the public security bureau. The committees' main tasks are to urge law enforcement agencies to uphold and exercise their functions and powers independently and in accordance with the law, to coordinate the working relationships of all departments, and to deal with important matters concerning politics and law as well as other major and controversial cases. Some political and legal-work committees coordinate the people's courts, people's procuratorates, and public security bureaus when the three departments have differing opinions, and make decisions for the three. This practice renders obsolete the existence of the collegial panel.

In a 1994 murder case in Chongqing, the police identified Tong Limin as the murderer, but the procuratorate felt the evidence to be insufficient. In 1998, the Chongqing Political and Legal-Work Committee called several meetings of the relevant department heads to review the Tong Limin case. They failed to reach an agreement, leading the committee to decide on the policy of "prescribing lesser punishment in case of doubt" and so demand that the court issue a guilty verdict but still keep the accused alive should circumstances require a change in verdict. The committee chairman said, "Should the verdict be incorrect, you will not take collective responsibility. All responsibility falls on the shoulders of the Committee. But any restitution payments will have to come from the procuratorate." In December 1998, the procuratorate issued an indictment. In October 1999, the court gave Tong Limin a suspended death sentence. After he had spent 2,773 days in detention, the case was reviewed and Tong Limin was declared innocent and set free in 2002.[7]

In all these cases, whether the defendants should be convicted is not decided at the court session but in the meetings of the political-legal work committee held beforehand, further illustrating the nominalization of criminal trials. Overall, as producing evidence, impeaching evidence, assessing evidence, and making judgment at the trial are all nominal formalities, it can be concluded that the criminal trial in China has lost its function.

Clearly, these wrongful convictions arose from errors committed at the investigation stage, but these "facts unclear, evidence insufficient" cases passed muster with both the procuratorate and the courts, flowing swiftly down the line in trial after trial, in the end becoming distinctly inferior products of the entire criminal justice system. This reflects a major deficiency in current Chinese criminal justice, namely that the three branches overlap more than sufficiently, yet check each other insufficiently or nominally. The main purpose of having three branches with separate powers in criminal justice is to ensure checks and balances, not to encourage total coordination. Only real checks among the three branches can help prevent further wrongful convictions.

Chapter Nine

The Nominalization of Courtroom Trials

1. The Function of Courtroom Trials

In developed countries governed by the rule of law, the core of criminal justice must be in the courtrooms. The collegial panel (or single judge) must be the actual decision maker. But in China, the importance of court hearings has been undermined; in other words, the courtroom trial has been defunctionalized or become a nominal proceeding.

At present, the courts determine the facts and make judgment not by hearing testimony and cross-examination and by examining physical and documentary evidence as it is submitted, but by examining a case file prepared before or after the courtroom trial. In other words, verdicts are not the products of a trial presided over by a judge but the products of "the judges behind the judges." Courtroom trials in China do not have a substantial role to play in criminal procedure and have become so inessential that they are now a mere formality. A major reason for this strange situation is that the trial committees overstep their boundaries.

Article 149 of the Chinese Criminal Procedure Law states the following:

> After the trial and deliberations, the collegial panel shall render a judgment. With respect to a difficult, complex or major case, on which the collegial panel considers it difficult to make a decision, the collegial panel shall refer the case to the president of the court for him to decide whether to submit the case to the judicial committee for discussion and decision. The collegial panel shall execute the decision of the judicial committee.

In practice, when the collegial panel meets with a "difficult, complex or major case," it will often submit the case to the trial committee for discussion because the verdict of the committee is more authoritative, and if the verdict should turn out to have been issued in error, the committee takes responsibility. In such cases, the verdict comes not from the trial judge but from judges who have not participated in the trial. In such cases, the opinion of the trial committee may not agree with that of the collegial panel, but the latter can only defer to the former, even if this results in wrongful conviction.

Courtroom trials ought to be the last line of defense against unjust verdicts, but they are now undermined to such a degree that they have become inessential. This not only damages the overall judiciary system but also prevents substantial justice, given that it often leads to wrongful conviction. The fact that what should be inadmissible evidence (such as a confession extorted through the use of torture) frequently makes it into the courts without obstruction is yet another indication of this defunctionalized process. Only by making the courtroom trial a valid and integral stage of criminal justice procedure can the Chinese criminal justice system strengthen its ability to avoid wrongful convictions.

As set forth in the introduction, false witness testimony is a major evidential cause of wrongful convictions—second only to false confession—as it can go through the proceedings and be used as a basis for judgments, mainly because most of the witnesses do not appear at the court for examination and impeachment. This illustrates one essential problem in Chinese criminal justice: the nominalization of courtroom trials.

In Chinese, adjudication by judges in the courts can be called, for short, "courtroom trials," which refer to

> legal proceedings that begin the opening of proceedings by the People's Court, with the participation of the public prosecutor, the litigants, and other participants in the proceedings, and also includes the reception to and interpretation of evidence and exposition of the facts presented by the two sides, the unfolding of argumentation in accordance with the law, and finally includes the determination of the guilt of the defendant based in accordance with the law, as well as whether punishment is warranted, and what, if any, punishment is appropriate.[1]

Since the essential function of the criminal procedure is to determine whether the defendants are guilty or not, the core stage of criminal justice should be the courtroom, and the substantive phase in the proceedings should be the trial. In China, unfortunately, the courtroom trial is in many cases merely a nominal formality. Judgments are not reached as a result of listening to and examining the evidence in the court, and in some cases, they are not even determined by the judges who sit in the trial but by the judges behind them. I pondered over the existing criminal trial system in China, asking myself whether it was really necessary to hold a courtroom trial at the price of human and financial resources when the judges could reach the same conclusion without hearing the case directly. In response to this question, I led a group of young researchers to conduct an empirical study on courtroom trials in criminal cases (hereafter referred to as "criminal trials") in China.

2. The Features of the Nominalization of Criminal Trials

Since the spring of 2009, members of the Empirical Study of Criminal Trials project at Renmin University of China Law School have conducted empirical research on the current situation and problems of criminal trials in China by way of distributing and collecting questionnaires, holding informal discussions, conducting interviews, auditing trials, and collecting case materials on the Internet. Members of this project audited 45 trials in Beijing and Hangzhou in 2009, and analyzed 292 actual criminal cases broadcast by the Internet program *Trial Now,* on the China Court Net website.[2] We found that to a significant extent, the nominalization of criminal trials in China has spread widely, which could be reflected in the whole proceedings of the court.

The Nominalization of Producing Evidence in Criminal Trials

The public prosecutor bears the burden of proving the guilt of the defendant in criminal trials. Accordingly, producing evidence by the public prosecutor is the essence of the whole of the criminal trial. In terms of the categories of evidence, documentary evidence submitted by the prosecutor takes precedence, followed by witness testimony. In the 292 criminal cases webcast on *Trial Now,* the prosecutors offered 1,924 pieces of documentary evidence, 6.59 pieces per case, with the most being 90 pieces for one particular case; they provided 1,286 pieces of testimony, 4.4 pieces per case, with the most being 31 pieces for one particular case.

Since it is easy to present documentary evidence at trial—that is, present original copies or duplicates—the nominalization of producing evidence mainly refers to the defect in witness testimony. The nonappearance of a witness in court makes the public prosecutor's burden of producing evidence exist only in name. In addition to the 1,286 pieces of testimony submitted by the prosecutors and the 27 pieces of testimony brought forth by the defenders in the 292 criminal cases, merely 39 witnesses attended the court, accounting for 3 percent of all the witnesses.[3] Limited by time constraints of the trials, prosecutors for the most part simply read some of the main points of the records in the case files. Consequently, for judges, defendants, and the defenders, it is difficult to comprehend the entire testimony without context. The defendant and defender have the right to introduce evidence of innocence during the trial, but in practice, they rarely exercise this right. Take the 292 web-broadcasted criminal cases as an example. Not only did defenders put forth evidence in only 34 cases—11.64 percent of the 292 cases—but the amount of evidence was pitiably low compared with that put forward by the prosecutors. Apart from the great disparity between the number of testimonies offered by prosecutors and the number offered by defenders, there are wide gaps between the other kinds of evidence produced by each side, such as the documentary evidence (1,924 copies by prosecutors, 64 copies by defenders), physical evidence (419 pieces by prosecutors, 18 pieces by defenders), and video documents (22 pieces by prosecutors, 1 piece by defenders). Moreover, the prosecutors produced 506 pieces of defendants' statements, 484 pieces of victims' statements, 358 pieces of experts' conclusions, and 204 pieces of records of inquest and examination; the quantity of the evidence introduced by defenders is negligible, but such a wide gap between the amount of evidence offered by prosecutors and the amount offered by defenders is normal. Although there are times when the evidence submitted by the defender is effective, it happens too infrequently to reverse the nominalization of the course of producing evidence in criminal trials. In other words, it is the production of evidence by the prosecutor that principally characterizes the production of evidence in criminal trials in China.

Given that prosecutors may produce evidence before and after the trial by transferring the case files to the courts, the production and submission of evidence at the trial becomes a mere ritual. Before the amendment of the Criminal Procedure Law in 1996, the pretrial transfer of case files to the court had been the practice in China. After a decision had been reached to prosecute the accused, the prosecutors would submit an indictment with all the files of the criminal case, including all the evidence, to the court. In fact, this "case-file transfer" system made the courtroom procedure merely functionary: the judges would have formed their opinion before the trial even began. Having drawn from the experience of the Anglo-American law system, China established the indictment-only system when revising the Criminal Procedure Law in 1996—that is, the prosecutor need only submit the indictment and the copies of primary evidence to the court, instead of transferring all the case records.[4] The principal official of the Law Committee of the People's Congress explains:

> In order to strengthen the course of trial and stimulate the functions of prosecution and defence, we have made the following amendments and supplements in the draft. . . . If the case is accepted by the people's court with the attachment of the list of evidence, a list of names of the witnesses, copies of the primary evidence or photographs, the people's court should hold a session to hear. The authenticity of the evidence should be tested after cross-examination at the court session rather than before the trial.[5]

However, owing to its failure to eradicate the judges' dependence on criminal case files, this reform has not yet elicited the expected effect.

Article 42 in Provisions on Some Problems concerning the Practice of Criminal Procedure Law, drawn up by the Supreme People's Court, the Supreme People's Procuratorate, the Ministry of Public Security, the Ministry of State Security, and the Law Committee of the People's Congress, provides that

> the evidence material, which the prosecutors prepare for showing, reading or broadcasting at the trial, should be submitted to the court exactly at the trial. If it is unattainable at the trial, the prosecutors should submit it within three days of adjournment. As to the testimony, which has been shown, read or broadcast at the trial without the attendance of the witness, if the witness has offered different testimony, the prosecutor should submit all the testimony to the court within three days after adjournment.[6]

According to this provision, the prosecutor still needs to submit the criminal case file to the court; however, the time of submission has changed—from before the trial to after the trial. At present, we practice the system of submitting part of the file before the trial and submitting the rest after the trial. When we discussed this as part of our research with the judges from

Hangzhou, some of them said that frankly, as long as the prosecutor submitted the criminal case files to the court, it would be impossible to avoid the nominalization of trials. The judges make their decisions based on the evidence in the files submitted by prosecutors outside the trial, rather than on the evidence put forth at the trial.[7] Due to the effective quoting of evidence found in the files submitted by prosecutors outside the trial, the course of quoting evidence at the trial has become nothing but a ritual.

The Nominalization of Impeaching Evidence in Criminal Trials

Impeaching evidence refers to challenging or questioning by the litigants and their legal representatives, including prosecutors, to the evidence put forth by the opposite side at the trial.

By pointing out evidentiary flaws, the act of cross-examination plays an important role in influencing attestation of evidence by the judge. Article 47 of the Criminal Procedure Code in China provides that testimony should not be grounds for a case unless it has been impeached by the prosecutor, victim, defendant, and defender, and verified after hearing the testimony of other witnesses. Correspondingly, Article 58 of the Interpretation on Some Problems in the Practice of the Criminal Procedure Code of the People's Republic of China, issued by the Supreme People's Court in 1998, prescribes that

> the evidence shall not be grounds for a case until it has been verified through the course of presenting, identifying and impeaching at the trial. The witnesses attending court shall be questioned by the prosecutor, victim, defendant and defender. Their testimony shall not be grounds for a case until verified.

Impeaching evidence by cross-examination should be an indispensable aspect of the criminal trial.

During criminal trials in China, after the evidence has been presented by one side, the judge asks for the opinion of the other side. Objections are rarely raised. Of the 292 cases we looked at, we found 5,817 pieces of evidence presented by the prosecutors and the accused. Of this, witness testimony had been questioned most frequently (16.67%); after this, documentary evidence (11.92%); victims' statements (9.83%); statement of the defendant and justification (7.53%); experts' conclusions (5.14%); video footage (4.34%); material evidence (3.18%); and then records of inquests and inspection (2.83%).

A majority of the queries related to the authenticity of the evidence, a minority to validity and relevance of the evidence.

Article 157 of the Criminal Procedure Law provides that

> testimony without the appearance of the witness at the trial, the experts' conclusions, records of inspection and other documentary evidence should be read at the trial. The judges shall hear the opinions of the public prosecutor, the parties involved, the defenders and the agents *ad litem*.

In consideration of the basic form of presenting evidence—that is, reading aloud from the records—the basic form of cross-examination in China is to question the evidence recorded on paper.

Impeachment of evidence clears up doubt. The substantive characteristic of cross-examination rests with questioning the evidence presented by the opposite side and with face-to-face confrontation. During the course of cross-examination, query and oppugner work together. The ultimate aim of cross-examination is to impeach evidence; therefore, questioning the one who has presented the evidence, including any witness or expert, is of importance. Merely submitting an opposing opinion should not be taken as effective cross-examination. Without the appearance of the witnesses, expert examiners, and the like, what remains is the evidence on paper, which thus reduces impeachment into a mere formality.

The Nominalization of Assessing Evidence in Criminal Trials

The assessment of evidence here refers to the judicial assessment of the admissibility, reliability, and weight of the evidence submitted. As the final phase of judicial proof, the assessment of evidence should be deemed the fundamental job of the court. Depending on the time and site, the assessment of evidence could be classified as assessment at the trial or assessment after the trial. The former means that at the court session, the judges assess the evidence introduced by one party and challenged by the other. For the latter, the judges complete the assessment of the evidence after the trial. In order to meet the requirement of criminal trial reform, assessment of the evidence should be done during the court session.

Producing evidence, impeaching evidence, and assessing evidence are the inseparable trinity of a criminal trial. Assessment of evidence makes the judicial decision-making process more open and transparent, thus improving the quality of justice. Moreover, it helps prevent corruption. Nevertheless, as judges worry about inaccurate rulings, or that rulings might be overturned, they find it difficult to complete the assessment of evidence during the court session. Consequently, the proportion of evidence assessment at trial is relatively low. In the 292 cases mentioned previously, only 62 (21.23%) of the judges ruled on the evidence presented at the trial. In addition, the rulings in 52 of those 62 cases could be considered insubstantial: there were no objections raised about the evidence from either side.

Furthermore, the Empirical Study on Criminal Trials project collected court records from 64 criminal cases broadcast by *Trial Now* from January 1 to June 31, 2009. Of those 64, the judges assessed the evidence during the trial in 30 cases, but only in 21 cases were the contents of the assessments found. The assessments involved questioning the authenticity of the evidence in 10 cases, the objectivity of the evidence in 2 cases, the legality of the evidence in 14 cases, the legal procedure of obtaining the evidence in 3 cases, the validity of the evidence in 16 cases, the relevancy of the evidence in 3 cases, and the weight of the evidence in 1 case. In 29 of the 30 cases, the judges ruled that the evidence submitted by the prosecutors could be accepted. No objections were raised by the defense. In only 1 of the 30 cases did the judge rule that the evidence introduced by the defender was rightly impeached when challenged by the prosecutor, thus dismissing the evidence as irrelevant. The defenders did raise objections to the prosecution evidence in 5 cases; in 2 of these, the judges gave no response, and in the other 3, the judges answered with "consideration would be given during the deliberation by the collegial panel after the trial." Thus, it could be concluded that most pieces of evidence were introduced without any objection from the opposite party, which resulted in the admittance by the judges of the evidence without proper assessment of its admissibility. When objections to the evidence were raised by the defense, the judges made their ruling on it after the trial, instead of during the court session.

It can be concluded that judicial assessment of evidence at the criminal trial is nothing but a nominal formality. On the one hand, the judges assess the evidence during the court session but give no ruling; on the other hand, assessment after the court session does not depend on the submission and challenge of evidence during the trial, instead depending on the documents in the case files. Just as Professor Chen Ruihua points out, "In spite of the appearance of the witness at court, judges in China still probably reject their oral testimonies and turn instead to the testimonies in the case files as the ground for the judgments."[8] Moreover, the empirical research held by

Professor Zuo Weimin indicates that the judges in China prefer to accept oral testimonies supported by the records or other evidence in the case files. In this pattern of judicial assessment of evidence, oral testimony would not have independent value, and it would make no difference whether the witnesses appeared in court or not.[9] With such a trial pattern, it is hardly surprising that the assessment of evidence at the court session has lost its function.

The Nominalization of Making Judgments in Criminal Trials

"Making judgment at the trial" refers to the process of the collegial panel reaching its conclusion based on the trial. Actually, the judgment could be made at the court session or after it. If the judgment is made in the name of the collegial panel but does not represent the panel's opinion, instead representing the opinion of other judges or persons, we should conclude that judgment making at the trial has lost its function or become a mere formality. Note the following examples:

(1) The presiding judge at any trial makes the judgment alone, which makes the collegial panel obsolete. The Criminal Procedure Law in China has provided for the composition and function of the collegial panel, which is composed of judges or of both judges and people's assessors. The panel tries the case, deliberates, and forms judgments together. However, in some courts, especially the primary courts at the basic level, the presiding judge may just use the name of the panel. The other members of the panel would participate in the court session but would not engage in any preparation or deliberation for the judgment. In fact, all decisions made in the name of the panel are made by the presiding judge. This is widely understood in the ordinary criminal trials in China. Some members of the collegial panel would just glance over the judgment, drafted by the presiding judge, and sign it. In some cases, panel members would sign it without having any idea of its content.[10]

Further, not all panel members' signatures could be found in the records of deliberations of the collegial panels in some primary courts. For instance, drawing on the records from one of the primary courts in Chengdu, the capital city of Sichuan Province, the researcher found that of 100 records, there were 26 documents without all the signatures from the collegial panel; and in 85 of the 100 records, there were no signatures from the court clerks. The records show that only after the presiding judge sent down a judgment were the collegial panels asked for their signatures; there was no proper deliberation among the panel. Even if the members of the panel had gathered to deliberate, any session lasted half an hour or less in most of the 100 cases; in fact, some comments in the records of these deliberations are identical to the words found in the judgments.[11] The loss of the panel's function could be due partly to the shortage of manpower available in the court, causing some judges to handle cases in a perfunctory manner. However, it is mostly due to the imperfect panel system, whereby there is neither proper adherence to the purposes of the panel nor proper rules set out for deliberation.

(II) The court's trial committee exceeds its duties and meddles in the affairs of the collegial panel. Article 149 of the Criminal Procedure Law in China provides the following:

> After the hearings and deliberations, the collegial panel shall render a judgment. With respect to a complex or major case, on which the collegial panel considers it difficult to make a decision, the panel shall refer the case to the president of the court for deciding whether to submit the case to the trial committee for discussion and decision. The panel shall implement the decision of the trial committee.

In practice, considering the authority of the decision made by the trial committee as well as the possibility of avoiding responsibility in the event of mishandling by the trial committee, the collegial panel prefers to submit the difficult, complex, or major cases to the trial committee for discussion and decision. In those kinds of cases, the real judges are not those who hear the cases. We describe this as "judges who hear the cases do not judge; judges who judge never hear the case" in China. Nevertheless, the collegial panels are sometimes obliged to obey the trial committee, even if they know the cases are being mishandled.

Early in the morning of April 21, 1998, a murder was committed in the city of Dandong, in Liaoning Province. Zhang Yiguo, an ordinary worker, was stabbed fourteen times. Police investigators determined that Li Yongcai, who had had a dispute with the deceased before the event, was the murderer. Because Li's defense attorney had, during court hearings, brought significant evidence to prove his client's innocence, the collegial panel ruled in his favor. However, the trial committee of Dandong City Intermediate Court determined after its own deliberations that while the evidence had been insufficient, Li Yongcai could still be found guilty, and so issued a suspended death sentence. The panel instituted the trial committee's decision. On February 3, 1999, Li Yongcai was sentenced to death with two years' suspension.

Two years and two months after he was wrongly convicted and locked in prison, Li Yongcai was released.[12]

In another case, Zhang Jinbo—a police officer in Harbin, the capital city of Heilongjiang Province—was accused of rape in 1995. Because the case relied only on the testimony of the alleged victim, as well as her daughter-in-law, a full determination was not forthcoming, and so the decision was reached during the "joint handling meeting," which involved the heads of the public security bureau, the procuratorate, and the court. The Nangang District Court found Zhang Jinbo guilty and sentenced him to ten years' imprisonment in 1998. He filed an appeal, which was then examined by judges of the collegial panel of the court of second instance. The panel found the case lacking sufficient evidence and found contradictions in the testimony supplied by the alleged victim. The panel thus issued an opinion concluding that the defendant was innocent. However, the trial committee of the court had a different decision. In the end, the presiding judge was forced to draw up a decision that rejected the appeal and upheld the original decision. Zhang Jinbo was held in custody until his release over 3,644 days later, when the case had been reviewed and his innocence declared in 2006.[13]

3. The Causes for the Nominalization of Criminal Trials

The criminal trial should be the decisive stage of criminal law proceedings. Unfortunately, in China, its function has become dispensable. This nominalization endangers both substantial and procedural justice. It is clear from the mishandled cases that criminal trials are not functioning. Surely, not all mishandled cases should be attributed to the nominalization of criminal trials, but it is clear that such mishandling inevitably leads to many tremendous miscarriages of justice. The fact alone that the use of torture to extract false confessions is accepted by the court—without obstacle—reflects the evil of the nominalization of criminal trials. To begin to promote change of this status, we shall analyze the causes for this phenomenon in China.

The File-Centered Judgment Model Resulting in the Nominalization of Criminal Trials

In tandem with the investigation-centered assembly-line model, the file-centered judgment model occurs automatically, because what is transferred in the assembly line are the case files, including the wide variety of evidence on record. The files from the investigation are not only the basis for prosecution but also fundamental to judgment. Almost all the evidence is in written form, whereupon the evidence review delineates these into inquiry records, interrogation records, inquest records, examination records, search records, identification records, and so on. Again, it makes almost no difference whether there is a courtroom trial or not. It has been asserted that the judges can concentrate better in their own offices than in court, therefore increasing efficiency. Thus, the file-centered judgment model can be held partly to blame for the nominalization of criminal trials.

Admittedly, using the hearsay records could speed up judicial work, but it is likely to lead to a miscarriage of justice. One of the misunderstandings in the concept of reviewing the records is the notion that attaching importance to the records is equivalent to attaching importance to the evidence; although the records may be taken as evidence, the evidence for a case is not just the records.

Another misunderstanding refers to the idea that records are equal to statements. We should not confuse what is written in the records with the statements of the victims, of the accused, and of the witnesses, even though their statements could be made into records. With regard to the oral or written statements, the subjects of proof are the victims, witnesses, and the accused, whereas for the records, the subjects of proof are the investigators who have drawn those records up. In the event that disputes arise as to the authenticity of the records, such as when a confession or evidence is withdrawn, the investigator who has drawn up the records should appear in court to clear up any confusion or conflict. The signatures of the victims, witnesses, and accused are used in the records as an important basis of authenticity, and videos or tapes made during inquiry or interrogation could verify the authenticity of the records. However, we should never equate the records with statements without any discrimination.

A third misunderstanding concerns the idea that all the records comprise original evidence. Some people believe that when comparing statements, the prior inquiry or interrogation records should be taken as the original and most reliable evidence insofar as they have been taken down in writing. This should be resisted, because what the inquiry or interrogation records prove is the statement rather than the wider facts. In common parlance, inquiry records cannot prove what the witnesses have known directly; they can only prove that the witnesses recounted what they knew. And interrogation records cannot prove what the accused have done; they can only prove that the accused said what they did. It is clear that those records should be classified as hearsay when it comes to proving facts.

As the most ancient and complicated rules of evidence in the Anglo-American legal system, the rules of hearsay are becoming absorbed by the continental legal system. Hearsay evidence is a statement made by a witness out of the courtroom. Rule 801(c) of the United States Federal Rules of Evidence defines *hearsay* as a statement other than one made by a witness while testifying at a trial or hearing, offering evidence to prove the truth of the matter asserted. In other words, any statement made by the witness outside the court should be taken as hearsay. For instance, A witnessed B killing C. The testimony made by A is hearsay evidence if A was absent from the trial and his or her testimony was read aloud during the trial. Hearsay evidence is generally not admissible. Rule 802 of the Federal Rules of Evidence prescribes that "hearsay is not admissible except as provided by these rules or by other rules prescribed by the Supreme Court pursuant to statutory authority or by Act of Congress."[14] The theory of hearsay-exclusion rules rests on its fallibility and the fact that it is difficult to review hearsay evidence. According to the rules of the common law system, the trustworthiness of testimony is guaranteed by the following three factors: first, the witnesses shall swear an oath as to the truthfulness of their statement; second, the witnesses shall make their statements directly facing the judge; and third, the witnesses should be interactively queried by the opposite party, or at least the opposite party should be given a chance to do so. Hearsay, as defined by the Anglo-American legal system as a statement made out of court, does not meet these three requirements. Therefore, hearsay may not be admitted as evidence. The main function of hearsay-exclusion rules is to ensure the appearance of witnesses at the trial.

Generally speaking, judgment in China is made on the basis of evidence that would be considered hearsay, and thus inadmissible, in the Anglo-American legal system. The absence of the witness in the courtroom trial provides further proof of the nominalization of criminal trials in China. The Chinese Criminal Procedure Law fails to make it consistently clear whether witnesses should testify in court. For example, Article 48 provides that "all those who have information about a case shall have the duty to testify"; Article 47 provides that "the testimony of a witness may be used as a basis for deciding a case only after the witness has been questioned and his testimony challenged in the courtroom by both sides, that is, the public prosecutor, the alleged victim as well as the defendant and defenders, and after the testimonies of the witnesses on all sides have been heard and verified." However, Article 157 provides that "the records of interviews of those witnesses who are not present in court, the conclusions of expert witnesses who are not present in court, and the records of inquests and other documents serving as evidence shall be read out in court." This obviously authorizes the nonappearance of witnesses while also making their testimony admissible as evidence. The acceptable absence of witnesses at court is yet one more factor leading to the nominalization of criminal trials in China.

The Administrative Decision-Making Model Resulting in the Nominalization of Criminal Trials

Administrative decision making refers to the realization of expected aims through the use of scientific theories and methods to analyze subjective and objective conditions systematically. In this way, government officials arrive at decisions relating to affairs of state. Serving as part of administrative management, administrative decision making should conform to fundamental principles, such as that of the lower administrative level subordinating itself to the higher level. In the organization mechanism of modern decision making, inner circles, which are referred to as "systems central to administrative decision-making" or "the administrative decision-making center," take responsibility for comprehensive policy decisions. The main task of the administrative decision-making center is to coordinate and control the entire process of making decisions regarding policy; that is, after recognizing the problems and the aims, the administrative decision-making center considers all alternatives before making its own decision. The administrative decision-making center exercises principal power and takes the major share of the responsibility.[15]

Adjudication, on the other hand, has two main tasks: to find facts that are accurate and pertinent, and to apply the laws correctly. The aim of a hearing is to find the facts in a case. As a specialized type of cognitive activity, the judicial officers' assertion of facts on the basis of evidence should be seen to be a reverse method of thinking, whereby the evidence is used to understand what happened in the past, while administrative decision making often deals with the actions in the future. The interests of all parties relative to any case, and these interests' influences on society, have usually been taken into account in the administrative decision. On the other hand, when judicial officers assert the facts of a case, the various interests and their influences on society become irrelevant and should not be taken into account until the judge hands down a sentence. Therefore, adjudication should mainly observe the principles and rules of its specialized cognitive activity, rather than the administrative decision-making principle of the lower level subordinating to the higher level.

However, common practice leans towards the so-called bureaucratization of justice in China. Judicial officials at all levels are primarily concerned with administrative decisions. The lower levels defer to the higher levels, and in important cases the highest officials must make the call. This is an unwritten factor underlying this type of administrative system, which continues to undermine courtroom trials. It was described in our empirical study of wrongful convictions as follows:

> In China today, courts may be presided over by a single judge, a collegial panel, or a judicial committee. Both the collegial panel and the judicial committee are examples of "democratic centralism" in decision-making. In actuality, they apply an administrative management model to decide on cases. During trials, the presiding judge or judges often report to the division chief judge and ask for instruction. The written verdict must be submitted to the division-chief judge and a deputy president of the court for approval. If the division chief or the deputy president does not agree with the panel's opinion, the verdict can be sent back with a request for a new deliberation, or simply turned over to the judicial committee for a decision. If the judicial committee feels it necessary, it may ask for instruction from a higher court. The panel must abide by any decision by the judicial committee or any higher court. Whether we speak of the procuratorate or the court, this bureaucratisation of the process, with its endless reports and approvals, is a typical example of an administrative-management model. A direct result of this model is that those who actually understand the facts of the case possess no authority over the verdict. Courtroom hearings become a formality. Improper interventions of all kinds find legal channels into the case, causing a serious threat to the fairness of the system, and imperceptibly adding to the risk of wrongful conviction.[16]

As noted, it has become common in China for trial committees to exceed their duties by meddling in judgment and in the political and legal committees that judge the cases before they go to trial. The reasons for this include the application of the administrative-management model, which affects trial committees at all levels, causing the leading officials of the courts to coordinate and control the process and results of judicial decisions. Consequently, administrative-management principles, such as the lower level subordinating to the higher level, or the decisions of major cases riding on the decision of leading officials, have been practiced as unwritten rules in China, which naturally could also be taken as an unwritten cause of the nominalization of criminal trials in China.

Chapter Ten

The Reduction of Punishment in a Case of Doubt

1. The Presumption of Innocence

From the establishment of the People's Republic of China until the 1990s, the Chinese judiciary consistently maintained that presumption of innocence was a principle applicable only to capitalist countries' criminal procedure. Chinese criminal procedure presumed neither innocence nor guilt but rather "seeking truth from facts." But even before the 1996 revision of the Chinese Criminal Procedure Law, some Chinese scholars suggested that, in fact, any criminal justice system that does not presume innocence presumes guilt.

In 1996, the existing Criminal Procedure Law that had come into force in 1979 was undergoing the process of amendment. One particularly controversial amendment was related to the presumption of innocence. For many years, the prevailing Chinese legal stance on the presumption of innocence was that it was a principle of capitalist law and that there should, in fact, be no presumption of guilt or innocence. The basic principle should be seeking truth from the facts. But prior to the amendment of the Criminal Procedure Law, some legal academics believed the question of the presumption of innocence could not simply be avoided. They argued that a country whose legal system did not apply the presumption of innocence had, in effect, a presumption of guilt. The presumption of innocence places the burden of proof on the prosecution, as the prosecution would have to demonstrate in court that the defendant was actually guilty. The presumption of guilt places the burden of proof on the defendant, as the defendant would have to prove in court that he or she was innocent. The presumption of innocence, it was argued, is a distillation of the judicial experience of human society and a symbol of a progressive and civilized legal system—in other words, China should learn from the experience of other legal systems.

In March 1996, the Chinese National People's Congress published its "Decision on the Amendments to the Criminal Procedure Law." Article 12 of the newly revised law set out the following rule: "No person shall be found guilty without being judged as such by a People's Court according to the law." The official of the Legislative Work Commission under the Standing Committee of the National People's Congress claimed that this rule was not a presumption of innocence; rather, it merely emphasized the authority of the court to convict. Nonetheless, scholars tended to believe that the new provision did possess the basic spirit of "innocent until proven guilty."

The presumption of innocence involves three levels of implicit meaning. First, before anyone can be found guilty in a criminal court, they are assumed to be innocent. Second, in a legal trial, the prosecution bears the burden of proof, and the defendant does not have any such responsibility: since defendants have no burden to prove their guilt, it follows that they have no burden to prove their innocence. Third, if the evidence provided by the prosecution does not meet the legal standards, the defendant is found not guilty; in other words, legal judgments should respect the principle of "no conviction without clear proof." Although the revised 1996 law did not provide clear guidelines on who should assume the burden of proof, Article 162 stated: "If there is insufficient evidence and thus the defendant cannot be found guilty, he shall be pronounced innocent on account of the fact that the evidence is insufficient and the accusation unfounded."[1] In advocating the principle of "no conviction without clear proof," this article embodied a certain spirit of the presumption of innocence. However, in practice, it tended to clash with traditional legal mind-sets, and this was related to the standard of proof in criminal cases.

2. The Standard of Proof in Criminal Trials

Neither the 1979 nor the 1996 versions of the Criminal Procedure Law directly stipulate positive provisions regarding the standard of proof for evidence in criminal proceedings. But based on formulations in related parts of the law, scholars generally summarize such standards by saying, "The facts of the case must be clear, and the evidence reliable and sufficient."

Law enforcement officials frequently refer to these explanations of the standard as "the two basics." The first person to use this expression was Peng Zhen, then chairman of the National People's Congress Standing Committee. In May 1985, in part of his remarks at a five-city security forum, he said, "Now, in some cases where the evidence is incomplete, there is no way to arrive at a verdict. But in truth, as long as there is reliable basic evidence, and the basic facts of the case are clear, a verdict can still be reached." From that point on, the standard for issuing a guilty verdict would forever be explained as "the basic facts are clear, and the basic evidence is reliable and sufficient."[2]

In addition, excessive zeal for fighting crime also caused law enforcement officials to relax standards of proof for evidence. Fearing that insufficient evidence would trigger the "no conviction in a case of doubt" rule, allowing criminals to go free, they instead applied the policy of "prescribing lesser punishment in case of doubt." This was especially evident in cases involving the death penalty. When the evidence was insufficient and there were doubts about the facts, the courts would not issue a death sentence to be carried out immediately but rather a suspended death sentence, or else life imprisonment, as a means of hedging their bets and in an effort to prevent wrongful conviction—though in some cases this manner of handling cases became the excuse for wrongful conviction.

In the wrongful conviction cases narrated previously, the defendants were accused of murder and so would generally have merited immediate death sentences if a guilty verdict had been returned, but applying the notion that insufficient evidence dictated lighter sentencing, Shi Dongyu, Du Peiwu, Tong Limin, Li Yongcai, Zhao Zuohai, and Zhang Hui were instead all handed suspended death sentences; Yu Yingsheng was given life in prison, and She Xianglin was sentenced to fifteen years in prison. As this makes clear, the policy of prescribing lesser punishment in case of doubt is itself misleading and may lead to more wrongful convictions.

3. The Dilemma of Wrongful Conviction versus Wrongful Acquittal

It is impossible to gain firsthand knowledge of a crime during the course of investigation, given that the crime has in fact been committed—in the past. Any evidence found allows only indirect knowledge. To investigators, the actual facts of the case must always remain "the moon in the water, the flowers in the mirror." Of course, the moon and flowers spoken of here have an objective existence, but what investigators can perceive has already been reflected and refracted through the water and the mirror. Thus, without evidence, investigators have no way to find the facts of past events. But knowledge of facts gained through evidence is not necessarily equal to the facts of the case as they happened. In situations in which the water is not clear enough or the mirror not bright enough, the moon and the flowers will appear distorted, sometimes so much so that there will appear to be two distinct moons or flower groupings. Which is the false one and which is the real one? The question will remain a mystery to the investigator. In other words, the criminal suspect might be guilty or not guilty. This is what is meant by "a case of doubt."

Shortage of evidence and unclear exposition of the facts introduce doubt into any investigation. Doubt tends to lead to errors in judgment, whether by investigators, the preliminary examiners, prosecutors, or judges, because they have to rely on the evidence submitted. These errors tend to be one of two basic types: believing a guilty party to be innocent, or believing the innocent to be guilty. "Never wronging the innocent, never freeing the guilty," cannot serve as more than an ideal, never to be fully manifested by the criminal justice system of any country. In cases in which doubt has been introduced, the judiciary must choose between wrongful release and wrongful conviction.

Traditional Chinese law would probably prefer wrongful conviction to wrongful release. Indeed, while few would now support the old saying "Kill 3,000 wrongfully rather than let a single one escape," few Chinese would be likely to agree with the Western precept "It is better that ten guilty persons escape than one innocent suffer."[3] Many law enforcement officers think that letting a guilty person escape may lead to public harm, and so is not in the best interest of the public; on the other hand, to punish the innocent harms only that individual. This, then, is the ideological underpinning of the policy of prescribing lesser punishment in case of doubt.

The notion of "no conviction in a case of doubt" gets at the gist of the principle of presumption of innocence and also represents a crystallization of much of judicial practice. The author certainly does not wish to argue that individual good does not defer to the good of the collective but that the conventional way of evaluating the relative risks of wrongful acquittal and wrongful conviction makes an error in calculation. As practical experience shows, wrongful acquittal entails only one mistake, while wrongful conviction entails two. Wrongful acquittal does no more than release, in error, a guilty party back into society, but wrongful conviction leaves a real criminal on the loose even as it punishes an innocent person in error. For example, while Shi Dongyu, Li Jiuming, Sun Wangang, and Zhao Zuohai were unjustly imprisoned, the real murderers in these cases, Liang Baoyou, Cai Xinwu, Li Maofu, and Li Haijin, remained at large. When Du Peiwu and the two Zhangs were imprisoned, the real murderers—Yang Tianyong and his gang, and Gou Haifeng—continued to pose a threat to society. And we may never know the identities of the real murderers in the cases of She Xianglin and Teng Xingshan. The danger posed by two mistakes exceeds that posed by one, which means that when faced with a case of doubt, the logical choice should be wrongful acquittal rather than wrongful conviction.

Shen Deyong, vice president of the Supreme People's Court, recently remarked:

> The rate of wrongful conviction is still unacceptably high, especially in the current situation in which the notion of presumed guilt has not been eradicated and the principle of presumed innocence has not yet been truly established. We must keep a clear awareness of this problem and strengthen still more the consciousness that will guard against wrongful conviction. We must work to prevent wrongful conviction just as we work to prevent floods and other disasters. It is better to wrongfully acquit than to wrongfully convict. If we wrongfully release one true criminal, the sky will not fall, but if we wrongfully convict one innocent citizen, especially if we wrongfully execute a citizen, then the sky will fall.[4]

Wrongful conviction overshadows the good work being done by the criminal justice system. Within this shadow lurk the flaws and deficiencies of the system, which must be shed light on in order to instigate and promote reform and improvement. In China, discoveries and revelations of wrongful convictions have, to a certain degree, begun to promote systematic reforms and improvements. For example, Article 53 of the 2012 edition of the Criminal Procedure Law stipulates more specific standards of proof for evidence, which should be reliable and sufficiently adhere to the following conditions: (1) all facts for conviction and sentencing are supported by the evidence, (2) all evidence used to decide a case has been legally verified, and (3) the evidence should support the arguments of the case beyond reasonable doubt. This rule will help put into effect the principle of presumption of innocence and eradicate the custom of prescribing lesser punishment in case of doubt.

In summary, there are ten major areas within the criminal justice system that may lead to wrongful conviction. Gaining awareness of these ten areas is the first step towards the prevention of wrongful convictions. From there we must come up with feasible and effective measures to protect against straying into these areas. The She Xianglin case was a good lesson. However, the miscarriage of justice was discovered many years later.

4. The Victim Coming back Alive

On March 28, 2005, Zhang Aiqing reappeared in Hechang Village. The news that She Xianglin's wife was alive spread quickly throughout the village. When she walked through the front door of her mother's house, her family was left speechless. Looking around, she said blithely, "It's Aiqing! I'm back!" Her mother threw herself into Aiqing's arms, and together they broke down in a tearful reunion. The rest of the family soon joined in.

Eventually, Aiqing's oldest brother said, "We were sure you'd died long ago."

Aiqing replied, "I was close to it, but I'm strong, and I managed to get back on my feet. Did you not get my letters? I've been writing to you for two years!"

Her brother said they had received the letters, but no one believed she had written them. The letters had been signed with her name, but they seemed out of character. They never explained where she was or what she was doing and only urged the family to take care of her daughter. The family had simply come to regard the letters as unpleasant pranks. Besides, the handwriting did not look like Aiqing's. When Mrs. Zhang asked her how she had spent all the missing years, Aiqing turned her head and glanced over her shoulder at the stranger who appeared in the doorway.

Aiqing's second brother said, "We were all scared when your letters came. We were afraid that someone was going to come for revenge. You know, like someone just out of prison, an acquaintance of She Xianglin who was sending us intimidating letters about your daughter."

Aiqing suddenly asked, "How is my daughter? And why is She Xianglin in prison?"

At this, the family looked at one another in silence, then Aiqing's oldest brother said, "It seems that She Xianglin has been treated unjustly."

When she heard the story behind his imprisonment, Aiqing's jaw became set, and tears started to roll down her face.

Her brother said, "We need to go and report this right away."

After the matter was reported to the local police station, it was immediately sent to the county police, where the news was treated very seriously. Its first priority was to conclusively identify the woman claiming to be Zhang Aiqing using scientific means. The next day, the DNA results confirmed her identity as the "deceased" Zhang Aiqing. The news traveled from the county police to the county Politics and Law Committee, and from there to the Jingmen City Politics and Law Committee. That night, the committee held a meeting, at which it was unanimously agreed that the matter had to be dealt with immediately.

On March 30, at an emergency sitting, the Jingmen City Intermediate People's Court repealed the ruling of first instance and the reconsideration ruling that found She Xianglin guilty of the murder of Zhang Aiqing. The court requested that the Jingshan County Basic People's Court reinvestigate the case and at the same time release She Xianglin on bail.

Two days later, on April 1, with his complexion pale and his hair thin, She Xianglin walked out of Hubei Shayang Prison. Many journalists were waiting by the prison gate, ready to capture this rare moment in Chinese legal history. When the reporters questioned him, She Xianglin described a confusing mix of feelings. He was both angry and grateful for Zhang Aiqing's "resurrection," but his immediate concern was for his daughter, who was hurrying home in the wake of her father's release on bail.

The story of a miscarriage of justice in which a supposedly murdered woman had come back from the dead attracted the attention of journalists across the country. They began to closely examine the original investigation and those involved. Lu Cheng, the deputy leader of the investigation team that had been assigned the case, had since been promoted to the position of deputy police chief in Jingshan County. In interviews with the media, he said he felt a deep sense of remorse. He regretted that no one had conducted a DNA test at the time, which would have made the case much clearer. Although Jingshan County had no such equipment at the time, the 126 Police Research Institute (now known as the Police Forensic Science Center) did. The misidentification of the body was the principal reason the case had turned into such a miscarriage of justice. At the time, Zhang Aiqing's family and relatives all seemed to believe that the dead body was hers. Lu Cheng believed it demonstrated the need to avoid placing too much emphasis on the testimony of witnesses. But even when questioned by reporters, he denied that the investigators in this case had ever used torture to extract She Xianglin's confession.

Reporters flocked to interview Zhang Aiqing to find out the reasons behind her disappearance. The attention took its toll, and her mental state became unstable once again. The local media put her family in contact with a psychiatric hospital that offered her free treatment. In the hospital, she spoke to reporters and said she had only come back to see how her family was, and that she had only expected to stay a couple of days. She had no idea that things would become so complicated. She especially wanted to see She Xianglin and speak to him face-to-face, but whether Xianglin was willing to meet her was another question. When she heard that he was out on bail and that he was very weak and refused to eat, she asked a reporter to send him a bunch of fresh flowers. She wanted to call him but didn't want to affect his mental state. After a while, and with some encouragement, she finally gave She Xianglin a call. She told him that even though this ordeal had brought him close to death, he had to keep up his spirits and strengthen his resolve. "Don't you remember the time when you had a fever of forty degrees but you still went to work? That was the first time you nearly died, so I know you can make it. You can overcome anything." Xianglin only listened, without responding. Finally, with tears in her eyes, Aiqing said softly into the phone, "I'm fine."

On April 13, 2005, the Jingshan County Basic People's Court heard the case. In front of She Xianglin and a mass of journalists, the presiding judge solemnly pronounced She Xianglin innocent.

When he left the court with his family and throngs of reporters in tow, She Xianglin went first to the cemetery to offer his respects to his mother. He kept saying that if it had not been for his wrongful conviction, his mother would not have had to shoulder such a heavy burden and die so early as a result.

When he first saw his eighteen-year-old daughter, he felt as if there were hundreds of things he wanted to say, but he didn't know where to begin. When Xianglin had last seen her, she had been six. She had grown up without her mother or father, and then without Mrs. She, her grandmother whom she had loved dearly. She had no friends in the tiny mountain village where she had lived, and after struggling through the first year of junior high school, she had dropped out. Soon after, she had gone with Xianglin's younger brother and his family to work—while still a child—in an electronics factory in Dongguan. Now that father and daughter were together, they silently embraced each other, leaving behind only tears.

After She Xianglin's case was overturned, local officials rushed to consult with him and his family to arrange compensation and government aid. The Chinese National Compensation Law had taken effect on January 1, 1995, and as most of the damages suffered by She Xianglin had occurred after the law had come into force, he was eligible for legal compensation. The compensation for erroneously judged criminal cases normally includes compensatory damages, medical expenses, dependants' living expenses, and the cost of lost labor. From April 11, 1994, when he was detained under the practice of "sheltered for investigation," to April 1, 2005, when he was released on bail, She Xianglin had been imprisoned for 3,995 days. The National Compensation Law states that "the compensation for a citizen who has had his or her personal freedom infringed upon should be calculated on the basis of the national average daily pay for the previous year." Consequently, having lost his personal freedom for eleven years, She Xianglin was entitled to 220,000 yuan (US$26,400). At the time, however, the National Compensation Law did not provide for damages for mental suffering.[5]

In September 2005, She Xianglin signed a compensation agreement with the Jingmen City Intermediate People's Court. The court agreed to pay 256,900 yuan (US$30,828) in damages to She Xianglin for the violation of his personal rights (this included a fee of 1,100 yuan for the burial of the unknown victim). In October, the She family reached a similar agreement with the Jingshan police. The police agreed to pay 226,000 yuan (US$27,120) in compensation to Xianglin, 4,000 yuan (US$480) to his brother for his imprisonment, and 220,000 yuan (US$26,400) to his family for the death of Mrs. She. The local Jingshan government also paid She Xianglin a 200,000 yuan (US$24,000) subsidy to help with his living costs.[6]

The two villagers from Yaoling Village who had been imprisoned on the basis of the certificate of sincerity also reached a compensation agreement with the Jingshan police: one received 22,000 yuan (US$2,640), and the other 3,000 yuan (US$360).

Although the government had undertaken the responsibility to provide compensation to the people affected by the erroneous decision, there were people directly involved in the case who needed to be held accountable for their lapses in judgment. In April 2005, the Jingmen City Politics and Law Committee established a work team to investigate the people responsible. Han Hua, who had been the deputy chief of the Jingshan police and the head of the special investigation team, had been transferred to the position of deputy president of the Jingshan County Basic People's Court. Lu Cheng, who had led the Jingshan police's criminal squad and who had been the deputy chief of the investigation team, had been promoted to Han Hua's old position. He Liang, one of the key members of the investigation team, had been promoted to the head of the criminal squad before he had died of liver cancer in 2001. Pan Jun, the other key member of the investigation team, was now an instructor in the county police patrol unit.

During the period that he was under investigation by the work team, Pan Jun complained many times of his mistreatment. On May 25, 2005, he went to a public cemetery in Wuhan after cutting his wrists with a metal can and wrote the words, "I have been wronged" on a gravestone in his own blood and hanged himself from a nearby tree. Although this incident was not reported in the media, it greatly alarmed the people involved in the inquiry. The work team came to a decision, which stated that the actions of the people involved in She Xianglin's case constituted extortion and dereliction of duty. While two of the principal people involved had already died, Han Hua and Lu Cheng would be dismissed from their current positions. And so, the investigation into the mishandling of She Xianglin's case was closed.

5. A Sweet and Bitter Life

Ultimately, She Xianglin was both fortunate and unfortunate: although he had been unjustly imprisoned, he was released and exonerated. Had Zhang Aiqing died or become so ill as to never return, then it would have been impossible for his verdict to be overturned. Zhang Aiqing, too, had mixed luck. Although her eventual reunion with her family and friends was a happy one, she had suffered during her time away. Gradually, she began to recount the things she had experienced in those missing years, though there were moments even she could not recall.

By the end of 1993, Zhang Aiqing had fallen ill, though she could not explain the cause. She was feeling an ever-increasing pressure, and that there were many things locked inside that she could not express to anyone. She experienced fluctuations in mood—moments when she felt intensely depressed and moments when she felt completely normal. She just wanted to leave and go as far away as she could. She roamed from place to place, "eating the wind and sleeping in dew," begging for food and drink. She couldn't remember exactly where she went, but it seemed she had been abducted and sold into slavery somewhere in Anhui Province. Eventually she escaped, and the entire experience empowered her, making her feel that she was a strong and vital person for having survived. She eventually found her way to the city of Zaozhuang in Shandong Province, where she happened upon a kind family that took her into their care.

At the time, the Fan family worked as caretakers at a forestry station run by the mining bureau. One day, the youngest son noticed a disheveled woman lying on a patch of grass in the woods, barely alive. The woman had a strange, unfamiliar accent, and though the young man could not understand everything she was saying, he worked out that she was asking for food. She seemed to be looking for her home, but she did not know where it was. Seeing how pitiful the woman was, he brought her home. The young man's parents were very kind—they took in the woman, who said her name was Zhang Aiqing, and gave her food and clothes.

The Fan family had four sons: the oldest was mentally disabled, the second and third had left home to start their own families, and the youngest had not yet married. Mr. and Mrs. Fan had no daughters, but they immediately treated Aiqing like one of their own. Once they realized that Aiqing's mental state was fragile, they spent thousands of yuan on a local doctor to help her recover. Aiqing was incredibly grateful to the Fan family, and once she had begun to recover, she helped out with the work, including the hardest and most tiring jobs.

Once Aiqing had lived with the Fans for some months and had come to understand how kind they were, she and the youngest son decided to get married. The next year, they had a son. Aiqing had told the Fans that she had been married before but that her original husband was no good.[7] The family looked after her carefully and knew to keep her calm, because the moment she got angry she would become ill and stop eating, drinking, and working. She would just lie on her bed and cry out for a home she could never identify. When she was healthy, Aiqing was smart and able. She raised pigs and chickens, and the family became increasingly prosperous. She was very good to her husband and his parents, often saying, "As a woman, treating your in-laws well is the same as treating your husband well."

After a few years had passed, Aiqing's body had fully recovered and her mental state improved. Her memory had gradually returned, and she could recall her hometown in Hubei and memories of her first husband and her daughter. She even remembered her exact address. She began to write to her oldest brother, though she never received a reply. Sometimes she would sit on her own, looking at a map, and daydream. Increasingly, she wanted to see her family and, most of all, her daughter, who was only six when she had left. When it came to She Xianglin, her feelings were complicated. Although there had been happy moments in their marriage, they were overshadowed by the painful experiences she had endured, and she felt a lingering sense of resentment towards him.

Aiqing was very happy with her new life, and the person she cared for most was her son. She thought he was particularly intelligent, and he reminded her of someone from her home province of Hubei. She thought that people from Shandong were very rigid and obsessed with rules. They were not flexible and resourceful, like people from her home province. Her son admired her, too. He said that in their home, Mum was the boss, he was second in command, and Dad was number three, because Dad was the stupidest. Aiqing's new husband was a man of few words, but he was not stupid. Whenever there would be a group discussion, he would stand to one side and not participate. When he heard his son's description of the family, he simply burst out laughing. And when Aiqing suggested they go back to her hometown in Hubei for a visit, he had no objection.

In early 2005, after the Chinese New Year, Aiqing sold ten of the pigs she had raised, which brought in more than 7,000 yuan, enough for her to start planning their trip. On March 27, she and her husband set off on the train for Hubei.

Zhang Aiqing became famous overnight. Reporters from all over the country came to the remote mountain village to interview her. She enjoyed being interviewed and spoke fluently and with ease. She spoke about her relationship with She Xianglin, her illness, her time drifting around, and her life with the Fan family. Aiqing had no qualms talking about Xianglin, even with her new husband by her side. She said that Xianglin was smart but that he had no sense of responsibility. She believed that human life was the sum of morality, ethics, and responsibility, and that he, unlike herself, did not meet those standards. If he had reflected on his actions for even a moment, then things would not have happened the way they did. She also thought that Xianglin had no sense of culture, and in reference to him, she said, "People who don't read, can't get anywhere."

She did, however, want to see him face-to-face, so that she could end things properly. While Aiqing was sympathetic to everything that Xianglin had suffered, she did not believe any of it to be her fault. Her mental condition had left her with no idea of what she had been doing in those days, and she never imagined that running away would have changed Xianglin's life so irreversibly. She wanted to explain to him why their relationship had failed—the prelude to the tragedy that befell them. But Xianglin was un-willing to meet, and she could not understand why. She decided to wait for the formal judgment on his case to be handed down before trying again.

When Aiqing saw her daughter for the first time in eleven years, she was relieved by how stable and calm she was—quite unlike her father. Aiqing asked her daughter whether she remembered how her mother had treated her when she was young. When she replied that she could not remember, Aiqing's heart turned cold. She realized that her daughter resented her. She understood that her daughter had had a difficult time, and that she had not fulfilled her responsibilities as a mother. Regardless, Aiqing refused to be-lieve she was to blame: it was all just a matter of fate. Perhaps it was better this way; if her daughter could not remember her, then maybe she would not think of her daughter any longer. She could concentrate on taking care of her son and being the best mother for him that she could be.

On the day of the trial, Zhang Aiqing did not go to the courthouse to hear the final verdict; she knew it was not the right occasion to show her face. She waited with her family, hoping that She Xianglin might appear. Later she heard a journalist say that Xianglin was heading to his mother's tomb to pay his respects, which she thought was very honorable of him. But when she found out that he was still unwilling to speak to her, she was stunned into silence. Eventually she let out a long sigh and muttered to her-self, "It's time to go home." She knew that too much had happened for her to be able to explain everything.

She spoke once more to a reporter, saying how grateful she was for the support of the Fan family over the years.

The reporter asked her husband to speak, but he just gave an honest smile and said, "My wife has said everything already. There's nothing I can say."

Aiqing began to talk about her son, becoming more and more excited and speaking faster and faster. Seeing that his wife was rambling, her husband rushed over and poured her a glass of water to distract her. When Aiqing had finished her drink, she seemed to assume an air of determination. She said that she could not stay in Hubei; her home was in Shandong. She was already speaking with something of a Shandong accent.

On April 15, Zhang Aiqing and her husband returned to Shandong. Before she left, she wrote a poem and asked a reporter to pass it on to She Xianglin.

The wind howls and the rain pours,
Sheltering in rubble, dreaming of past springs.

He Jiahong

You glimpse a sign showing a bouquet of roses,
and you struggle towards it.
When you are confused, please pick a maple leaf
and decorate it with roses. This will be its radiant day.
Pages turned over are like ruins. Please cherish the world.
We are not lucky, but we are proud;
in our short years, we have tasted bittersweet life.[8]

Part Three

New Developments in the Criminal Justice System following the Zhao Zuohai Case

(Back from the Dead III)

> We cannot see history, and some truths might be lost forever. We can only try to recover them with pieces of evidence. How to obtain and use the evidence constitutes procedural justice, without which the people will lose confidence in social justice.
>
> *He Jiahong,*
> *China Daily, 2015-04-30*

Chapter Eleven

The Exclusionary Rules against Illegally Obtained Evidence

1. Another Victim Back from the Dead

Wrongful convictions occur in the course of the criminal justice system's fight against crime. However, the generation of a wrongful conviction is in itself a crime, one that harms or even kills innocent citizens in the name of the law. Such a crime presents an even greater threat to society: it not only damages individual rights and causes the people involved to suffer a great wrongdoing, but also is destructive to the public good, to the legal system, and to social order. The implications could go so far as to cause the public to lose its faith in the law, or in its own government. However, as mentioned before, discoveries and revelations of wrongful convictions have, to a certain degree, promoted systematic reforms and improvements.

In 2001, the Legislative Work Commission under the Standing Committee of the National People's Congress invited a selection of legal scholars and experts to discuss and draft the rules of criminal evidence, as part of an amendment to the Criminal Procedure Law, and one major issue concerned the use of torture and the exclusionary rule. In 2003, the Standing Committee of the NPC put the amendment to the Criminal Procedure Law into their legislative agenda; however, the committee failed to act for years, until another case of wrongful conviction was discovered.

On February 15, 1998, in Zhaolou Village, Zhecheng County, Henan Province, a villager reported the disappearance of his uncle, Zhao Zhenshang, who had been missing since October 30, 1997, and who was suspected of being murdered. As a result of a quick investigation, a man named Zhao Zuohai was arrested a week later, on the basis that he and Zhenshang had fought shortly before the disappearance. But after twenty-plus days' detention, Zuohai was released due to lack of evidence.

On May 8, 1999, a local villager found in a discarded well a decomposed corpse with no head and severed limbs. The body was believed to be that of Zhenshang. The following day, public security officers again arrested Zuohai, and from May 10 to June 18, Zuohai was interrogated continuously and admitted his guilt no less than nine times; however, the police could not find the missing parts of the corpse. Zuohai confessed that he had buried the head in his family's graveyard, but the police found nothing after carrying out an excavation. Another issue was that the identification of the corpse was still in question: DNA tests were inconclusive.

In January 2001, the Supreme People's Procuratorate issued its "Notice Regarding Taking the Next Step to End and Rectify Unlawfully Extended Custody," which called for a comprehensive approach to ending the practice. During this period, the Zhecheng County Public Security Bureau handed the Zhao Zuohai case over to the Political-Legal Work Committee for deliberation. In July, the committee convened a joint case-handling meeting, but finding themselves unable to gain a consensus, they put it aside.

On May 31, 2002, in Weifang City, Shandong, the National Procuratorate Rectifying Unlawfully Extended Custody Experience Exchange was convened, at which meeting the high-level leaders in the procuratorate urged their agencies across the country, at all levels, to apply greater intensity of purpose to the project of resolving unlawfully extended custody cases, with the aim of rectifying all instances of this by the end of June 2002. In the wake of the meeting, Zhao Zuohai's case was put on the list of cases targeted for rectification. In October 2002, the Political and Legal-Work Committee of Shangqiu City held a joint meeting of the three branches and then made a decision to "issue an indictment within twenty days."

On October 22, 2002, the People's Procuratorate of Shangqiu City filed the case for prosecution of Zuohai for murder in the Intermediate People's Court. On December 5, the court convicted Zuohai of murder and sentenced him to death with two years' probation. Zuohai did not appeal, and on February 13, 2003, the High People's Court of Henan Province confirmed the conviction after reviewing the death penalty. Two years later, the sentence was reduced to life imprisonment.

Years later, on April 30, 2010, the "victim" showed up in Zhaolou Village. Zhenshang explained to the shocked villagers that he had run away after the fight with Zuohai and had led a vagabond life in big cities by collecting scraps and running a small business. But recently he had not felt well, and so he returned to the village to live out the remainder of his life.

His reappearance was reported to the authorities, and in a matter of days the retrial commission organized by the High Court overruled the conviction against Zuohai and released him. On May 9, Zuohai walked out free after eleven years' imprisonment, and subsequently received compensation from the state of 650,000 yuan.

When Zhao Zuohai was exonerated, the police used DNA testing to identify the corpse as a missing villager of another township, Gao Zhi, who disappeared on September 12, 1998. In late May 2010, the police found and arrested the three true perpetrators separately.

After Zhao had been released the chief protectorate remarked, "Our biggest mistake here at the Procuratorate was not steadfastly maintaining our original opinion."[1] Certainly the decision to end unlawfully extended custody was correct, but the judiciary in some areas took the course of issuing indictments and guilty verdicts on doubtful cases. It did not wish to let the guilty go free, and as a result, unlawfully extended custody led to wrongful conviction.

2. The Two Provisions on Criminal Evidence

Influenced by the wrongful conviction of Zhao Zuohai, on June 13, 2010, the Supreme Court, the Supreme Procuratorate, the Ministry of Public Security, the Ministry of State Security, and the Ministry of Justice jointly issued Provisions on Issues concerning the Examination and Evaluation of Evidence in Death Sentence Cases and Provisions on Issues concerning the Exclusion of Illegally Obtained Evidence in Criminal Cases. Implemented on July 1, 2010, the two provisions stress the importance of the exclusionary rule of illegally obtained evidence, and the latter stipulates the issue of exclusion of illegally obtained evidence more specifically. Article 1 of the Provisions on Issues concerning the Exclusion of Illegally Obtained Evidence in Criminal Cases provides:

> The confession of a suspect or defendant obtained by unlawful means such as torture, and the statement of a witness or victim obtained by unlawful means such as force or threat, are illegal testimonial evidence.

Article 2 provides:

> Those pieces of illegal testimonial evidence ascertained according to law shall be excluded and not be used as the basis for determination in the case.

Article 14 provides:

> Where the collection of a physical evidence or documentary evidence is obviously in violation of the law, and may affect the impartiality of the court, a supplementary correction or reasonable explanation shall be made, otherwise the evidence shall not be used as the basis for determination in the case.

The Provisions on Issues concerning the Exclusion of Illegally Obtained Evidence improves the operability of the rules in several ways. First, it establishes the priority principle of procedural review of illegal evidence. Article 5 of the provisions states:

> Where a defendant or the defender argues before or during trial proceedings that the defendant's pretrial confession had been obtained by illegal means, the judges shall make a courtroom investigation after the public prosecutor has finished reading the bill of prosecution.

That is to say, the issue of whether the investigators have obtained the confession illegally, such as through the use of torture, should be reviewed first by the court; it should not be reviewed together with the substantial issues in the case, such as whether the defendant is guilty or not. In other words, the issue of illegal evidence belongs to the admissibility of evidence, not the reliability or the value of evidence.

Second, it makes the allocation of the burden of proof clear for the issue of illegal evidence. Article 6 of the provisions states:

> Where a defendant or the defender thereof argues that the defendant's pretrial confession has been obtained by illegal means, the court shall ask him to provide clues or evidence with regard to the person(s) involved in the alleged illegal activities, as well as the time, place, way and contents thereof.

Article 7 states:

> Where, upon investigation, the court has any doubt over the legal-
> ity of the collection process of the defendant's pretrial confession,
> the public prosecutor shall provide the interrogation transcripts, the
> original audio or visual recordings of the interrogation or other evi-
> dence to the court . . . to prove the legality of the collection.

If there were a dispute over the use of torture, the defense should bear the
primary burden of proof, after which the prosecution should bear the final
burden to prove the legality of the evidence. Such a rule can be regarded as
the reversion of the burden of proof.

Third, it makes clear the standard of proof for the use of torture. Article
10 of the provisions states:

> Where, during court proceedings, any one of the following circum-
> stances occurs, a defendant's pretrial confession may be introduced
> and cross-examined: (1) Neither the defendant nor the defender
> thereof has provided any clue or evidence to prove that the confes-
> sion had been illegally obtained; (2) Though the defendant and the
> defender thereof have provided a clue or evidence to prove that the
> confession was illegally obtained, yet the court has no doubt over
> the legality of the collection process; or (3) The evidence produced
> by the public prosecutor is reliable and sufficient enough to rule out
> the possibility that the confession had been illegally obtained.

Article 11 states:

> If the prosecutor fails to provide evidence to prove that a defendant's
> pretrial confession had been legally obtained or if the evidence they
> provide is not reliable or sufficient, the confession shall not be used
> as the basis for determination in the case.

The proof of torture provided by the defense should be so great that the
judges would have some doubt on the legality of the evidence, which can be
understood as the standard of proof of "forming a reasonable doubt." And
the proof of the legality of evidence provided by the prosecution should be
reliable and sufficient, which can be understood as the standard of proof of
"beyond a reasonable doubt." The former is lower and the latter is higher,

which should be beneficial to the application of the exclusionary rules against illegally obtained evidence.

Despite this, and after the promulgation of the two provisions on criminal evidence, the satisfactory application of the exclusionary rules against illegally obtained evidence has not yet been seen in China. Our survey of criminal judges in a court in the city of Guangzhou, Guangdong Province, in order to assess the application of the two provisions on criminal evidence, gave us the following results:

(1) Before the application of the two provisions on criminal evidence, the cases in which the defense argued during the trial proceedings that the defendant's pretrial confession had been obtained by illegal means was about 25 percent of the total cases tried by the court; after the application, it was about 30 percent. Among these, 55 percent of the defenders could provide some clues or evidence with regard to the person(s) involved in the alleged illegal collection or to the time, place, way, or contents thereof. But, ultimately, only 5 percent of such arguments were sustained by the judges.

(2) The surveyed judges believe that among those cases they have tried, there were about 10 percent that may have involved the use of torture, but use of torture had been found in only 1 percent of the cases.

(3) Among those cases the judges have tried, approximately 10 percent of the interrogation records are flawed, such as by a mistake in the time of interrogation or the interrogator's name, or by the absence of the interrogator's signature or the record informing the defendant of his or her procedural rights. Among these, 85 percent were taken as the basis of determination in the case after the "supplementary correction or reasonable explanation."

(4) Among those cases the judges have tried, about 5 percent of the interrogation records were not checked and confirmed by the defendants with their signatures and fingerprints, but about 90 percent of such records were taken as the basis of determination in the case.

(5) Among those cases the judges have tried, about 50 percent of the physical and documentary evidence was obtained through the suspect's statements or identification; among them, there were about 5 percent of statements alleged to have been given under duress, with about 10 percent due to use of threats, inducement, or deceit, but about 80 percent of such evidence was taken as the basis of determination in the case.

(6) Among the physical and documentary evidence provided to the court by the public security organs, about 15 percent was flawed, such as having no signature of the investigator or the witness on the examination or inspection records; no detailed description of the characteristics, quantity, or quality

of collected items; or no note to prove that the copy of a document is identical to the original one, or no explanation of the process of making the copy. Among these, about 80 percent were taken as the basis of determination in the case after "supplementary correction or reasonable explanation."

(7) Before the application of the two provisions on criminal evidence, when it was required to prove the legality of the evidence collection process, the prosecution took the way of adding an explanatory letter with an official seal in about 85 percent of the cases.[2] After the application, that number was about 80 percent.[3]

This survey data indicate that there was no obvious change of the application of the exclusionary rules against illegally obtained evidence after the promulgation of the two provisions on criminal evidence. Here we see the gap between the law on paper and the law in action.

3. The New Amendment to the Criminal Procedure Law

The amendment to the Criminal Procedure Law was finally passed by the National People's Congress in March 2012 and came into effect on January 1, 2013. One priority of the amendment is to deter and restrain torture and other illegal means to obtain evidence by the exclusionary rules. Article 50 of the amended Criminal Procedure Law basically copied the original provision in previous laws that "extracting confessions by torture, and the use of threat, inducement, deceit and other unlawful methods to collect evidence are strictly prohibited, and no one shall be compelled to prove his or her guilt." The amendment added some provisions similar to those in the Provisions on Issues concerning the Exclusion of Illegally Obtained Evidence in Criminal Cases. Article 54 of the new Criminal Procedure Law states: "The confession of a suspect or defendant obtained by unlawful means such as torture and the statement of a witness or victim obtained by unlawful means such as force or threat shall be excluded. The collection of a physical evidence or documentary evidence is in violation of the legal procedure, and may seriously affect the judicial justice, a supplementary correction or reasonable explanation shall be made, otherwise the evidence shall be excluded."

From these provisions, as well as in the two provisions on criminal evidence, we can see that the exclusionary rules put illegal evidence into two types. The first type is that of mandated exclusion with an explicit list, including the confession of a suspect or defendant obtained by torture and the statement of a witness or victim obtained by force or threat. The second type is that of discretionary exclusion, for which the judge shall ask for a supplementary correction or reasonable explanation, and then make a decision whether it is excluded or not. This type mainly includes the physical evidence and documentary evidence collected in violation of the legal procedure, as well as the confessions obtained through threatening, inducing, or deceiving; the statements obtained through inducing or deceiving; and the physical evidence or documentary evidence obtained as the fruit of a poisonous tree.

At first glance, these exclusionary rules against illegally obtained evidence are clear and explicit. However, after making a close analysis, we may find that there are still some ambiguities among them. For example, what is torture or force? What is threatening, inducing, or deceiving? What are other illegal means? For example, in the case of Zhao Zuohai, the investigators interrogated him for continuous days and nights, and when Zuohai felt drowsy, they let off a firecracker over his head. Is such interrogation considered torture? During the interrogation, the investigator told Zhao Zuohai, "If you don't tell the truth honestly, I'll drive you out and kick you off the car and shoot at you, then I will say you are trying to run away." Is this threatening? In the case of She Xianglin, since She could not describe the process of killing correctly, the investigator hinted, "If you put the corpse in a pond, we can dry the pond and find the corpse!" Is this inducing? As is well known, when they do not have enough evidence for their case, lots of investigations like to tell the suspects, "We have collected enough evidence, and others have told us all. What will you say?" Is this deceiving?

The exclusionary rules against illegally obtained evidence should have some basic characteristics, such as specificity, operability, and predictability. Among these, specificity is the key point, which serves as the basis for operability and predictability. The more specific the rules are, the more operable and predictable they will be. In a sense, the specificity of the rules of law symbolizes the level of the technique of legislature as well as the perfection of the legal system. However, influenced by several factors, such as the ambiguity of the concepts, the polysemy of the language, and the changes in social language, generally speaking, the rules of law should have some openness regarding interpretation—that is, a relative clarity of main meanings with a relative ambiguity of bordered meanings. That is to say, on an abstract level, they are relatively specific; on a concrete level, they are relatively ambiguous.

In addition, in order to meet the requirements of universal and long-term application, it is necessary for the rules of law to have some flexibility. The exclusionary rules against illegally obtained evidence need some flexibility so that judicial personnel can make a decision about whether evidence should be excluded or not in accordance with specific conditions. The factors judicial personnel may consider are as follows: the severity of violation of the law for collecting the evidence, the severity of infringement on human rights for collecting the evidence, the seriousness of the crime in the case, the proof value of the evidence, the subjective state of the person obtaining the evidence, the influence of the behavior for obtaining the evidence on the judicial justice, the influence of the behavior for obtaining the evidence on the environment of law enforcement, the influence of the behavior for obtaining the evidence on the social interests, and so on. Many factors need to be considered, and many standards need to be upheld; however, these factors can change, and these standards have ambiguity. Legislators cannot make these stipulations precisely in advance. However, leaving all these problems to be solved at the discretion of the judges will lead to chaos in the rules' application, especially in the present judicial environment in China. Thus, figuring out how to apply the exclusionary rules against illegally obtained evidence has become an important problem for judicial personnel to face.

The preceding data indicate that there was no obvious change in the application of the exclusionary rules against illegally obtained evidence after the promulgation of the two provisions on criminal evidence. Even with the amendment to the Criminal Procedure Law, there is still a long way to go for China to turn the laws on paper into the rules in action.[4] Sometimes, people may have very different understandings of the laws on paper, and the right to silence is a good example.

4. The Right to Silence in the Amended Criminal Procedure Law

The readers of this book may have seen a difference between Article 50 of the 2012 Criminal Procedure Law and the relevant article in the 1979 or 1996 Criminal Procedure Law. The 2012 law added a sentence to the provision: "No one shall be compelled to prove his or her guilt." This is a significant improvement in Chinese law, because it implies that China has adopted the "voluntariness" standard for admitting confessions in criminal proceedings, which should be an important part of the exclusionary rules against illegally obtained evidence. However, there are still conflicting views about its meaning—especially its relationship to the "right to silence."

At present, the more popular view is that this clause does not establish a right to silence—or, in other words, criminal suspects and defendants do not enjoy a right to silence. Those holding this view probably believe that the Miranda warnings in the United States are the standard for determining whether a right to silence has been established, but this view is flawed.[5] There is no question that the establishment of the Miranda warnings—or rights, as they are sometimes known—has exerted a great influence on the right to silence in the United States and around the world. Thanks to American films and television, the phrase, "You have the right to remain silent" has become popularized and has led people to understand that in the face of police interrogation, one has the right to remain silent. In terms of promoting more civilized criminal justice in a humane society, the positive contribution of the Miranda case and its outcome is incalculable. But the American right to silence did not begin with Miranda.

The Fifth Amendment of the United States Constitution, which went into effect in 1791, provides: "No one in any criminal case may be compelled to be a witness against himself." Therefore, "voluntariness" has become the standard by which the American courts judge whether a person's confession may be admitted as evidence. A suspect facing police interrogation has the right to remain silent. Accordingly, it is clear that America's right to silence was established in 1791. The 1966 decision of the United States Supreme Court requiring Miranda warnings did not create the right to silence for suspects and defendants but merely provided protection for that right. As Fred Inbau, the famous twentieth-century American criminal law professor, pointed out, the reason members of the libertarian faction, with Chief Justice Warren as their representative, wanted to establish these rules "was certainly not borne of a notion to protect the rights of the innocent" but was "a product of the philosophy of pursuing equality." They reasoned that "the wealthy, the educated and the intelligent might become aware through outside sources of their right to remain silent but, on the contrary, the poor, the uneducated or the unintelligent might not be aware of these rights. Accordingly, all those in detention or other forms of custody were entitled to be warned of their right to remain silent."[6]

As per the principle of American governance—the separation of powers—the Supreme Court may, through case law, interpret the Constitution and provide guarantees for the proper implementation of constitutional rights; however, the court cannot add to the rights guaranteed by the Constitution. Otherwise, the court would infringe upon the power of the legislature. Thus, in the United States, the right to silence comes from the Fifth Amendment to the Constitution and not the Miranda decision. During police interrogations, when the police advise a suspect of his or her right to remain silent, they are not conferring this right upon the suspect but are merely reminding him or her about this right. It is a mistaken view that the Miranda warnings established the American right to silence; rather, their historical significance is due to the fact that they changed an implicit right to silence into an explicit one.

By a so-called implicit right to silence, I am referring to the fact that the relevant legal provisions did not use the phrase "right to silence" but that one could deduce such a right from the relevant legal provisions—that is, the Fifth Amendment's rules concerning compelled self-incrimination, which guarantees that suspects and defendants enjoy a right to silence. By an explicit right to silence, I mean that the relevant legal provisions expressly use the phrase "right to silence," and that law enforcement officials must immediately advise suspects and defendants of their right to silence.

No system is perfect. Each one has its advantages and disadvantages, and there are advantages and disadvantages to an implicit right to silence as well as an explicit one. Undoubtedly, an explicit right to silence can more effectively protect a suspect's lawful rights, prevent confession due to torture, and raise the interrogation procedure to a more civilized level, but it may also limit investigative options and afford the guilty an opportunity to avoid punishment. In reality, the suspect—the subject of interrogation—falls into one of two categories: the innocent or the guilty. According to the psychology of interrogation, the truly guilty (by this I mean the factually guilty, not necessarily the legally guilty) are in an internally contradictory state of mind, in which they are facing a choice: to confess or not. In some sense, an interrogation is a battle of wits and will between the interrogator and the factually guilty suspect. If the law requires investigators to clearly advise the suspect of his or her right to remain silent, then some guilty defendants will make the choice to simply remain silent, or when asked a difficult question or a question that causes him or her to hesitate about whether to answer, the suspect might assert his or her right to silence and easily create a mental wall of defense. Experience shows that for those guilty suspects who are somewhat mentally weak, the initial interrogation presents the best opportunity to break down any psychological defenses. If the investigator must clearly advise the suspect of his or her right to silence, then the best opportunity to solve the case may be lost. This is because from the point of view of the investigation and trial, what may be lost is not only the suspect's confession but also the opportunity to obtain hidden physical and documentary evidence to which the confession may lead. On the other hand, an implicit right to silence may not protect a suspect's rights as effectively as an explicit right to silence, and the concept of compelled self-incrimination may be difficult to grasp in practice; however, an implicit right to silence may be more balanced in furthering the goals of fighting crime and enhancing efficiency of the criminal justice system.

In sum, the American example of using the Miranda rule to protect the right to silence is not the only way to guarantee the right and may not necessarily be the best way to protect it. China needs to work hard to choose its proper position when facing the conflicting values of protecting human rights and fighting crime. In China's current social conditions, an implicit right to silence strikes the right balance, and Article 50 of the amended Criminal Procedure Law provides the legal basis for this kind of right. Regardless of whether the legislators were self-aware or not, writing "no one shall be compelled to prove his or her guilt" into the law indicates that China has recognized that suspects and defendants are afforded a right to silence. Making this clear is of paramount importance, for on the one hand it shows the progress of the Chinese Criminal Procedure Law, and on the other it clarifies that suspects and defendants have a right to remain silent during police interrogations.

Perhaps some people will say that because the amended Criminal Procedure Law, in Article 118, retains the requirement that during interrogation, the suspect "should provide truthful answers to the investigators' questions," the suspect does not enjoy a right to silence. I agreed with those who advocated eliminating this clause from the amended Criminal Procedure Law; however, since the legislators chose to keep this language, we must provide a rational explanation for it. One piece of legislation cannot sustain provisions in direct conflict with each other. Therefore, one cannot interpret the amended Criminal Procedure Law as both providing that no one can compel a person to incriminate himself and, at the same time, requiring that a criminal suspect provide truthful answers to investigators' questions. The former provides for a right to silence, while the latter does not permit the suspect to remain silent. This is an irreconcilable contradiction. I believe that a rational interpretation is as follows: when facing an interrogator's questions, a suspect may choose to answer, or he can remain silent. If he chooses to answer, he must answer truthfully. In other words, he has a right to remain silent, but he does not have a right to lie.

China has already established an implicit right to silence regime through legislation, but there is still a lot of work to be done to transform that system from one that should exist to one that exists in fact. First, the legislative body and judicial organs should make clear in their interpretations and regulations of Criminal Procedure Law that criminal suspects and defendants have a right to remain silent during police interrogations. Second, the judicial organs should perfect the exclusionary rule, which is related to the right to silence, and specify the circumstances under which the obtained confession must be excluded. Judicial precedents might be helpful in this regard, such as the guiding cases issued by the Supreme People's Court in recent years. In sum, allow the Chinese right to silence to live up to its name: that is a must.

The effective exclusionary rules against illegally obtained evidence will help prevent wrongful convictions; however, the legislative purpose of these rules is not to exclude evidence but to include more of it. The implementation of the rules will promote the evidentiary investigation abilities of law enforcement and judicial officers. Since the basic task of the police officers, the procurators, and the judges in a criminal case is the handling of evidence, it is most important that they improve the process of evidence collection as well as the examination and evaluation of evidence. In order to effectively prevent wrongful convictions, the abilities of police, procurators, and judges must rise to a higher professional standard in this particular regard.

Chapter Twelve
From Investigation Centeredness to Trial Centeredness

1. Reform of the Criminal Procedure System

The year 2013 seemed to be the year of wrongful convictions for the Chinese criminal justice system. On March 26, the High People's Court of Zhejiang Province announced that Zhang Hui and Zhang Gaoping, incarcerated since 2003 for rape and murder, were innocent; on April 25, the Intermediate People's Court of Pingdingshan, Henan Province, made the same proclamation about Li Huailiang, who had been incarcerated since 2001 for the rape and murder of a young girl; on July 2, the High People's Court of Zhejiang overturned the guilty verdict handed down by the lower court to the five defendants—Tian Weidong, Chen Jianyang, Wang Jianping, Zhu Youping, and Tian Xiaoping—for the robbery and murder of Xu Caihua, a female taxi driver in Xiaoshan in 1995; on August 13, the Intermediate People's Court of Bengfu, Anhui Province, overturned the 1996 conviction of Yu Yingsheng, who had been incarcerated on conviction of killing his wife.

We have a very good slogan in criminal justice: "To make no innocent person convicted and to let no guilty person escape." It is a dream impossible to realize. In the criminal justice system of any country, wrongful convictions cannot be avoided absolutely. Investigators, prosecutors, and judges can never have direct perception of the facts in any case. The facts all happened in the past. Legal officers are not gods or immortal beings. They cannot know everything or cross the "time tunnel." They can only find facts based on limited and insufficient evidence, and unavoidably make mistakes. We are not exculpating legal officers but confronting the inevitability of wrongful convictions and analyzing their causes to ensure a reduced and, it is hoped, minimized rate of mistakes. We are not making excuses for wrongful convictions but letting people know the causes of those wrongful convictions in an effort to establish a better criminal justice system in order to prevent such miscarriages of justice from continuing in our society. While we may not be able to completely eradicate cases of wrongful conviction, we must spare no efforts to guard against them.

In order to prevent wrongful convictions, we should push forward the reform of the Chinese criminal procedure system. We have made some progress with the amendment to the Criminal Procedure Law in 2012, but we should go further. In October 2014, the Fourth Plenum of the CPC Central Committee made a decision to promote the rule of law in China. The decision calls for the reform of the criminal procedure system towards the model of trial centeredness. On April 10, 2015, the Chinese central leadership published its Implementation Plan to Carry Out the Decision of the Fourth Plenum of the Party's 18th Congress to Deeper the Reform of the Judicial System and the Social System. One priority of the plan is to promote the reform of the criminal procedure system towards the model of trial centeredness.

As discussed in chapter 9, the Chinese criminal procedure assembly-line model has the feature of investigation centeredness, and the nominalization of criminal court trials is the result. In order to fulfill the mission of promoting the reform towards a trial-centered procedure, both policy makers and enforcers of judicial reform need to first change their old mentalities.

2. Investigation Centeredness versus Trial Centeredness

With reference to the process of the development of the judicial system, we can see that the function of criminal investigation has been departing gradually from the adjudicative function. In early human society, in both Eastern and Western countries, the investigation function was subsidiary to adjudication. In other words, judges performed investigation of the case, and normally this was done through questioning litigants and witnesses during trial. For example, Di Renjie, Bao Zheng, and other famous judges in Chinese history were responsible for investigating cases, and they also proved to be the "experts" in resolving them. As society developed, and especially as the professional division of labor in society became finer and more detailed, the function of criminal investigation gradually transitioned from adjudicators to special state officers. As a result, judges are now only responsible for adjudication. As investigation and adjudication have become two fundamental stages of criminal justice activities, one question arises: Which stage is more important? Or, to put it in another way, which stage should be the core of the criminal justice process? In answering this question, it is beneficial to refer to the historical development of the criminal procedure system in Western countries, especially those countries that use the continental legal system.

Beginning in the twelfth century, European continental countries gradually changed their criminal procedure system from an "accusatorial model" to an "inquisitorial model." Under this system, the procedure of trying criminal cases could be divided into two stages: preliminary trial and adjudication. The mission of the preliminary trial was to investigate the facts of the alleged criminal acts, whereas the mission of adjudication was to determine the guilt of the accused. Although those who were responsible for preliminary trial and adjudication were all court officials, as far as their functions were concerned, there was a clear division of labor between the two groups of people.

During the preliminary trial stage, the basic method used by judges to investigate cases was to try the accused, and the trial was conducted in secret, where extortion of confession by torture was common. The various kinds of evidence obtained by the judge at the preliminary trial—mainly written testimonies and oral evidence—were used not only as the bases for prosecution but also as the bases for the trial judge to determine the guilt and the sentence of the accused. During the trial, the judge listened to the opinion of the prosecution, which was prepared by the prosecutors based on the materials considered during the preliminary trial. After that, the judge would give the defendant a final trial based on the relevant materials, without calling any witnesses to testify. After this, judgment was handed down; thus, adjudication was merely a formality, and judges' examination of the evidence existed in name only.

At the same time, common-law countries such as the United Kingdom formulated the "adversarial model" on the basis of the "accusatorial model," whereby both the prosecution and the defense could investigate the case and collect evidence. The rights to investigation of both parties were equal, at least theoretically. Generally speaking, the prosecution directed the police to investigate and collect evidence, while the defense would carry out the investigation and collect evidence on their own or hire private detectives to do so on their behalf. Adjudication was the most important part of the criminal trial. Whether the evidence collected by the prosecution and the defense could be used as the basis for determining a case was decided by the judge. Also, the facts of the case could be determined only by the judges (or the jury) based on the examination conducted by the court.

From this, we can see that the continental legal system has an investigation-centered tradition, whereas the Anglo-American legal system has a trial-centered tradition. Under the former, investigative officers are the key figures in a criminal trial. A case would be considered resolved once the investigative officers had completed their investigation, with the judges' adjudication simply a kind of procedure without much meaning. In the latter kind of system, judges are the central figures in a criminal trial, and cases will only be considered resolved after being adjudicated by them.

However, as social development and the mind-set of the judiciary changed, the focus of the criminal trial in countries using the continental legal system gradually changed from investigation to adjudication. France is one example. Since around the seventeenth century, prosecutors had played an important role in criminal investigation. In the nineteenth century, judicial police with the characteristics of modern police also became a major force in criminal investigation. Under the system of demarcation of the powers of investigation, prosecution, and adjudication, although the prosecutors might supervise and guide the investigative activities of the police, and the judges of a preliminary trial had to examine the evidence collected by the investigative officers before trial, the work of collecting evidence was still mainly vested in the police. The examination of evidence by the trial judge had thus become more meaningful. Since the mid-twentieth century, under the influence of the theories of judiciary fairness and protection of human rights, the trial-centered theory has become accepted, and the direct and oral principle in criminal evidence law is a reflection of this idea.

Under the investigation-centered approach, judges' assessment of evidence during trial does not have any meaning in substance; therefore, there is no need to emphasize direct examination by judges. Nor is it necessary to exclude written testimony obtained by investigative officers before trial; however, under the trial-centered approach, given that the determination of the case has to go through the process of adjudication, the questions as to whether the evidence is directly presented in court and whether it is directly examined by the court have important meanings. In addition, under the contemporary judicial system, only judges can decide whether the accused are guilty. Neither the police nor the prosecutors can do that. From this, we can see that changing from an investigation-centered mentality to a trial-centered

165

mentality complies with the trend of development of the judicial system in human society.

For a period of time after the establishment of the People's Republic of China, China's criminal justice system was also an investigation-centered system. Especially under the guidance of the principle of using class struggle as the framework, adjudication naturally became ancillary to investigation, and it was not surprising that the president of the court had to accept the guidance of the head of the public security bureau. In modern states incorporating the rule of law, however, the core of the criminal trial should be adjudication, and the power of criminal adjudication should belong to judges. Therefore, the direction of China's criminal justice system reform should change from being investigation centered to being trial centered.

In China today, the trial-centered concept has been accepted by the legal profession to a certain extent, and the general public has also gradually recognized the leading role of judges in a criminal trial. However, many investigative officers have not yet moved on from investigation-centered thinking and practices. For example, some investigative officers believe that as long as they can catch a suspect and obtain a confession, the case should be considered resolved and the investigation complete. In practice, in cases on which the public security bureau has completed investigation, the defendant may not be convicted in court. Although it is not necessarily true that the public security bureau has made mistakes in investigation in those cases and caused the court not to convict the accused, it has been discovered that in a large number of cases, the investigative officers did make some mistakes in collecting evidence. Certain cases become "half-cooked rice" simply because investigative officers are too keen to obtain confessions, thus making them overlook the need to collect important physical evidence. The reason why certain cases cannot be determined is the failure of investigative officers to recognize the importance of preserving the evidence, which eventually leads to the loss of the legal value of such evidence. Therefore, investigative officers should adapt to the requirement of the modern trial-centered system, change their mind-set, raise their awareness of evidence and evidence collection, understand their position clearly, and perform their work with due care and diligence.

Changing from an investigation-centered to a trial-centered mind-set could also help curb the use of torture to extort confession. Under the trial-centered system, the confession given by a criminal suspect during the investigative stage has only limited value during adjudication; what is crucial instead is the statement of the accused in court. Thus, investigative officers would be prevented from thinking their work is complete once they have obtained a confession of guilt, motivating them to focus on the collection of other evidence to support the confession. As the impact of the criminal suspect's confession reduces, the investigative officers' motivation to practice the use of torture should be weakened. In conclusion, insistence on an adjudication-centered mind-set may help ensure that investigative officers handle cases in accordance with the law, thus raising the quality of criminal investigation.

3. The Principle of Direct Hearing and Oral Testimony in Criminal Trials

To satisfy the requirements of substantial and procedural justice, as it should be, the trial is essential to criminal procedure, with collegial panels or a single judge acting as the real decision maker in adjudication.

It is not easy to change the criminal procedure model in China. As mentioned previously, it is necessary to change mind-sets from investigation centeredness to trial centeredness. It is necessary also to improve the legal system in general, paying attention to issues such as the deliberation procedure of collegial panels, and to encourage the increased use of single judge trials to relieve the stress of staff shortages. Transformation should not be expected at once, but there should be some major impetus to promote reform. And to restore the substantive function of criminal trials in China, the principle of direct hearing and oral testimony should be established.

The principle of direct hearing and oral testimony at trial consists of two basic aspects. The first is that adjudication should be made by those who have sifted through the evidence themselves, rather than by those who have never done so in person. The second relates to producing and impeaching evidence delivered orally. This is the opposite of a trial reliant on records. Used by continental legal systems, this principle achieves the same effect as the rules of hearsay used in Anglo-American legal systems. Article 250 (the directness of evidence review) in the Law of Criminal Procedure in Germany provides that "if personal feelings are used to attest to the reality of the facts, the witnesses should be required to attend court to allow for cross-examination at the trial."[1]

The principle of direct hearing and oral testimony could serve as a guarantee of justice. As the adjudicator, the judge should be required to personally review the evidence submitted at the trial. Accordingly, only by producing and impeaching the evidence given orally at the trial can judges establish their "intimate conviction" of the authenticity and admissibility of the evidence. In addition, the principle of direct hearing and oral testimony could meet the requirements of procedural justice. The process of giving direct testimony, direct impeachment, and direct assessment—namely, verbal testimony at court—allows for the opposition to confront any witness face-to-face, and the judge reviewing the oral testimony and its possible impeachment—in person and with immediacy—could not only improve the transparency of judgment by preventing judicial officials from prejudging cases before trial but also protect the legal right granted to litigants, especially the right to challenge any witnesses face-to-face and the right to a fair trial.

The principle of direct hearing and oral testimony is compatible with the concept of the trial-centered procedural model. In the investigation-centered procedural model, the review of evidence at trial by judges is not essential. Consequently, there is no need to emphasize whether the judges hear testimony in person at trial or not. At the same time, the documentary verbal evidence obtained by investigators before the trial could still be acceptable. As far as the trial-centered procedural model is concerned, and owing to the ascertainment of facts that should be completed during the process of testifying, whether or not evidence is put forward in court and whether or not evidence is reviewed personally by judges would make a significant difference. It deserves to be noted that the principle of direct hearing and oral testimony lays stress on the review of evidence by judges in person and the idea that only judges who have presided over a trial themselves can participate in its adjudication. In Taiwan, the appeal court would rule a judgment illegal if judges who had not sat in on the trial participate in making the judgment.[2]

Although it is still relatively difficult to establish the principle of direct hearing and oral testimony comprehensively in China, we should advocate a progressive transition as follows.

First, it should be set out clearly that witnesses are required to testify at court if one of the parties challenges his or her testimony. Without a doubt, the economic guarantee and safeguard of witnesses appearing in court should be prescribed as well. The amendment to the Criminal Procedure Law, passed by the National People's Congress in March 2012, has a better provision on this issue, but it still allows judges a lot of room for discretion.[3] In terms of testimony free from controversy, the judge could easily assess this evidence when court is in session. In contrast, if any testimony has been challenged, the judge should assess it on the basis of the version rendered by the witness who would testify at court. There should be no need to review the records of inquiry or testimony in the case files made before the trial. This would remove the judges' dependence on previewing case files and lead to the restoration of the substantive function of the courtroom trial in China.

Second, it should be set out clearly that only the judges who have heard the case could pass judgment. Any judge who has not personally heard the case should only be able to lend opinion on the application of the law rather than render any decision on the ascertainment of the facts. As mentioned previously, in practice in China, trial committees could be conceived as being the actual decision makers, in spite of their members never reviewing the evidence at the court in person. Obviously, this goes against the principle of direct hearing and oral testimony. On the premise that trial committees could not be dissolved, the trial committee's extent of power should be limited to legal issues, or the application of the law, while the factual issues in the case, or the finding of the facts, should be decided by the collegial panel, whose members would have heard the case themselves. Issues concerning the application of the law consist of those regarding substantive as well as procedural law, which include the rules of evidence. For example, it could be submitted to the trial committee to decide whether a confession obtained from the accused using psychological or other forms of torture could be excluded on the grounds of extortion. However, whether the confession and other evidence proves the allegation could be decided by the collegial panel alone after deliberation, and neither be decided by the trial committee nor by the political-legal work committee. In advancing reform, the relevant leaders should change their mind-sets to respect the rules of adjudication, abandon their administrative decision-making habits, and make the judges who hear the cases become the real decision makers.

In order to change the situation of the nominalization of criminal trials and to prevent wrongful convictions in China, we must push forward judicial reforms, such as these: the party's political and legal work committees should not interfere with the judiciary pertaining to individual cases, the trial committees of the courts should not hold deliberations on the factual issues of the cases, the defense lawyers should play a more active role during criminal trials, and the people's jurors should play a more substantive role in influencing adjudication.[4] I believe this last one could serve as the entryway for judicial reform and deserves more detailed discussion.

Chapter Thirteen

Reform of the People's Juror System

In both the decision of the Fourth Plenum of the CPC Central Committee in October 2014 and the implementation plan of the central leadership in April 2015, the reform of the people's juror system is emphasized. In fact, it is an issue I have been focusing on in my legal research for many years.

1. People's Juror versus People's Jury

In the early 1990s, when I was studying at Northwestern University School of Law in Chicago, I attended court several times, including a jury selection procedure. The U.S. jury system impressed me deeply. Later, the O. J. Simpson "trial of the century" captured the interest of the Chinese, who as a result began to pay attention to the jury system. At this point, I published several articles in local newspapers to introduce the jury system and began to think about reform of the people's juror system in China.

The people's juror (or people's assessor) system, established in the 1950s, is similar to that in the continental legal system used in countries such as France and Germany. Normally, in this system, a collegial bench is formed to sit in on any trial and to adjudicate. The bench is composed of one judge and two people's jurors, or two judges and one people's juror. The members jointly take part in the trial and enjoy equal rights apart from acting as the presiding judge. After the Culture Revolution in 1970s, the system began to confront dilemmas. On the one hand, judges complained that it was difficult to find qualified jurors: some of them were unable to play a real role in the trial because of their lack of competency or their failure to understand their responsibility. On the other hand, jurors complained that they were being overlooked by judges or that they felt themselves to be considered nothing more than cheap labor. As a result, the people's juror system became a mere formality, with jurors' roles compared to "the ears of a deaf person."

At the end of the twentieth century, reform of the juror system became a hot topic in Chinese legal circles. By that time, I had published several papers and had begun to be interviewed as an expert on the topic. After several years' discussion, the Standing Committee of the National People's Congress adopted the Decision on Perfecting the System of People's Jurors, which came into force on May 1, 2005, and emphasizes the importance of people's jurors and provides some measures to safeguard the system.

Since then, people's courts all over China have made efforts to select and train jurors; therefore, cases with jurors directly participating at the trial have accelerated significantly.[1] Of the 292 cases mentioned in chapter 9, people's jurors took part in 177 (60.62%). The one-plus-two (1 + 2) model, namely, the collegial panel consisting of one judge and two people's jurors, accounted for 130 cases (44.52%); the two-plus-one (2 + 1) model—the collegial panel consisting of two judges and one people's juror—made up 47 of the cases (16.10%). Despite this, the overwhelming majority of people's jurors played passive roles at the trial: in 98.31% of the 177 cases, the people's jurors posed no questions; in 69.47% of the 177 cases, the people's jurors had no communication with the presiding judges. It is common for people's jurors to be present without really listening, or to listen but not participate in the decision-making process.

Therefore, the decision to select and train jurors has not resolved the problems of the people's juror system, which is fundamentally to "accompany rather than try" and which exists in name only. The decision also fails to reflect the core value of the peoples' juror system: to promote judicial independence and justice through public participation. Therefore, I led a group of scholars to research jury systems around the world in order to provide some suggestions for reform. In 2006, we published the fruit of this research, *Which Direction Shall the Chinese People's Juror System Go?*[2] Of course, no system is perfect; every system has its merits and demerits. But as a result of this comparative study, I assert that the direction of reform should be from "peoples' juror" to "peoples' jury." However, it has been very difficult to persuade the decision makers in the Chinese judiciary to accept this idea. Learning from the reform of France and Japan, I then made another suggestion: to increase the number of jurors at trials.[3] Taking into account that

Chinese courts find it difficult to adopt the jury system at present, I further amended my suggestion for reform, calling for more jurors to participate in the trials of important cases—for example, to set up a trial bench of one judge with six jurors.[4]

If we want the people's jurors to function as "promoting impartial justice," the number of people's assessors should be increased in the collegial panel, and the Criminal Procedure Code of China should be revised. The original provision states:

> Trials of cases of first instance in the Primary and Intermediate People's Courts shall be conducted by a collegial panel composed of three judges or of judges and people's assessors totaling three. . . . Trials of cases of first instance in the Higher People's Courts or the Supreme People's Court shall be conducted by a collegial panel composed of three to seven judges or of judges and people's assessors totaling three to seven.

This provision should be revised to:

> Trials of cases of first instance in the Primary People's Courts shall be conducted by a collegial panel composed of three judges or of judges and people's assessors totaling three. Trials of cases of first instance in the Intermediate, Higher, or the Supreme People's Court shall be conducted by a collegial panel composed of three to seven judges or of judges and people's assessors totaling three to seven.

This version would make some room for useful experiments in reform. Some intermediate people's courts may hold a court by the one-plus-six $(1+6)$ or the two-plus-five $(2+5)$ models, with the collegial panel consisting of one judge with six people's jurors or two judges with five people's jurors, to hear complicated and major cases.

This revision could bring about reform within the legal framework as well as oversee such reform. Thus, an out-of-control jury, which has been raised as a possible point of concern, would not be an issue. The leaders of higher people's court, those who are determined to reform, could select a qualified intermediate people's court as the pilot unit to hear some complicated and major cases by seven-member collegial panels. Relevant regulations would be set out. First, defendants would be ensured of their right to option: the court would ask for the consent of the defendants. If consent is withheld, the cases would be heard by the three-member collegial panel, as before. Second, the people's jurors would be selected at random at court. Once having decided to hear cases by a seven-member collegial panel, the court could pick twenty candidates from the list of people's jurors present at the people's court and direct them to participate in the selection at the courtroom on the trial date. During the selection process, the judge could roll-call at random to ask whether the jurors believed in their own impartiality. These possible jurors could be given the opportunity to excuse themselves from the panel, but the basis of application for withdrawal should be supported by valid and specific reasoning. Withdrawal from responsibility to sit on the panel should be limited to three times for each juror. The five or six people's jurors should take an oath testifying to their understanding of their responsibilities, then hear the cases as members of the collegial panel. Third, the rules for the people's jurors taking part in the trials would be clearly set out. For example, they could be required by prosecutors and defenders to explain the relevant issues and review all the evidence in person. Fourth, the rules for deliberation of the collegial panel would be made clear as well. For instance, the people's jurors could be empowered to express their opinions freely and before the judge(s) in the process of the deliberation. After their full deliberation, the collegial panel would pool their opinions to vote, and convict only when five or more members find the defendant guilty. After the vote, the judgment would take effect regardless of any approval from the Judicial Committee. These are my suggestions, and any pilot program should make rules in consideration of the particular circumstances. On the basis of summarizing the experiences of all the programs, the Supreme People's Court could mark out the right cases for which a seven-member collegial panel could be used and then make the rules for trials requiring a collegial panel. Publicizing the rules nationwide would make the judges, people's jurors, prosecutors, lawyers, defendants, and public familiar with the trial model and would help it to prevail.

Such reform of the people's juror system would reverse the nominalization of criminal trials in China. When the seven-member collegial panel serves as the real decision makers, the courtroom trial will become the substantive stage of criminal proceedings. Holding this kind of trial is so challenging that judges who lack professional quality and experience would be found hardly competent. At the same time, with the function of the trial restored, a more highly capable prosecution and defense would be required, which would help enhance the professional skills of prosecutors and defense lawyers.

While we scholars were calling for the establishment of the jury system, some judicial authorities in China started to reform boldly. For instance, in June 2009, the Henan High People's Court decided to select six intermediate people's courts in Zhengzhou, Kaifeng, Xinxiang, Sanmenxia, Shangqiu, and Zhumadian as experimental zones. According to reports, from June 2009 to March 2010, courts in Henan heard a total of 107 criminal cases through the "people's jury" system and achieved sound social effects. Since there is no legislative basis for the reform, this people's jury can operate only as an observer, providing points of reference and opinion. Greatly inspired by this, I organized a publicly held mock trial to illustrate the advantages of a jury trial. The case of lawyer Li Zhuang provided a great opportunity.

2. A Special Criminal Case of a Defense Lawyer

In the summer of 2009, Bo Xilai, the then party secretary of Chongqing, launched an anti-Mafia campaign in the city. From then until the spring of 2010, according to some reports, the Chongqing police captured more than four thousand underworld criminals, including more than sixty core gang members. Among them, the spotlight was turned on Gong Gangmo, the former general manager of Chongqing Yingang Motor Sales Company. He was arrested in June 2009 for allegedly organizing and leading an underworld organization. He was also accused of murder. Even so, the arrest did not attract widespread attention; he became famous because of his defense lawyer, Li Zhuang.

Li Zhuang worked for the Kangda Law Firm in Beijing. He was hired as Gong Gangmo's counsel and met him in the Chongqing detention center on November 25 and 26 and on December 4, 2009. However, on December 10, Gong told the police that Li had encouraged him to fabricate testimony against the police: to accuse them of torturing him into a confession. On December 12, Li was taken from Beijing to Chongqing by the Chongqing police, and was detained the following day. He was formally arrested two days later, charged with inducing a witness to give false testimony and obstructing justice. The case was transferred to the Jiangbei District People's Procuratorate of Chongqing on December 17, and the prosecution was submitted to the Chongqing Jiangbei People's Court the next day.

The trial opened on December 30, 2009. On January 8, 2010, the court found Li Zhuang guilty of the two charges and sentenced him to thirty months' imprisonment. He appealed, and on February 3, the second instance trial of Li Zhuang was opened in Chongqing's First Intermediate People's Court, where Li Zhuang announced the withdrawal of his appeal and pleaded guilty. A week later, the court sustained the guilty verdict but mitigated the sentence to one year and six months. After hearing the ruling, Li Zhuang became very emotional, accusing Chongqing prosecutors of bad faith and claiming that his previous guilty plea was false. However, this was the final judgment of the court and became effective immediately.

The rise of the political star, Bo Xilai, the success of the largest anti-Mafia campaign, and the conviction of a defense lawyer—these three elements attracted widespread attention in China.[5] For a while, Li Zhuang became nationally known, with legal professionals taking notice of this case for a particular reason: it illustrated the professional risk of defense lawyers and the controversial offense of fabricating evidence by lawyers in Chinese criminal law. Article 306 of the Criminal Procedure Law of China states:

> In criminal proceedings, a defendant or legal agent who destroys or fabricates evidence, or helps a litigant to do so, or threatens or entices a witness to change his true testimony or commit perjury, shall be sentenced to imprisonment or custodial labor of no less than three years, and shall be sentenced to imprisonment for three to seven years if the circumstances are serious.

Article 306 has been criticized by some lawyers and legal scholars in China, who have argued that the Criminal Procedure Law already includes the general provision pertaining to the offense of perjury; therefore, the offense of fabricating evidence specifically by lawyers is inappropriate and makes lawyers a special target. In reality, police officers and prosecutors, for example, might also threaten or entice witnesses to change their testimony or give false testimony, yet there is no corresponding special provision for them set out in the Criminal Procedure Law. It is clearly a discrimination against lawyers, with a negative impact on the development of the legal profession in China. Indeed, the criminal defense rate in China has been falling, and the number of criminal defense lawyers has dwindled. A widespread notion in the legal profession is that

> if you are going to practice law, don't be a lawyer. If you are a lawyer, don't take a criminal case. If you are taking a criminal case, don't

collect evidence. If you are collecting evidence, don't take witness testimony. If you cannot follow these rules, you should take yourself to the detention house.

During the National People's Congress in 2010, a group of representatives submitted a proposal to abolish the offense of fabricating evidence by lawyers, but failed to garner sufficient support. The subsequent case of Li Zhuang brought this issue to public attention again, with some comparing the role of lawyers in China to the role of lawyers in Western countries, such as the United States.[6]

As a law professor, I had been paying close attention to the trial process of the Li Zhuang case. Although he was not someone I particularly liked, his fate was related to the fate of Chinese criminal defense lawyers, even the fate of the rule of law in China. What could I do? Probably because I am not only a jurist but also a novelist, I often have some novel ideas about legal issues. And, indeed, an idea did come to mind: to organize a mock trial for the Li Zhuang case, to be held on the Internet. I knew it would be tricky and risky, but it would be worthwhile, and I did have special reasons for doing it.

3. A Jury Trial of a Mock Court

On January 12, 2010, I registered a blog on JCRB.com, affiliated to the Supreme People's Procuratorate, and contributed some entries. Consequently, the idea to organize an online mock jury trial came to my mind. The Li Zhuang case happened to provide me with inspiration. I understood that the case was politically sensitive, so I had to be extremely careful. After serious thought and thinking of it as playing a game, I decided to organize a mock jury trial to hear the Li Zhuang case. On March 21, 2010, I posted the following announcement on my blog:

> I am setting up a mock court in the Kingdom of Justice, to try Li Zhuang by jury. This is just a game, without any other purpose. And it is a mock trial: we cannot use the result to influence the trial held in the real world. I shall appoint myself as the sole judge.

The game will be composed of ten steps:

S1, selection of the prosecutors and the defense lawyers
S2, selection of a nine-person jury
S3, opening statements
S4, the introduction of evidence by the prosecution and cross-
examination of this evidence by the defense
S5, the introduction of evidence by the defense and cross-
examination of this evidence by the prosecution
S6, the introduction of rebuttal evidence, and cross-examination
of the evidence
S7, closing arguments
S8, the judge's instructions to the jury
S9, deliberation by the jury
S10, announcement of judgment.
All participants shall follow the rules of the game, which will be
announced by the court before each step.

I felt somewhat anxious after posting the announcement, because I could not anticipate how netizens would react and because I prefer to use my real name when I am writing. But as it turned out, many netizens sent messages of support. Others thought the trial to be meaningless; still others warned me not to play with fire. I had already consulted the heads of JCRB .com, who were hosting my blog; they realized the risks but still gave me the green light.

Overall, I was encouraged by the number of reactions I was receiving and I invited the netizens to apply for the various roles of counsel for the prosecution, counsel for the defense, or member of the jury. I promised that as a token gesture of remuneration and in acknowledgment of their enthusiasm and regard to fair play, each person chosen would be given a signed copy of the crime novel I had written. Because netizens often disguise their identities online, Article 4 of the Application Rules allowed applicants to wear a disguise if they so chose, but required them to declare whether they had any experience of legal practice, such as serving as a judge, prosecutor, or defense lawyer. Article 5 stipulated that anyone involved in the Li Zhuang case in the real world would be disqualified.

Within three days of the call for applications, twelve netizens applied for the role of prosecutor, and the number of applications for the roles of defense counsel and juror were seven and twenty-two, respectively. Many netizens expressed their interest in following the course of the mock trial. As the self-appointed judge, I selected four applicants to play the role of public prosecutor and four as counsel for the defense, depending on the answers they submitted. The former were mostly incumbent prosecutors; the latter mostly practicing lawyers. I also appointed a chief prosecution attorney and a chief defense attorney in accordance with the application sequence. Then I asked the jury applicants to answer five questions, including Could you guarantee participation at every stage of the mock trial? and Could you pledge to give a fair judgment? Based on their answers, seventeen names appeared on my jury list and became prospective jurors. I next asked them to attend jury selection "in court."

During voir dire, I asked each prospective juror six questions on the basis of the questions suggested by the prosecution and the defense, including:

1. Which one is more important in criminal prosecution, the public interest or the protection of the rights of the accused?
2. Do you have any friend who is a lawyer?
3. Would you call the police if your mobile phone had been stolen or if you had been cheated out of hundreds of yuan?

After they had answered, I permitted the prosecution and defense to challenge the qualifications of the candidates. Both sides used what is called "challenge for cause" three times and a "peremptory challenge" twice. After a careful examination, I ruled that all four peremptory challenges were effective, as were three challenges for cause from the defense and one challenge for cause from the prosecution, ruling two of the prosecution's challenges to be invalid. According to my rules, prospective jurors that had been challenged effectively could still serve as substitute jurors in the mock trial. Finally, I announced a list of nine jurors and appointed juror number one as the foreperson.

I set up several sections on my blog for people involved in the trial to discuss the case and exchange views: the prosecution section, the defense section, the juror section, the media section, and the observer section. Yang Jianguo, a doctoral candidate at the Law School of the People's University, served as the court clerk and bailiff, and was in charge of answering participants' questions and sweeping away unrelated and inappropriate messages.

Some netizens created media, such as See See TV (a pun on CCTV) and Crazy TV, to report on the mock trial. Microblogging was not yet prevalent, so they often reported on their own blogs, covering interviews and whistle blowing on prosecutors and defenders. Even though I forbade jurors to be interviewed, a small number of jurors still appeared on "TV." Reporters revealed that prosecutors had already united as one and assembled in an "ocean-view villa" to prepare for the trial. The defense appeared to be rudderless and showed signs of infighting. Some reports said that the reason the prosecution peremptorily challenged two prospective jurors was because of "family problems." One defense lawyer suddenly disappeared because he had accepted an interview by See See TV, while a judge's mobile phone was either powered off or out of the service zone, reporters added. Some of the stories might have been false, but it made the trial much more interesting. We had a surge of visitors to the blog, and the click-through rate (CTR) soared rapidly.

Journalists in the real world displayed an interest in covering the mock trial at the very beginning, just after the initial information was leaked out. They never followed through, but they told me later that they believed it would be better not to cover the story for "special reasons." Actually, I thought it was a good thing that the trial attracted little outside attention, because all I wanted was for the experiment to run smoothly.

4. The Prosecution versus the Defense

The long-awaited online mock trial of Li Zhuang finally began. First and foremost, I would like to declare that Li Zhuang was unable to appear in court for obvious reasons. Luckily, the absence of a defendant would not influence the proceedings of the mock trial because of its virtual nature. Besides, testimony from both sides could not be presented directly to the judge and jurors or be cross-examined face-to-face. In other words, we could not follow the principle of direct hearing and verbal testimony in this mock trial. We had to arrange for the prosecution and the defense to make statements in court separately because both sides could not guarantee that they would be available online or "appear in court" at the same time. Prosecutors made an opening statement and read out the indictment on March 30. One day later, defenders issued their defense statements. However, an incident occurred, and I had to issue the following statement:

> Friends, I am sorry to inform you that because of some unusual reasons the mock trial of Li Zhuang will be postponed with the time

of its reconvening to be determined. I profoundly regret and apologize for any inconvenience and worries caused. Here and now, as a judge, my feelings are mixed. Originally, all I wanted was to play a game with friends online and I never imagined this trial would alarm anyone. A kind-hearted man has advised me to stop now, and not become addicted to online games. It is unwise for at some point it may spill over into reality and I could get myself burned. "If you have time, play more badminton because your health is much more important," he said. Compared to such a euphemism, others seemed to be impolite. I received a call from a stranger with a northeast accent who claimed to be a member of the underworld. "Do you know you have offended my boss? All the shit you have done online! Do you know your leg is worth 200,000 yuan?" the man roared. Then he even outlined some specifics of my family. I wrote down his number 13718517094 and called the police.

Reactions online were shocked, angry, and regretful. I announced another statement the next day:

Friends, I apologize to all of you for the joke I made yesterday. Happy April Fool's day! But please let me be clear that within that note only the postponement of the trial was untrue. All else had basis in fact, including the threatening phone call. The police should have the phone record and the number is real. I posted the number online to remind other friends to be vigilant. After this, I was resolute: I would rather be beaten to death than be frightened to death. Nobody can stop me from proceeding with this mock trial.

The reactions online were jubilant. After that, the trial proceeded smoothly. First, prosecution lawyers spent two days submitting fifteen pieces of evidence against Li Zhuang focusing on the charge of fabricating evidence, and eight pieces of evidence on the charge of unduly influencing the witnessing. The prosecution lawyers also handed in four pieces of comprehensive evidence. It took the defense one day to cross-examine all the evidence submitted. They put forward a total of twenty-seven challenges, seven of them regarding the admissibility of the evidence and the others challenging the reliability of the evidence. For the challenges to the admissibility of the evidence, I ruled in support of four of them. In other words, four pieces of evidence submitted by the prosecution were excluded. Afterwards, the defense spent another two days before submitting their own eleven pieces of evidence in support of their argument. Six of these pieces focused on the former charge, and five the latter. The time the prosecution took to cross-examine the evidence was the same as the defense had taken. The prosecution challenged the admissibility of six pieces of evidence. I only supported one of them.

After ensuring both sides had finished arguing their cases, I announced the time had come for closing statements. At first, I gave one day to the prosecution and one day to the defense. An additional day was given to prosecutors to make their closing statement.

The courtroom session ended. I gave jurors their instructions, emphasizing the importance of the principle of legality and the presumption of innocence, and explaining the burden and standard of proof in criminal trials. Then I published the rules of deliberation for this mock trial: jurors should deliberate in the "jury room" (the jury section on my blog); each juror should speak at least once in the jury room; each juror should comment on both charges; the views the jurors state in the jury room do not stand for their final opinion; and the duration of deliberation was from midnight on April 19 to midnight on April 20.

Our netizen followers eagerly awaited the verdict, as did we all.

5. The Verdict and the Discussion

I posted an announcement on my own legal blog on April 22, 2010, as follows:

> Jurors, your decision will be historic in the Kingdom of Justice. Whether or not your decision is just will depend on the assessment of the netizens and future generations. Please vote publicly. In this case, Li Zhuang is charged with two offenses: inducing witness to give false testimony and obstructing justice. Each juror should vote twice: once for each charge. You do not need to give any reasons for voting one way or the other.
> Votes must be submitted from 20:00 to 21:00, 22 April.

After the vote and on behalf of the mock court, I announced:

> According to the jury rules, only when more than two-thirds of the total jurors (in this case no less than 6 jurors) vote for guilty, can

Li Zhuang be convicted. For the first charge, inducing witness to give false testimony, the vote was 9–0 for "not guilty"; for the second charge, obstructing justice, the vote was 8–1 for "not guilty."

As the sole judge, I ruled the verdict to be legal and effective immediately. The jury returned a verdict of not guilty for Li Zhuang, which is the judgment of the court. The mock trial of the Li Zhuang case was concluded.[7]

Based on the data provided by JCRB.com, thousands of bloggers participated in this mock trial and left messages during the period of the forty-two-day trial. The CTR of relevant blogs soared to 100,000. The mock trial became a hot topic among legal professionals.

When the trial ended, we set up an online survey. Twenty-two online users were willing to participate. Among them, sixteen were satisfied with the trial proceedings, while six felt them to be acceptable. None were discontent. For the verdict, nine people were satisfied, ten felt it to be acceptable, and three felt discontent. Some users said that the mock trial might profoundly influence judicial reform in China. Others said that such a comparison might give us incredible insight into the flaws of our Chinese trial system and may help promote reform of the people's juror system and amendment of the Criminal Procedure Law.

On May 3, the Institute of Evidence of the Renmin University of China School of Law and JCRB.com held an academic conference in Beijing on The Mock Trial of the Li Zhuang Case and the Reform of Chinese Trial System. About one hundred people attended, including professors, judges, prosecutors, lawyers, and the media. Some of the participants of the mock trial of the Li Zhuang case also attended the conference, which enlarged both the social and the political influence of the mock jury trial. The discussion went further, to include the topic of the problems existing in the Chinese criminal justice and the ways to push forward judicial reform.

I am very encouraged by the changes occurring recently in China. For example, the Central Political-Legal Work Committee of the CPC released its Rules for Conscientiously Preventing Wrongful Convictions in August 2013. It is the policy of the committee to reaffirm the handling of criminal cases in accordance with the law, to strengthen criminal defense, and to prohibit the party's political-legal work committees at local levels from interfering with the judicial work in individual cases. In December 2013, the Supreme People's Court decided to select some ten courts to be used experimentally nationwide for the purpose of reform of the people's juror system.

Chapter Fourteen
Reform of the Criminal Retrial System

1. The Ambiguousness of Facts and the Antagonism between Parties in Redressing Wrongful Convictions

Wrongful convictions are frequently covered up, easily concealed amid the magnitude of correct verdicts. Some dormant, or cold, cases do occasionally rise to the surface, gain the attention of law enforcement or the public, and so encounter an opportunity for rectification. In China, the cases of Teng Xingshan, She Xianglin, and Zhao Zuohai, for example, were all exposed to the world when the alleged victim came "back from the dead." Indeed, cases of wrongful conviction often lay dormant for long periods before they are discovered. As part of our empirical study, my team gathered fifty-five sets of case materials from wrongful conviction cases in China that had the rulings overturned and which resulted in compensation issued by the national government between 1995 and 2007. Among these cases, one salient trait was clear: violation of the prescribed custody in forty-eight cases involving sixty people. The average custodial period was five years. The case with the most egregious example of this was that of Li Huawei of Liaoning Province, accused of premeditated murder and held in custody for sixteen years. The shortest time involved was the case of Zhu Mingli of Sichuan Province, accused of rape and held in custody for 372 days. Five people had been in custody for over ten years, fifty persons between five and ten years, and twenty-five fewer than five years.[1]

The Ambiguousness of Facts Surrounding a Conviction

Adjudication is a reverse mental activity, in that it uses evidence to prove the facts of past events. Likewise, wrongful conviction is frequently only apparent many years after the event, which means that discovery of the miscarriage of justice is a second reverse mental activity performed on a past mental activity. Given the passage of time and change of location, the difficulty of the mental work involved is understandable, even if there is new evidence or newly discovered evidence. Certainly, in some wrongful conviction cases newly discovered evidence is substantial, even ironclad, but in the majority of wrongful convictions, new evidence does not constitute 100 percent proof of guilt or innocence and so adds varying degrees of ambiguity or uncertainty. Let us look at the case of Hugejiletu.

On April 9, 1996, in the Saihan district of Hohhot City, Inner Mongolia, a young woman was raped and murdered in a public restroom. A police investigation determined the suspect to be a man going by the surname of Hugejiletu, who had first reported the crime. A confession was obtained from him. The Hohhot Intermediate People's Court, relying mainly on this confession, sentenced Hugejiletu to death for the crimes of rape and murder; this sentence was approved by the Inner Mongolia Autonomous Region High People's Court. Hugejiletu, only eighteen years of age, was executed on June 10, 1996. The proceedings had gone so quickly that there were only sixty-two days between investigation and execution!

We have no way to confirm his guilt with certainty, because the evidence includes some material that helps his case, and other material that damages it. Even though there may be evidence to show his guilt, there is also evidence clearing him of guilt. This is what we mean by uncertainty surrounding a conviction. As mentioned previously, as far as law enforcement is concerned, the facts of a case that occurred in the past are like the image of the moon reflected in the water. Without evidence, law enforcement officials have no way of determining the facts, but facts determined through evidence do not necessarily correspond to the objective facts. When the water is murky or choppy, the action of refraction and reflection distorts the image, sometimes so much so that the resulting image is totally different from the reality. In the case of Hugejiletu, the water is turgid, which is to say, the evidence itself suffers from defects and uncertainty. First of all, there is no direct evidence to prove that he carried out the crimes. Second, the evidence is incomplete and even features a mutually exclusive chain of evidence. Finally, there are many problems with the key pieces of evidence. However, the evidence does not eliminate the possibility that Hugejiletu was in fact guilty. Thus, there are two moonlight images in the water: in one, Hugejiletu is guilty, and in the other, he is not. Which one reflects the truth? We do not yet know.

The Antagonism between Parties in Correcting the Possible Wrongs

It is human nature to pursue one's own interests and to try to avoid harm. It is instinctive to deny or cover up our mistakes. For this reason, those whose work leads to wrongful convictions frequently do not wish to admit to this; some will even go to great lengths to prevent the cases from being overturned. Thus, work on such cases becomes a struggle, both overt and covert, between two collective and competing interests, especially in China. Let us look at the Hugejiletu case again.

In 2005, alleged serial rapist-murderer Zhao Zhihong, in prison for another crime, confessed of his own accord that he had raped and murdered a young woman in a public restroom at the location in question. Given the time and the location, this must have been the crime for which Hugejiletu had been executed. According to an investigating officer of the Inner Mongolia Autonomous Region Public Security Bureau, during his trial, Zhao Zhihong related consistently—four times—the details of raping and murdering the young woman in the Hohhot public restroom. Despite the passage of over nine years, Zhao remembered the location of the crime, the victim's height and facial and body characteristics, and the circumstances of her death, including the position of the body; his memory was accurate. On October 30, 2005, Zhao led the police to the location of the crime. Even though the restroom had been demolished, Zhao was still able to point out its original position. In November 2006, Zhao went on trial before the Hohhot Intermediate People's Court, but charges raised by the prosecution did not include rape-murder relating to the April 9 incident. After the conclusion of the trial, Zhao released an appeal for redemption from his detention center, once again narrating the details of the 1996 rape-murder. Zhao wrote, "Since my arrest, having been educated by the government, I want to find the conscience of a real human being as my life comes to an end." For this reason, he demanded that the courts reexamine the case, "in order to allow me to face the end of my life without regret."[2] The case soon generated much public attention. Hugejiletu's parents, who had always maintained their son's innocence, filed appeals and petitions with much greater intensity after hearing the news. However, six years passed, and the relevant agencies did not respond with any clear conclusions. It was said that officials associated with the case reasoned that "the evidence to overturn the conviction was insufficient," and that there was no ironclad evidence of a wrongful conviction.

At the time of the crime, guilt could be determined based on the defendant's confession alone, but closer to the present, a wrongful conviction could not be established by defendant testimony alone. At the time of the crime, there was no demand for ironclad evidence of guilt; now, it was required to overturn the conviction. It was an embarrassing predicament.

It is clear that "insufficient evidence" was a pretext for not overturning the convictions of Hugejiletu, and that a much deeper factor of this decision was the relevant officials' fear of and even resistance towards the responsibility to investigate and uncover wrongful convictions.

2. The Analysis and Restatement of Chinese Standard for Proving Wrongful Conviction

In the course of determining wrongful conviction, both ambiguity and antagonism can be encountered; to overcome this, there should be a unified and clear standard of proof, else the determination would differ according to those involved, or to details of the event, the time, or the place. Some wrongful convictions are determined with relative ease, unimpeded, while others are pushed forward step by painful step. Some people will use the excuse that the standard of proof is not clear or else apply their own interpretation of the standard to obstruct the determination and rectification of a wrongful conviction, leading to endless appeals and petitions.

Determination of the true facts behind a case of wrongful conviction is not always a black-and-white process; sometimes there is a gray zone, meaning that there is no way to determine with accuracy whether the defendant is guilty or not. In other words, the line between good guys and bad guys is not clear cut but rather fuzzy and vague. As a result, coming up with standards regarding the rectification of wrongful convictions becomes problematic. In what follows, I will discuss the standards for determining the facts leading to wrongful conviction cases. This discussion represents the level and degree of knowledge that law enforcement officials must bring to their roles within the judiciary.

Chinese law lacks clear-cut standards for proving wrongful conviction but does stipulate the conditions for enacting a retrial. And since retrial is the first step towards redressing wrongful conviction, criteria for retrial and standards for proving wrongful conviction are closely connected. Article 242 of the 2012 revision of the Criminal Procedure Law states:

> If a petition presented by a party or his legal representative or his near relative conforms to any of the following conditions, the people's court shall retry the case: (1) There is new evidence to prove that the confirmation of the facts in the original judgment or ruling is definitely wrong; (2) The evidence upon which the conviction was made and the punishment was meted out is unreliable or insufficient, or should be excluded according to law, or the major pieces of evidence for proving the facts in the case contradict each other; (3) The application of law in making the original judgment or ruling is definitely incorrect; or (4) The judges in trying the case committed acts of embezzlement, bribery, or malpractices for personal gain, or bent the law in making judgment.

Article 243 states: "If the president of a People's Court at any level finds some definite error in a legally effective judgment or ruling of his court as to the determination of facts or application of law, he shall refer the case to the trial committee for deliberation." Paragraphs two and three of this article also use the term "definite error." According to the rules stipulated here, standards for proving wrongful conviction have been interpreted to be standards of definite error.

Before discussing these standards further, I want to explain the method of proving wrongful conviction in China. Based on the different ways wrongful conviction is discovered and proved, we can classify the methods for proving wrongful conviction into two types: direct proof and indirect proof.

The first method means using evidence to prove that the accused did not commit the criminal act for which they have been convicted. This situation is common to cases in which the alleged victims have "come back from the dead," as in the case of She Xianglin (see part 2) and to instances in which major evidence from the original trial has been reexamined and subsequently rejected, as with the American Innocence Project.

The second type (indirect) includes methods for counterproof, meaning proof that another person has committed the crime, thus indirectly proving the defendant from the original trial to be not guilty. This situation is common to cases in which a suspect or defendant in another case confesses that he is the true perpetrator in the original case, as in the case of Hugejiletu, and in which evidence proves the existence and guilt of the true perpetrator, as in the case of Shi Dongyu. It is also common to cases in which new evidence comes to light that clearly indicates an error in the original verdict, as in the case of Du Peiwu. Such scenarios also occur in combination.

As stated earlier, in some cases proof of wrongful conviction may be ironclad, as with the case of She Xianglin. However, not every case must achieve such a high standard. The definite-error rule is sometimes interpreted to be equal to the standard that demands "clear facts in the case, with full and reliable evidence" to issue a guilty verdict, with the result that the accused is often required to provide evidence full and reliable enough to prove his or her innocence, or else full and reliable enough to prove that another person is the true perpetrator. This interpretation is mistaken, or at least inappropriate.

First of all, "definite error" cannot be understood to mean that all the facts leading to a determination of guilt are incorrect, but rather that errors may exist in some of the facts. For example, in the case of Shi Dongyu, the original verdict had been based on forensic testing of blood type to determine the traces of blood on the defendant's clothing to be that of the victim, Guan Chuansheng. Later, a second test showed the original test results to have been erroneous, and that the defendant's clothing had no blood from the victim on it.[3] This is a determination of definite error. This standard neither demands full and reliable evidence that Shi Dongyu was not the murderer, nor does it require full and reliable evidence that Liang Baoyou was the murderer.

Second, item 2 of Article 242, as stated previously, stipulates that a case should be retried if "the evidence upon which the conviction was made and the punishment was meted out is unreliable or insufficient, or should be excluded according to law, or the major pieces of evidence for proving the facts in the case contradict each other." The law certainly does not require reliable and sufficient evidence, but rather should be seen as holding to a standard of finding "evidence either unreliable or insufficient." This is similar to the "formation of a reasonable doubt" standard in the United States and the United Kingdom, and also to the German "overturn the intimate conviction" standard.

Finally, when using counterevidence to prove that the claimant is not guilty, proving that another person is the true culprit certainly goes hand-in-hand with proving the conviction to be wrongful. However, the two standards are not equivalent. Excluding the possibility that the suspects committed the crime together, the probability that one of the two suspects committed the crime may go up or down. For example, in the Hugejiletu case, if the probability that Zhao Zhihong committed the rape and murder was 20 percent, then the chance that Hugejiletu committed the crimes would have been 80 percent. And if Zhao's odds reached 80 percent, then there would have been only a 20 percent chance that Hugejiletu could have been the perpetrator.

On November 19, 2014, the High People's Court of Inner Mongolia made a decision to retry the case of Hugejiletu. On December 15, 2014, the High Court declared Hugejiletu's innocence. After eighteen years, the wrongful conviction was finally corrected. However, it was too late for Hugejiletu and his family.

The rules regarding the standard for proving wrongful conviction in Chinese law are not clear enough and need to be enhanced with interpretation by relevant judicial agencies. It may be beneficial to set out the standards in levels. The first standard relates to calling for a retrial or registering a wrongful conviction case, somewhat similar to the definite-error standard explained previously. The second level is the standard determining wrongful conviction in retrial, which can be formulated as "preponderant evidence," meaning that the evidence in toto proves the probability the claimant is not guilty to be greater than the probability of guilt. The third level is the standard for determining state compensation, which can be formulated as "evidence being reliable and sufficient," meaning that reliable evidence sufficiently proves that the claimant is indeed not guilty.

The standard of proof associated with determining state compensation should be higher than the standard of proof associated with determining a wrongful conviction. It is more appropriate. On the one hand, the application of the comparatively lower standard for proving wrongful conviction can give the innocent more chances for rectification. On the other hand, the application of a higher standard of proof for providing state compensation may prevent such compensation from becoming an obstacle to rectification. It will also reduce government expenditure associated with compensation, providing for wiser use of taxpayer money.

Additionally, a system of accountability or liability of the parties involved in determining a wrongful conviction will raise the quality of the judiciary and law enforcement, as well as the general morale of the legal profession. It can also, however, become an obstacle to rectification of wrongful conviction, and so the standards of accountability should be distinguished carefully from the standards for determining a wrongful conviction. In short, determining a wrongful conviction can follow the principle of "no-fault liability," but determining the accountability of the people involved must follow the principle of "fault liability."

3. A Well-Known Case on the Horns of a Dilemma

At around 5 p.m. on August 5, 1994, a woman by the surname of Kang, who worked at a hydraulic-parts factory in Shijiazhuang, Hebei Province, was raped and murdered in a cornfield by the side of a road in the outskirts of the city. Based on tips from the public, police identified Nie Shubin as a suspect and obtained a confession to the crime. On March 15, 1995, the Shijiazhuang Intermediate Court found Nie Shubin guilty of premeditated murder and sentenced him to death. They also found him guilty of rape and sentenced him to fifteen years in prison for that crime, with the primary evidence being his confession. On April 25, the High Provincial People's Court of Hebei released its final verdict approving the death sentence, and two days later Nie Shubin was executed.[4]

In March 2005, alleged serial rapist Wang Shujin was arrested for other crimes and, while being interrogated, confessed that he had raped and murdered a young woman in a cornfield by the side of the road in the outskirts of Shijiazhuang. His narration of the crime and knowledge of its location, which he identified, agreed with details of the rape-murder of the female surnamed Kang. Nie Shubin's mother had never believed that her son, who had always been an honest and timid boy, could have committed rape and murder, and so upon hearing this news made even more insistent appeals on her son's behalf, nevertheless to no avail.[5] A police officer involved in the case said:

> If this had happened ten years ago we might well have determined Wang to be the murderer with only his confession to go on, and no other corroborating evidence. But cases can no longer be made with confession alone, not to mention this case has already been closed, and one person has been executed.[6]

On June 25, 2013, the second-instance trial of Wang Shujin for rapes and murders finally began. Eight years after Wang's shocking confession, the Hebei High People's Court tried the case again at the Handan Intermediate People's Court. The event garnered much public attention. Arguments in the retrial instigated a fresh outlook: the defendant maintained that he was indeed the true culprit in Kang's case, while the prosecution making the charges maintained that he was not. Public attention focused not on whether Wang Shujin was guilty but on whether Nie Shubin was guilty.

In the courtroom on June 25, the prosecution supplied four reasons why Wang Shujin could not have raped and murdered the victim surnamed Kang. First, Wang Shujin's testimony regarding the body did not correspond with the facts of the case. The corpse was clothed with a white undershirt; the neck had been obscured by cornstalks, which when removed revealed a flower-printed shirt. Wang Shujin's testimony lacked these details. Second, Wang's testimony as to the method of the murder did not correspond with the facts. The cause of death was strangulation, but Wang said he had first choked the victim, then stomped on her chest until she died. But apart from the shirt wrapped around the victim's neck, there were no bone fractures found at the autopsy. Third, Wang's testimony as to the time of the victim's death did not accord with the facts. Fourth, Wang's description of the victim's height was incorrect. The prosecution also pointed out that when the events occurred, Wang was at work at a factory nearby and familiar with the area around the crime scene, and when law enforcement authorities were examining the crime scene, a considerable number of public onlookers had gathered around. In this way, Wang could have learned some of the details of the case.[7]

So is Wang Shujin the true culprit or not? We have no way of knowing. Based on the case presented by the prosecution, there is insufficient evidence to prove him guilty, not guilty, or innocent. It is possible that he is lying— if, indeed, Wang could be so conniving. However, it is common for the actual criminal to make some errors when recounting the events of the crime; plus, it should be remembered that Wang's confession came more than ten years after the crime had been committed. Moreover, in the meantime, he had committed rape and murder on three other occasions and rape on two other occasions. It would have been surprising if some of his testimony had not been confused, some of the details mixed up in his memory. In sum, given the evidence at hand, it cannot be certain that Wang Shujin committed the murder and rape against the victim surnamed Kang, nor can it be certain that he did not. Roughly, let us assume that the chance Wang did commit the crime was about 60 percent. In other words, the chance that he is the true culprit is slightly higher than the chance that he is not.

In Chinese Criminal Procedure Law, the standard for proving a defendant guilty of a crime is that "the facts of the case be clear, the evidence reliable and sufficient." In terms of probabilities, the chances that the defendant committed the crime must reach at least 90 percent. According to the principle of presumption of innocence, or "no conviction in a case of doubt," whenever the chances that the defendant is guilty drop below 90 percent, the court should find the accused not guilty. In the case at hand, and if it can be assumed that Wang Shujin's chance of being the true culprit is only 60 percent, the court should find Wang "not guilty" in the case of the rape and murder of the victim surnamed Kang. However, the next question is, What can be done in the case of Nie Shubin? Some believe that Nie's case cannot be overturned as long as Wang Shujin cannot be identified as the true culprit. But not being able to confirm Wang Shujin as the true culprit is not equivalent to confirming Nie Shubin as the true culprit. When using counterevidence to give indirect proof of wrongful conviction, an increased chance of one suspect committing the crime corresponds to a decreased chance that the other suspect committed the crime. In this case, if there were a 60 percent chance that Wang Shujin committed the crime, and if this were not enough to determine his guilt, then Nie Shubin's 40 percent chance is also not enough to determine Nie's guilt.

On January 27, 2013, the Hebei High People's Court opened trial proceedings against Wang Shujin in the Handan Intermediate People's Court for the crimes of rape and murder. The court ruled that the evidence was insufficient to prove that Wang Shujin committed rape and murder against the victim surnamed Kang, and so rejected the appeal and reaffirmed the original verdict, convicting him on the other five charges of rape and murder. Wang Shujin was sentenced to death.[8]

On December 12, 2014, the Supreme People's Court of China made a decision to appoint the High People's Court of Shandong Province to review the case of Nie Shubin. On April 28, 2015, the High Court held a special hearing on the case, for which the Court invited fifteen representatives of the people, including law professors, journalists, members of the people's congress, and local residents. It was the first time Chinese courts had held such a hearing in a criminal case, and it may illustrate the direction of the related judicial reform.[9] On June 11, the High Court decided to extend the review time for three months, until September 15, 2015. However, on September 15, the High Court announced another extension for three months. Many people are still waiting to see . . .

Chapter Fifteen
Changing the Mind-Set for Criminal Justice

According to an article in the August 13, 2013, issue of the *Legal Daily*, the Central Political-Legal Work Committee has recently released its Rules for Conscientiously Preventing Wrongful Convictions. This document faced up to the most outstanding problems in the criminal justice system, reaffirming the handling of cases in accordance with the law, developing the work of defense attorneys, upgrading the evaluation of evidence, and issuing no sentence in doubtful cases. The document also affirmed the need for explicit standards by which to determine wrongful conviction, as well as explicit procedures for correcting mistakes, and the need to establish robust accountability mechanisms for wrongful convictions. The Supreme People's Court and the Supreme People's Procuratorate are presently formulating directives regarding the prevention of wrongful convictions. While we may not be able to completely eradicate cases of wrongful conviction, we must do everything in our power to guard against them.

In the reforms discussed in previous chapters, the enactment of relevant laws and the establishment of relevant institutions are necessary, as is the insistence on certain principles of criminal justice. However, the most crucial aspect of reform lies in the change in the mentalities of judicial and law enforcement officers. The spirit and principles of criminal justice can only be implemented in judicial practice through the acts of these officers, and their acts are performed under the direction of certain kinds of mentalities. From the illustrations in parts 1 and 2, we can see that the traditional mentalities of Chinese judicial and law enforcement officers are quite far from the rule of law. Therefore, adjusting and modifying these mentalities are important and inevitable challenges faced by China's judicial and law enforcement officers.

1. Changing from the Mind-Set of Unitary and One-Sided Values to the Mind-Set of Multiple and Balanced Values

In every country, the criminal justice system exists among conflicts between various interests and values, such as the conflict between personal and public interests, the rights of the defendants and the rights of the victims, the pursuit of the truth and the reduction of costs in judicial activities, and strengthening the procedural safeguards and raising the efficiency of the criminal justice system. These conflicts are not controlled by the will of the people. The criminal justice system of every country has to find a position for itself amid these complicated and conflicting relationships, and as each society develops, this kind of value determination will also develop and change.

From the perspective of the initial stage of the division of labor in society, the original function of the criminal justice system was to fight crime. Therefore, for quite a long time in the history of every country, fighting crime had been regarded as the fundamental value of the criminal justice system. Whether during the time of the ancient Eastern civilization or during medieval Western culture, wide application or even the legitimization of extortion of confession by torture was one of the examples demonstrating such values. However, as society developed and human beings became more civilized, there were growing concerns for protection of human rights, to the point where it has become one of the values and goals of criminal justice activities.

The focus on the protection of human rights in the criminal justice process is, of course, to protect the rights of the suspects or the defendants. Because they are the targets of the criminal justice system, their rights are easily sacrificed at the expense of crime fighting. However, the rights of the victims should not be put aside and ignored. It is true that in certain circumstances, the aim of protecting the rights of victims is in line with society's interests—the aim of fighting crime—or we may say that the protection of rights of victims can be covered under the interests of the society as a result of crime fighting. In certain circumstances, however, these two aims may be divergent. This is because what individual victims pursue in some specific cases may not necessarily reflect the needs of society at large in terms of crime fighting. From this perspective, we can understand that the criminal justice system faces a kind of triangular relationship, involving the interests of society, the rights of the accused and their families, and the rights of the victims and their families. In establishing a criminal justice system, every country must consider how to position the system given this triangular relationship.

Some countries still believe fighting crime to be the fundamental if not the only aim of the criminal justice system, with other interests and values subordinated to that cause. Some go so far as to assert that in order to fight crimes, the law enforcement and judiciary may use whatever means they deem necessary and ignore any costs incurred, real or otherwise. On the other hand, some countries regard the protection of human rights—especially the rights of the accused—to be the fundamental goal or the highest aim of the criminal justice system, with other interests and values subordinated if needed to preserve and protect human rights, and that in order to protect human rights, the efficiency of the judiciary may be sacrificed and criminals allowed to escape justice. Excessively emphasizing the protection of the rights of the accused affects the efficiency of crime fighting. As we all know, there are many social factors that contribute to the acute problems of drug- and violence-related crimes in the United States. However, overemphasis on the protection of the rights of the accused, which is disadvantageous to fighting crime, is also a factor that cannot be denied.

Undoubtedly, being influenced by traditional values, along with the mind-set of emphasizing the interests of society and maintaining objectivity and fairness, and being subjected to the habitual way of thinking in class struggles, such as "the contradiction between ourselves and enemies," China's criminal justice system has been putting more emphasis on the necessity of fighting crime; thus, it fails to pay enough attention to the protection of the rights of the accused.[1] The progress of human society should reflect a respect for human rights. Therefore, one of the aims of the reform of China's criminal justice system is to strengthen the protection of the rights of the accused. In recent years, China has made remarkable progress in human rights protection. Under these conditions, some judicial officers have begun to be aware of the disadvantages of overemphasizing crime fighting and have instead begun to focus on the importance of the protection of the rights of the accused. In other words, the mind-set of the Chinese has begun to change.

To recognize the value of the protection of human rights in the enactment of criminal evidence law, judicial and investigative officers are required to change their biased thinking and practice. It is now looked down on to use the attitudes and means that were formerly applied to "class enemies" to treat criminal suspects and defendants, or to adopt the thinking and practice related to military struggle to direct criminal investigations. Even if we put the principle of presumption of innocence aside, from a practical perspective the accused are not necessarily guilty. As far as proof of guilt is concerned, criminal suspects and defendants have only the possibility of being convicted and should receive fair treatment in the trial process. Therefore, the judiciary that exercises power on behalf of the state should respect the basic rights of the accused.

The value orientation of a country or a society is affected by many factors, including historical and cultural traditions, the psychology of the people, political and economic systems, and the society's intrinsic morality. And it is true that there are great value differences between the East and the West. In reforming the evidence system and enacting legislation concerning the gathering and introduction of evidence, China must learn from the experiences of foreign countries while protecting its unique characteristics. This is not to say that China should preserve certain characteristics simply for the sake of it, or preserve backward characteristics. The actual condition in China should instead be examined to study seriously the experiences and lessons of foreign countries. Experiences and knowledge from other countries should not be transplanted without due consideration. We should have the courage to confirm those aspects of traditional Chinese culture that are positive and beneficial to development, and use, promote, and develop such native resources without being blindly influenced by the experiences of those outside our borders.

In searching for the path for reform of China's criminal justice system, we should abandon the old values and mind-sets associated with criminal justice but also refrain from going from one extreme to another. To rectify the previous attitude of being concerned only with fighting crime rather than protecting human rights, China should not one-sidedly emphasize the importance of protecting the rights of the accused. China should not sacrifice the fundamental need for fighting crime in exchange for an acclamation of protecting human rights. The criminal justice system is not an arbitrary institution to be held aloof from the world; it shoulders the mission of fighting crime and protecting citizens.[2] To strike a balance between the values inherent to successfully fighting and deterring crime and protecting human rights by way of establishing a right to silence in China is a good example on this point.[3] We should not forget that the criminal justice system also shoulders the functions of maintaining social order, protecting the life and property of citizens, and fighting and preventing crimes. In other words, China should pursue a civilized application of the law and should recognize the need for the protection of the legal rights of the accused, as well as those who are duly convicted; at the same time, it should remember that, after all, the fundamental mission of the criminal justice system is fighting crime and protecting the people.

Besides, different participants in the criminal justice system may have different value orientations. Investigators and prosecutors should focus on crime fighting and protection of the people as their main goals, and the protection of the rights of the criminal suspects and the defendants should be ancillary. Defense lawyers should focus on the protection of the rights of the criminal suspects and the defendants, and the protection of the interests of other people and public interests should be ancillary. Judges should be maintaining judicial fairness as their main goal, and crime fighting and human rights protection should be ancillary. To sum up this analysis, judicial and investigative officers should change their previous value orientation as to the overemphasis on fighting crimes, and seek to strike a balance among the various values and beliefs.

2. Changing from the Mind-Set of One-Sided Emphasis on Substantive Justice to the Mind-Set of Emphasizing both Substantive and Procedural Justice

Maintaining social justice and realizing judiciary fairness are the fundamental goals of the criminal justice system. To a certain extent, what the judiciary themselves pursue is justice.

The compositions of Chinese characters have symbolic meaning, and the word *law* has the meaning "even or level as water" and "getting rid of unevenness." Similarly, the ancient Greek concept of justice is illustrated by a centuries-old statue holding scales in one hand and a sword in the other. Across the ages, there will have been different understandings of the meaning of judiciary fairness, yet even if we put aside differences, such as those that pertain to a class-ridden or a supposedly classless society and those relating to ideology, there are multiple meanings of judiciary fairness. One-sided emphasis on substantive justice and one-sided emphasis on procedural justice should be the two best representatives of the multiple nature of judiciary fairness.

So-called substantive justice requires the judiciary to demonstrate the spirit of justice and fairness in trial outcomes. So-called procedural fairness requires the judiciary to insist on the principle of propriety and equality in the criminal justice process. While the former is mainly concerned with the outcome, the latter is mainly concerned with the process. If we treat the judicial system as a factory, then the examination of substantive justice is just like the examination of the product being manufactured, and the examination of procedural justice is just like the examination of the manufacturing process. In normal circumstances, in order to ensure the quality of the product, a scientific and reasonable manufacturing process has to be followed, and this scientific and reasonable manufacturing process should lead to the production of a product that meets certain standards. The indices for these two kinds of examinations are different. If we simply consider substantive justice, then as long as a product meets the required standards, it may be considered "justice" regardless of the process used to manufacture it. On the other hand, if we simply consider procedural justice, then so long as a scientific and reasonable manufacturing process was used to produce the product, it will be considered "justice" regardless of its quality.

Substantive justice and procedural justice are two correlated but different concepts. On the one hand, they are united and support each other under judiciary fairness; on the other hand, they have different values and standards. Although the insistence on procedural justice can normally ensure substantive justice, procedural justice is still quite different. The insistence on procedural justice does not necessarily lead to substantive justice, and procedural justice is not the only way to achieve substantive justice. In certain circumstances, substantive justice and procedural justice may oppose each other or be in conflict. The pursuit of substantive justice may harm procedural justice, and the insistence on procedural justice may lead to the sacrifice of substantive justice.[4]

In establishing its criminal justice system, every country has to expressly or implicitly define and balance the relationship between substantive and procedural justice. Of course, different countries have different approaches to dealing with these issues, and sometimes the differences are very great. One extreme approach is to simply emphasize substantive justice and ignore procedural justice. In short, despite the procedure and the means used, as long as the result is just, judiciary fairness is considered to have been achieved. This was once a tradition of the trial system in countries using the continental legal system, and it remains the guiding principle for the criminal justice system in some countries today. Another extreme approach is to simply emphasize procedural justice, or even sacrifice substantive justice at the expense of achieving procedural justice. This approach is based on the judicial tradition of emphasizing the rules of procedure, practiced in common-law countries such as the United States.

Practical experiences in China have proven that the mere pursuit of substantive justice does not only ignore or trample on the legal rights of the litigants but also twists the concept of judicial justice: substantive justice and procedural justice should have equal weight. Of course, the mere pursuit of procedural justice is also wrong. Everything has a limit, and any act that exceeds its limit will become a show—a mere performance to make others see that you have done the act. Despite the fact that such acts can help stabilize society, their disadvantages should not be overlooked, because the sacrifice of substantive justice undoubtedly makes judicial fairness lose its original meaning. Evidence is the basis for judicial officers to determine the outcome of trials, and it is also a bridge leading to substantive justice. Based on this meaning, we can say that evidence has the function of realizing substantive justice; however, when we enact criminal evidence legislation, we should consider not only the requirement of substantive justice but also the requirement of procedural justice.

"Emphasizing substance and ignoring procedure" is one of the characteristics of the traditional legal culture of China; therefore, both the judiciary and the general public in China believe that substantive justice is the basic component of judicial fairness. In recent years, under the motivation of the study of jurisprudence, an increasing number of people have learned the value of procedural justice, especially the meaning of emphasizing procedural justice in criminal justice activities. However, the practice of mere pursuit of substantive justice still has the potential to influence law enforcement and judicial officers. Due to this, we should stress the importance of procedural justice in criminal evidence system reform. Emphasis on the importance of procedural justice does not mean we should rule out the value of substantive justice completely. Nor does it mean that we should merely pursue procedural justice. We should establish the judicial mind-set of giving equal emphasis to both substance and procedure in practice.

3. Changing from a Fact-Finding Mind-Set to a Mind-Set of Proving the Facts

Under the trial-centered system, judicial and law enforcement officers should raise their awareness of the correct means of gathering evidence and what kind of evidence is admissible. Changing from a fact-finding mind-set to one that focuses on proving the facts has an especially significant practical meaning for investigative officers. In judicial activities, the concepts of finding and proving are easily and often confused. Fact finding comes from investigation, such as that conducted by criminal investigators, prosecutors, and adjudicators looking for evidence of guilt or innocence. Proving refers to showing evidence or illustrating facts in the case by using the evidence that has been found.

Finding and proving are correlated but also distinct: finding is the basis of proving; proving is the purpose of finding. However, proving is not the same as finding, and finding cannot replace proving. To put it another way: finding is to make oneself understand, while proving is to make others understand. Only when one understands can one make others understand. However, even though one understands does not mean that others will understand. These two cannot be mixed up, and their relationships cannot be reversed. In the law of evidence, distinguishing between these two concepts is very important. As far as judicial activities are concerned, very often it may seem easy to understand a concept or a piece of evidence relating to a cause of conviction or exoneration; however, unless this concept or evidence can be understood by others, it is useless. If investigative officers have already thoroughly investigated the facts of the case, they must also prove the case by using evidence recognized by the law, and this, in many cases, is not an easy task.

Some experienced investigative officers memorize or simply write a few words in a notebook to describe what they have discovered, including the interviewees' narrations related to the case and the details of discovering physical evidence. If the aim of handling a case is to find the facts, then this may be a convenient and effective method. If the aim of handling a case is to prove the facts, then such a method is inappropriate, for what is in the mind of the investigative officer and in his notebook may not have the "competence of evidence." Changing the focus in the practice of criminal investigation from finding to proving is beneficial to raising investigative officers' awareness of the evidence and their handling of cases in accordance with the law. To investigative officers, it is undoubtedly much more difficult to prove than to find: the requirement concerned is higher. However, this will lead society to be more in line with the rule of law.

4. Changing from the Mind-Set of Relying on Testimonial Evidence to the Mind-Set of Emphasizing Physical Evidence

As far as the methods of judicial proof are concerned, human society has experienced two major evolutions: the first one was from a "proof by holy evidence" to a "proof by human evidence" method; the second one was from a "proof by human evidence" to a "proof by physical evidence" method. Accordingly, the historical development of the method of judicial proof can be divided into three stages, namely proof by holy evidence, proof by human evidence, and proof by physical evidence (or scientific evidence).

The so-called proof by holy evidence method is based on a god indicating evidence. It involves using certain designated methods to invite a god to help in deciding a case. It also uses certain designated methods to reveal the orders of the god, using them as the basis of adjudication. The method of proof by holy evidence includes swearing to the god and trial by ordeal. "Swearing to the god" is exactly what it sounds like: swearing to the god so as to prove the truth in a case. "Trial by ordeal" means that the party concerned will accept certain kinds of physical torture or tests so as to prove that his or her case is truthful.

In trial by ordeal, the function of judicial officers in determining the facts of the case is not important. The basic function of the judge is not to investigate the facts and apply the law on this basis; instead, it is to act as the host of such arbitration ceremonies. To a certain extent, courts during this period were not judicial institutions established with the purpose of investigating facts of the case. They were simply tools used to invite a god or gods to indicate the facts of the case, and places with strong religious characteristics, established for the purpose of obtaining the "orders of the god." As a result, judicial decisions were considered to be orders from the god. The parties concerned did not convince judges to accept their claims by making use of evidence and justifications. Instead, they prayed to the god and urged the god to prove their claims to be correct or truthful. Under these social conditions, trials were considered to be held to solve disputes between private individuals, and the state demonstrated control over judicial activities mainly by preventing the parties concerned from using the law as a tool of revenge. Therefore, authoritative judgment was much more important than reasonable judgment, and the understanding of the people towards the concepts of reasonableness and justice would have been subordinated to their belief in and respect for the god.

In contrast, in ancient China, there were methods of judicial proof similar to trial by ordeal, such as the "god sheep" used by Gao Yao, the official responsible for administering justice in the time of Emperor Shun (?–2037 B.C.). When Gao adjudicated criminal cases, he would ask for the so-called god sheep to be placed in front of the defendant. If the god sheep used its horns to butt the defendant, it meant the accused was guilty; if the god sheep did not butt the accused, it meant the accused was innocent. Although it is true that trial by ordeal—including trial by fire and trial by water—never became popular in mainstream Chinese society, variations were popular among some ethnic minority groups and used until the early twentieth century: the Tibetans used trial by boiling oil, the Jingpo used trial by boiling water, the Yi used trial by holding a plough, the Dai used trial by hanging a dustpan, and so on.

Trial by ordeal is irrational; therefore, as society developed and knowledge increased, it gave way to more rational methods. In many countries, adjudication was no longer considered to be an arbitration of a dispute between private individuals but a tool for rulers to control and suppress the activities of citizens. Therefore, the ruling classes began to feel discontent with those irrational methods, especially as the outcome reached was difficult to predict. As a result, they required judicial officers to exercise greater powers in making decisions during trial. In 1215, a Catholic church in Europe expressly prohibited the use of trial by ordeal in the trials conducted in its ecclesiastical court. By the end of the thirteenth century, trial by ordeal had become obsolete in relation to judicial proof. During the time when proof by holy evidence was the main method of judicial proof, proof by human evidence also existed, though it played only a minor role. This was because the ultimate decision in judicial proof was vested in god. As trial by ordeal was being extinguished and the method of judicial proof was becoming more rational, the proof by human evidence method gradually became the major basis for judges in adjudicating cases and handing down judgment.

During the time when the proof by human evidence method was the primary method of judicial proof, there was no doubt that the statement of the parties concerned—especially the statement of the defendants in criminal cases—was deemed the most important evidence. In criminal cases, the methods of adjudicating and interrogating cases with the main purpose of obtaining confession from the defendant naturally became the major method of judicial proof. As a result, extortion of confession by torture certainly occupied a position in the history of the criminal justice system. Since the thirteenth century, European countries had widely adopted the inquisitorial trial approach, and many countries had even expressly provided in the law that the confession of the defendant should be considered the most effective evidence. Therefore, extortion of confession by torture had become a means for making defendants speak. During that time, according to the law of the European church and the laws of some European countries, the court might try a defendant as long as it had some materials or clues against the defendant. In addition, the court was allowed to use whatever means of interrogating the defendants in order to obtain evidence concerning the motive and the purpose of committing the crime, as well as details as to the process of committing the crime. The judges would mainly rely on that evidence to decide the guilt and the sentencing.

The proof by human evidence method was at the core of the evidence system in ancient China. The trial system in ancient China had the characteristics of the inquisitorial approach; therefore, its evidence system had many similarities with that of countries of the continental legal system. During the more than four thousand years of history from the establishment of the Xia Dynasty to the decline of the Qing Dynasty, the evidence system in China had three major characteristics: first, the confession of the defendant had heavy weight in determining guilt, and there was an insistence on the principle of "confession must be obtained for conviction"; second, interrogation with torture was the legally prescribed means of obtaining confession, and there were often express provisions as to the conditions, methods, tools, and extent of torture in the law; and third, judicial officers still enjoyed great discretion in evaluating evidence, though there were provisions such as "conviction should be based on more than two witnesses" and "confession must be obtained for conviction."

At the time when extortion of confession by torture was used as the major method of judicial proof, judicial officers in all parts of the world were exploring the more scientific method of "proof by human evidence." For example, judicial officers in ancient China developed some scientific interrogation methods, such as "using five physical reactions in hearing cases" and "roundabout interrogation"; Western scholars began to invent some scientific interrogation techniques, such as use of the polygraph. At the same time, it became more usual to introduce various kinds of physical evidence into judicial proof.

The use and the promotion of the use of physical evidence in judicial proof often go hand in hand with the invention and development of scientific technologies. Although physical evidence exists objectively, it cannot go to the court to prove the facts of the case by itself. It has to rely on human beings to explain the facts of the case as reflected by it. In other words, the messages conveyed by physical evidence have to be interpreted, and certain scientific knowledge is required in order to do so. Therefore, physical evidence and scientific technologies are closely related to each other. In most circumstances, physical evidence cannot have any effect on proving once it has departed from scientific technologies. Thus, physical evidence and the results of the relevant evaluation can be considered to be scientific evidence.

In the development of human history, various techniques used to evaluate physical evidence have been used randomly and developed separately. Since the eighteenth century, scientific techniques relating to physical evidence have gradually formed their systems; hence, the function of physical evidence has been growing in importance. Undoubtedly, the development of scientific methods of judicial proof flourished in the nineteenth century in two main ways: first, the emergence of forensic medicine provided effective methods in proving the facts of cases scientifically; and second, the invention of various technologies in human individualization provided scientific means for investigating and finding the facts of cases.

Since the twentieth century, scientific technologies for judicial proof have developed rapidly. After graphology, anthropometry, and fingerprinting, technologies such as footprint examination, tooth-mark examination, voiceprint examination, and lip-print examination became weapons added to the warehouse of evidence that could be allowed as judicial proof. DNA fingerprinting, which emerged in the 1980s, has led to a great leap forward in the development of judicial proof. Indeed, physical evidence has now become the new king of evidence in some technologically advanced countries.

Judicial proof has entered an era in which physical evidence is the major component of scientific evidence. Rapid scientific development, judicial activities, and the environment in which they are carried out are becoming more scientific in nature. Therefore, to realize judicial fairness and to raise the efficiency of the judiciary, we have to rely on scientific technologies and raise the scientific standard of the method of judicial proof. In short, we have to change the focus of judicial proof from reliance on testimonial evidence to reliance on physical evidence.

However, even now, some investigative officers in China continue to rely on testimonial evidence, or at least they have not abandoned their preference for using testimonial evidence in investigation psychologically. When handling cases, they often only want to obtain evidence from suspects and witnesses, and fail to be aware of the need to find and collect various kinds of physical evidence. In many cases, physical evidence can be found at the crime scene; however, due to Chinese investigative officers' preference for using testimonial evidence, they miss the chance of collecting physical evidence to prove the facts of the case, thus leading to investigation without proving the case or, worse, conviction of the innocent. To criminal investigation officers, putting the emphasis on using physical evidence rather than testimonial evidence not only complies with the trend in the development of judicial proof but is consistent with the trend in the development of a civilized society based on the rule of law.

Postscript

The Fourth Plenary Session of the 18th CPC Central Committee concluded in Beijing on October 23, 2014. The communiqué issued after the meeting lays out the general objective of building a system serving "the socialist rule of law with Chinese characteristics" and a country under "the socialist rule of law," in order to fully advance the rule of law in China.

"Rule of law" differs from the concept of "rule by law" that was formed in 2011, marking the rise of law governance in China. Of course, it will take more than one meeting to realize the goal, but this meeting is likely to become a milestone in the further development of the rule of law in China. The realization of the rule of law will largely lie in the sound implementation, in the next few years, of the decisions made at the meeting.

There are two stages to advance the rule of law: the first is law legislation; the second is law enforcement. Without laws, there would be no basis for the rule of law, but the existence of laws does not always lead to the rule of law. To evaluate the rule of law in a certain country, the most important standard is law enforcement rather than legal legislation. Therefore, the committee emphasized that "the life of a law lies in its implementation" and "realizing scientific legislation, strict enforcement, judicial justice, and cultivating law-abiding citizens."

The goal of having citizens "fully abiding by the law" aims at helping the general public form a law-abiding consciousness and set of behaviors, instead of exerting the rule of law as a kind of belief on them.

In reality, "fully abiding by the law" is impossible. If 80 percent of citizens in one country develop the habit of abiding by the law, then the country can fairly be called a "nation under the rule of law."

The proportion of citizens abiding by the law in China is probably now under 20 percent. That figure is reflected by the amount of violations of traffic regulations in daily life.

So can people be helped to develop a habit of abiding by the law? As an old Chinese saying goes, "A country cannot be always strong, nor weak. The one with a lot of law-abiding people will be strong, otherwise, it will be weak." In other words, if the law-abiding citizens gain power in the country, then the country will stay powerful; on the contrary, if the law-abiding citizens are reduced to the vulnerable group and always suffer losses for abiding by the rules, then the country cannot remain strong.

The main problem in Chinese society is that law-abiding people are not strong enough. Therefore, China should build a social environment to cultivate powerful law-abiding citizens in order to build a modern country under the rule of law. Moreover, the rule of law can only be achieved through the compliance of all Chinese citizens, regardless of their status and wealth. If privileged drivers can ignore traffic regulations, then others will follow suit. If a government official treats the Constitution as nothing, then the general public will not respect it.

Therefore, government officials should become role models for the public; only in this way will more and more people be convinced to abide by the law. When most government officials and the general public form law-abiding habits, then China can realize its rule of law. The goal is not far from us, but the question is, How fast can we act to achieve it?

In China, the tradition of placing power in the hands of a strong leader has a long and deeply rooted history. Although Chinese feudalist societies produced such legalist icons as Shang Yang and Shen Dao, with their maxim "Rule according to law," the more dominant position was held by Confucius, whose maxim was "Government is a human matter." That ideology has allowed a particularly stubborn "strongman complex" to develop in China.

The strongman ideology gets some things right, at least in the abstract. History shows that when a good emperor leads good ministers, it is indeed possible for the country to be functional, prosperous, and peaceful. The difficulty is that good emperors and officials are hard to find and have relatively short lives. It is simply too dangerous to base the security and well-being of the nation and its citizens on such a weak foundation. Yet the Chinese system presumes that the person or group holding power is good and so lacks provisions against those who abuse their authority. Just a single emperor going bad is enough to send the system into a vicious cycle of corruption.

Since the 1970s, there have been many indisputable legislative successes in China, which have brought the country from anarchy to relative lawfulness. Nevertheless, the Chinese have not yet cultivated behavior conducive to the rule of law. The state of Chinese society is not one of insufficient legislation but of legislation insufficiently applied and adhered to. In other words, the reality in China today is that the laws are often ignored. To give one example, "Red light means stop, and green light means go" is a rule known to every child, yet on city streets in China, it is common to see drivers, bicyclists, and pedestrians run red lights. It should perhaps come as no surprise that government officials also dare to run red lights.

As system operators, many officials continue to think that power stands above the law, and so certain people stand above the law; internal policy is above the law, as are the demands of superiors. In many places, the officials in charge operate according to this principle: if there is no instruction, the law is followed; if there is an instruction, then the instruction is followed, not the law. Selective application of the law is also a sign that the law is not being followed strictly enough. Some officials turn their backs on the basic principle that all are equal in the eyes of the law and instead treat people differently based on who they are.

In China, there has long been an emphasis on *guanxi,* or relationships, between people. Certainly all people who live in societies become involved in all manner of relationships, good or bad, close or distant. The law is not opposed to relationships; on the contrary, the law is meant to set behavioral norms and standards for them. But what this author refers to by the term *guanxi* is that sort of relationship that "opens doors to hidden paths," and this sort of *guanxi* goes against the spirit of the law.

The Chinese emphasis on *guanxi* to accomplish various tasks dates from the mid-1970s. Gradually, it seemed that *guanxi* was necessary to accomplish anything desirable, like entering university, seeing a doctor, finding goods to purchase, eating at restaurants, getting a job, asking for a raise, being promoted, or doing any kind of business. *Guanxi* was even more critical to government bureaucracy. Thus, taking sides and forming cliques became and continues to be a common feature of socioeconomic life in China.

In a society that places such high emphasis on *guanxi,* the laws are often overlooked, because when *guanxi* is available, the rules can be ignored; that is, they can be applied when they are needed and not applied when they are not. This is especially true when rules are unclear or never made public. There will be a difference in the treatment of those who have *guanxi* compared to those who have none. Those with none will have a hard time of it even if their demands are simple. And those who have *guanxi* may find that their needs are met smoothly even when they are far from reasonable. The result is that the people will do anything to obtain or construct *guanxi*. Also, the sheer use value of *guanxi* keeps increasing, from purchasing rationed meats to land- and resource-development deals, from amounts in the tens of yuan to hundreds of millions of yuan. Never strong in the first place, laws and customs weaken further in Chinese society as its members consider the law to be of little consequence or use. Those who ignore the rules are counted all the bolder for it, while those who find ways around them are admired for their talent.

The Fourth Plenary Session of the 18th CPC Central Committee lays out the general objective of building a modern state with the rule of law. The Ming Dynasty statesman Zhang Juzheng once said, "Of all things under Heaven, the difficulty is not in establishing law, but in enacting it." The best measure of a country's progress toward the rule of law is not legislation, not the laws on the books, but the enactment of the law in real life, the place it holds in the eyes of the people.

He Jiahong
Beijing, China
September 2015

NOTES

Preface

1. The CPL was revised in 1996 to allow the defendant the right to a lawyer when the investigation has concluded and the case is transferred to the procuratorate for public prosecution. The law was revised again in 2012 to allow the defendant (or suspect) the right to a lawyer when he or she is interrogated for the first time or taken into custody.
2. It is the case of Shi Dongyu, which is elaborated in the introduction of this book.

Introduction: Empirical Studies on Wrongful Convictions

1. See Guo Xinyang, *Critical Evaluations of Wrongful Convictions* (Beijing: Publishing House of the People's Public Security University of China, 2011), 213–222.
2. There are thirty-two regions in China, not including Hong Kong and Macau, in the PRC. It is very difficult to conduct such surveys without the help of local people. We found some people to help us distribute the questionnaires in those nineteen regions only.
3. The five choices of this question intersect, but answers can reflect cognitive attitudes of the questioned to these common problems in witness testimony reality.
4. Among the 137 cases, 70 are cases of murder (including rape-murder and robbery-murder), 22 are cases of rape, 24 are cases of robbery, 17 are cases of injury, and 4 are cases of explosion. There are 164 defendants in the 137 cases; 158 of them are male, and 6 female. On average, each defendant has been wrongfully incarcerated for four years. See Liu Pinxin, ed., *Criminal Wrongful Conviction: Factors and Strategies* (Beijing: China Legal Publishing House, 2009), 169–170.
5. (1) Li Huawe in a murder case in Liaoning Province in 1986, incarcerated that same year, sentenced to death with a two-year suspension in 1990, exonerated in 2002; (2) Teng Xingshan in a murder case in Hunan Province in 1987, sentenced to death and executed in 1989, redressed in 2006; (3) Shi Dongyu in a murder case in Heilongjiang Province in 1989, incarcerated that same year, sentenced to death with a two-year suspension in 1991, exonerated in 1995; (4) Yang Yunzhong in a murder case in Heilongjiang Province in 1994, incarcerated that same year, sentenced to life imprisonment in 1998, exonerated in

2002; (5) She Xianglin in a murder case in Hubei Province, incarcerated that same year, sentenced to fifteen years' imprisonment in 1998, exonerated in 2005; (6) Tong Limin in a murder case in the city of Chongqing in 1995, incarcerated that same year, sentenced to death with a two-year suspension in 1999, exonerated in 2002; (7) Yang Mingyin in a robbery-murder case in Hunan Province in 1995, incarcerated in 1996, sentenced to sixteen years' imprisonment in 2000, exonerated in 2006; (8) Liu Minghe in a murder case in Anhui Province in 1996, incarcerated in 1996, sentenced to life imprisonment in 1997, exonerated in 2001; (9) Sun Wangang in a rape-murder case in Yunnan Province in 1996, incarcerated that same year, sentenced to death with a two-year suspension in 1996, exonerated in 2004; (10) Guo Xincai in a murder case in Shandong Province in 1996, incarcerated that same year, sentenced to death with a two-year suspension in 1998, exonerated in 2001; (11) Du Peiwu in a murder case in Yunnan Province in 1998, incarcerated that same year, sentenced to death with a two-year suspension in 1999, exonerated in 2000; (12) Qin Yanhong in a rape-murder case in Henan Province in 1998, incarcerated that same year, sentenced to death in 1999, exonerated in 2002; (13) Chen Shijiang in a murder case in Shandong Province in 1998, incarcerated that same year, sentenced to death with a two-year suspension in 2001, exonerated in 2006; (14) Zhao Xinjian in a rape-murder case in Anhui Province in 1998, incarcerated that same year, sentenced to death in 2001, exonerated in 2006; (15) Liu Ritai in a series of murder by poisoning cases in Fujian Province from 1997 to 1999, incarcerated in 1999, sentenced to death in 2000, exonerated in 2003; (16) Wang Xueyi in a murder by poisoning case in Gansu Province in 2000, incarcerated that same year, sentenced to death with a two-year suspension in 2001, exonerated in 2003; (17) Tan Fuyi in a murder case in Beijing in 2000, incarcerated that same year, sentenced to death with a two-year suspension in 2001, exonerated in 2003; (18) Deng Liqiang in a murder case in Guangxi Zhuang Autonomous Region in 2001, incarcerated that same year, sentenced to death in 2002, exonerated in 2003; (19) Li Jiuming in a murder case in Hebei Province in 2002, incarcerated that same year, sentenced to death with a two-year suspension in 2003, exonerated in 2004; (20) Li Julan in a murder by poisoning case in Shaanxi Province in 2002, incarcerated that same year, sentenced to death in 2003, exonerated in 2005. See Guo, *Critical Evaluations.*

Part One: The Misleading Roads Illustrated in the Teng Xingshan Case

1. Yang Fengkun, ed. *Collected Cases of Justice Rectified,* original text by Song Ci of the Southern Song Dynasty (1127–1279) (Beijing: Masses Publishing House, 1980), 4.

Chapter One: The Setting of Inappropriately Tight Deadlines for Solving Criminal Cases

1. See "Mandated Death Case Breaking," *Legal Daily,* November 5, 2004; "Zhou Yong-kang Demands Nation-Wide Law Enforcement Push to Solve Cases, Nation-Wide Improvement to Crime-Fighting Capability," *Legal Daily,* November 6, 2004.
2. See Chao Getu, "Mandated Death Case-Breaking, Madman Found Guilty Mistakenly," *Southern Weekend,* May 6, 2010.
3. In Chinese, the term *public security bureau* is used to refer to local police forces. "Public security bureau" and "police" are used interchangeably in the text.
4. During the Strike-Hard era, it was common to see petty crime punished harshly. For example, in 1983, a middle-aged woman named Ma Yanqin, who organized a private dance, was accused of "promoting illicit sexual relations" and sentenced to death by a court for the crime of hooliganism; in 1984, a twenty-year-old Beijing resident, Niu Yuq-iang, was given a deferred death sentence for the crime of hooliganism after stealing a hat, smashing a glass, and fighting. He was the last person in China to be sentenced to death for hooliganism.
5. China first implemented a resident-identity-card system in Beijing in 1984. On April 6, 1986, the State Council approved the Ministry of Public Security's notice Request for Consultation on Several Issues Pertaining to Resident Identity Cards, and later that year they published Regulations for the Trial of Resident Identity Cards in the People's Republic of China. This commenced the process of implementation of the household regulation supervision system, a process that continued until the 1990s in various parts of China.
6. Zhou Ying, ed., *Criminal Investigation* (Beijing: Law Publishing House, 1982), 30.

Chapter Two: The "From Confession to Evidence" Model of Criminal Investigation

1. See the 1979 version of the Criminal Procedure Law, Article 35. The text is preserved in the 1996 version as Article 46 and in the 2012 version as Article 53.
2. At this time, courts in the United Kingdom and the United States were already using DNA identification, but this process was hardly known in China.

Chapter Three: The Misinterpretation of Scientific Evidence

1. The 2012 revision to the Chinese Criminal Procedure Law substitutes "expertise opinions" in place of "expertise conclusions," which should be of some aid in preventing the confusion of these two types of evidence.
2. See Guo, *Critical Evaluations,* 216.
3. See Waltz, Jon R., *Introduction to Criminal Evidence,* 3rd ed. (Chicago: Nelson-Hall, 1991), 335–336.

4. See "Lie Detection Instrument Comes to China," *Beijing Evening News,* July 23, 2000.
5. After Du Peiwu was exonerated in 2000, the lie-detection specialists who administered the test were widely criticized. One of the lie-detection specialists sent a letter to me, outlining her opinion of what she knew of the case. She averred that Du's answers had been inconsistent. Although he exhibited signs of having told lies, he showed signs of telling the truth when he answered questions directly related to his case. She says she noted this in the final report on the lie-detector test, but her concerns were overlooked by investigators who simply wanted proof that Du had been telling lies.
6. On June 14, 2000, Kunming police arrested Yang Tianyong and associated gang members for crimes including murder and car theft, and discovered that it had actually been Yang and his gang who had killed the two police officers in April 1998—a conclusion supported by material evidence, including a gun, an ammunition magazine, and a microcassette recording. On July 7, the Yunnan Provincial Law-Politics Committee convened a meeting that ordered a review of the Du Peiwu case. On July 11, the Yunnan Provincial High People's Court declared Du not guilty. See Guo, *Critical Evaluations,* 140–152; see also the entry for "Du Peiwu" in *Baidupedia,* http://baike.baidu.com.
7. See Guo, *Critical Evaluations,* 405–409; see also the entry for "Li Jiuming" in *Baidupedia,* http://baike.baidu.com.
8. On April 7, 1998, Bengbu Municipal Intermediate People's Court found Yu Yingsheng guilty of murder, and sentenced him to death with a two-year suspension. He appealed. On September 14, Anhui Provincial High People's Court determined that Yu's case exhibited unclear facts and insufficient evidence, and so set aside the earlier verdict and ordered a retrial. On September 16, 1999, the Intermediate Court convicted Yu and handed down the same sentence as the original. Yu appealed for the second time. On May 15, 2000, the Provincial High Court remanded the case for the second time. On October 25, the Bengbu Court again found Yu guilty of murder, but this time he was sentenced to life in prison. Yu appealed again. On July 1, 2002, the High Court rejected this appeal and upheld the original judgment. On December 8, 2002, Yu Yingsheng filed a complaint against the judgment to the High Court. On August 9, 2004, the High Court rejected Yu's complaint. Yu Yingsheng filed another complaint, this time to the Anhui Provincial People's Procuratorate, which reviewed the case carefully and found the facts unclear and the evidence insufficient, to the degree that the defendant should be declared not guilty. After review and negotiations, the Provincial Procuratorate submitted the case to the Supreme People's Procuratorate. After investigation of the case and consultation with experts, the Supreme People's Procuratorate issued a protest to the Supreme People's Court according to trial supervision procedure. On August 13, 2013, the Bengbu Intermediate People's Court retried the case and declared Yu Yingsheng not guilty, based on the principle of "no conviction in a case of doubt."
9. On May 8, 2013, the Complaint Department of the Supreme People's Procuratorate invited five legal scholars (including this author) to discuss a case of verdict protestations, which happened to be that of Yu Yingsheng. The scholars looked into the case carefully, and each prepared individual commentary. The scholars unanimously believed

the evidence used to convict Yu Yingsheng to have been insufficient and, in fact, far from what would be sufficient to prove that another person had not committed the alleged crime. The scholars unanimously recommended that the Supreme Procuratorate issue a protest to the Supreme Court to demand a retrial. The details presented here are based on the case files examined during this event.

10. According to a news report in the *Jinghua Times,* December 4, 2013, the police of Anhui Province had found the true perpetrator with a match of DNA testing.

Chapter Four: The Continued Use of Torture to Extract Confessions

1. See Guo, *Critical Evaluations,* 141.
2. Ibid., 407.
3. Ibid., 148.
4. See the entry for "Li Jiuming" in *Baidupedia,* http://baike.baidu.com.
5. "Misfeasance of investigators" includes extorting confession by torture and fabricating evidence; "misfeasance of judicial officers" includes judges prohibiting cross-examination in session and failing to arrange witnesses to appear in court; "deficient expert conclusion" refers to illegalities in the procedure or form of the conclusion.
6. In fact, almost every wrongful conviction has some kind of ignorance of innocence evidence. For our analysis, what we especially marked as cases of ignorance of innocence evidence are cases in which the defendant counsel had clearly pointed out the evidence.
7. The murder conviction of Fan Chengkai in Jilin was the result of unclear legal provisions on the issue of proper or improper self-defense at that time.
8. This author served as a part-time deputy director of the Department of Anti-dereliction of Duty and Infringement on Human Rights from June 2006 to December 2008. See He Jiahong, ed., *Forum on Evidence,* vol. 12 (Beijing: Law Press, 2007), 156–161.
9. See Zhou Ying, ed., *Criminal Investigation* (Beijing: Law Publishing House, 1982), 30.
10. Ibid., 47–51.
11. The 1979 Criminal Procedure Law stipulates, "The People's Courts must pass a carbon copy of the indictment to the defendant within seven days, at the same time informing the defendant of his right to entrust a person to be his defender." In the 1996 revision of the law, Article 33 states, "From the day that a case has been accepted for public prosecution, the defendant has the right to entrust a person to be his defender." The 2012 version of Article 33 states, "After the criminal suspect is interrogated by an investigation organ for the first time or from the day on which compulsory measures are adopted against him, he may entrust a person to be his defender. During the investigation, only a lawyer may be entrusted to be his defender. The defender has a right to entrust a defender at any time. After the criminal suspect is interrogated by an investigation organ for the first time or from the day on which compulsory measures are adopted against him, the suspect should be informed of his right to entrust a person to be his defender." These updates to the law show progress in the Chinese Criminal

Procedure Law, but the right to have a defense lawyer present during interrogation has not yet been instituted.

12. For the author's research on this subject, see, for example, "The Admission and Evaluation of Evidence: Remarks on the Language in the 'Two Rules on Evidence,'" *Study of Law* 3 (2011): 138–156.

Chapter Five: The One-Sided and Prejudicial Collection of Evidence

1. See Liu Pinxin, ed., *Criminal Wrongful Conviction*, 169–176.

2. On the evening of May 18, 2003, Zhang Gaoping and his nephew Zhang Hui were driving a truck from She County, Anhui, to Shanghai. A woman from their town, surnamed Wang, was riding with them as far as Hangzhou. On the morning of the next day, Wang's body was discovered in a canal by the side of Liusi Road in the West Lake District of Hangzhou. Investigation determined the two Zhangs to be suspects. On April 21, 2004, the Hangzhou Intermediate People's Court sentenced Zhang Hui to death as the principal in the crime, and sentenced Zhang Gaoping to life in prison as the accomplice. On October 19, the Zhejiang Province High People's Court, the court of second instance, gave Zhang Hui a stay of execution; Zhang Gaoping was sentenced to fifteen years in prison. In November 2011, the Zhejiang Provincial Politics-Law Committee initiated a review of the case. When DNA data—collected from analysis of human tissue found under the victim's fingernails—was entered into the public security bureau's DNA database, it was found to match the DNA of Gou Haifeng. Gou had previously been convicted of murdering a female university student named Wu and sentenced to death, with an execution carried out in 2005. In April 2012, the Zhejiang High Court opened a new trial, and on March 26, 2013, it formally declared Zhang Hui and Zhang Gaoping not guilty.

3. See Zhou Xifeng, "The False Imprisonment and Release of the Zhangs," *Xiaoxiang Morning News*, March 27, 2013; Pan Congwu, "Lack of Direct Evidence Worst Feature of the Zhejiang Zhang Wrongful Conviction Case," *Legal Daily*, April 4, 2013.

4. See Kong Qingyun, ed., *The Theory and Practice of Lawyering* (Beijing: China People's Public Security University Publishing House, 1987), 1–7. In "Report on the Legal Industry and Social Responsibility in China (2013)," the National Lawyers' Association states that there were 232,384 lawyers in mainland China by the end of 2012, meaning 1.6 lawyers per 10,000 people. The ratio of lawyers to population is highest in Beijing, where there are 11.7 lawyers per 10,000 people, and lowest in Tibet, where there are 0.6 lawyers per 10,000 people (http://www.acla.org.cn).

5. Article 1 of the 1980 Provisional Regulations for Lawyers stated: "A lawyer is a national legal worker." Article 2 of the 1996 Lawyers Law stated: "A lawyer is a professional who provides legal services to society." The 2007 revision of the Lawyers Law stated, in Article 2, that a lawyer was "a person involved in the supply of legal services." Before the reform of the lawyer regulation system in 1993, law firms were all state owned, and lawyers were all employed and paid by the state. After reform, some areas established

law firms owned by cooperatives, individuals, and joint partnerships. In "Report on the Legal Industry and Social Responsibility in China (2013)," the National Lawyers' Association published figures stating that by the end of 2012, there were 19,361 law firms in mainland China. Of these, most were joint partnerships (13,835, making 71.5% of the total); there were 3,993 individually owned law firms (20.6%) and 1,504 state-owned law firms (7.8%). The remaining 29 were collectively owned law firms and were changing into either partnerships or proprietorships (http://www.acla.org.cn).

6. At the time of Teng's arrest, the PRC's 1954 Rules for Re-Education through Labour still applied. Section 56 of these regulations stated: "Prisoners may not see family members more than twice each month, and each visit must not exceed thirty minutes. . . . Those awaiting trial require administrative or judicial authorisation to see family members."

7. On June 11, 2001, I participated in a China-EU Human Rights Dialogue in Beijing, which took the death penalty as its main topic. Speaking as a Chinese expert, I made a statement, "The Death Penalty and Public Opinion." At the time, I did not support the abolition of the death penalty in China, my main reason being that an absolute majority of the Chinese people did not support it. In order to prepare this statement, I implemented a survey of students at the Renmin University of China Law School. Results showed that 87 percent of students did not support the abolition of the death penalty, with only 13 percent in favor. On April 25, 2013, I was invited to a forum on the problem of the death penalty by the French embassy in China, where I presented a paper titled "Misjudged Criminal Cases and the Death Penalty." In this presentation, I stated that I believe that it is impossible for China to abolish the death penalty immediately, but that we should promote its abolition with great force, so that even more of our fellow citizens understand the way in which it is abused. Because of the possibility of erroneous judgments in our criminal legal system, we cannot guarantee that decisions involving the death penalty are correct and verifiable. Consequently, China should abolish the death penalty. On October 12, 2013, as a commemoration of the World Day Against the Death Penalty (October 10), I repeated the survey about the abolition of the death penalty in class at the Renmin University of China Law School. This time, 40 percent of students did not support the abolition of the death penalty, 16 percent supported its abolition, and 44 percent supported its gradual abolition over the next twenty years.

8. Influenced by the wrongful conviction of Teng Xingshan, on January 1, 2007, the Supreme People's Court regained all review power in cases involving the death penalty.

9. Zaoshen, the god of the kitchen, is celebrated on the twenty-third day of the twelfth lunar month, a date known as "Little New Year."

10. Teng Xingshan's given name means "flourishing good."

11. This story of Teng Xingshan is based on reports in newspapers, periodicals, and the Internet. Direct quotations are sourced from the transcripts of the case files. Some sources cannot be identified for reasons of confidentiality. In this text, while Teng Xingshan is a real name, the other people involved have been given aliases. See Guo

Xinyang, *Critical Evaluations*, 438–445. Also see the entry for "Teng Xingshan" in *Baidupedia*, http://baike.baidu.com.

Chapter Six: The Bowing to Public Opinion in Contradiction to Legal Principles

1. See the entry for "Sun Wangang" in *Baidupedia*, http://baike.baidu.com. On January 3, 1996, a female university student was raped and murdered in Qiaojia County, Yunnan Province. An investigation determined Sun Wangang, the victim's boyfriend, to be the main suspect. He was detained, and a confession was obtained through interrogation. On September 20, the Zhaotong Prefecture Intermediate People's Court declared Sun guilty of murder and sentenced him to death. Sun appealed. On September 19, 1997, after retrying the case, the Zhaotong Court again delivered a death sentence. Sun appealed again. On November 12, the Yunnan Provincial High People's Court handed down a suspended death sentence. Afterwards, the real murderer was identified, and a new trial was ordered. On February 10, 2002, the Yunnan High Court declared Sun Wangang not guilty and released him.

2. See the entry for "Zhang Jinzhu" in *Baidupedia*, http://baike.baidu.com.

3. See the entry for "Li Changkui" in *Baidupedia*, http://baike.baidu.com.

4. The People's Republic of China is divided into thirty-one provinces, autonomous regions, and municipalities. Hubei is one of these provinces, and it is further divided into 13 prefecture-level divisions, which administer 102 counties, which in turn administer 1,234 towns and villages. Villages and towns are managed by village committees and led by village heads (or mayors).

5. This value is based on the average historical exchange rate in 1994. In 1990, 1 Chinese yuan was worth 0.21 U.S. dollars. After economic policy changes in the early 1990s, the yuan's value dropped to 0.11 U.S. dollars in 1994. Its value has remained relatively stable since then, gradually rising throughout the 2000s to 0.16 U.S. dollars in 2012.

6. The average per capita national income in 1990 was US$350, equivalent to 139 yuan per month, though this figure does not reflect the income disparity between urban coastal regions and rural areas.

7. Although the state has relied on this 1975 document as a justification for its actions, the origins of the document are unclear. "An official document of this importance should have been published in the State Council Gazette, but it is not included there. Nor is it found in such comprehensive compilations as the *Complete Book of Laws of the People's Republic of China*." Tao-Tai Hsia and Wendy I. Zeldin, "Sheltering for Examination (*Shourong Shencha*) in the Legal System of the People's Republic of China," *China Law Report* 7, no. 95 (1993).

8. "Notification Regarding the Merger of the Two Measures of Forced Labor and Sheltering for Examination into Re-education and Rehabilitation through Labor," February 29, 1980.

9. After the problems with arbitrary detention came to light in the 1980s, the Ministry of Public Security released two notices on the matter: "On the Strict Control of the Use of Shelter and Investigation" (1985) and "Specific Provisions on the Basis for and Review of Shelter and Investigation" (1990). When She Xianglin's case was under investigation, lawyers and legal academics were discussing the abolition of sheltered investigation. Some called for it to be stopped, as they believed that it led to abuses of power and was constantly subject to malpractice. Others called for its retention, arguing that it was an excellent method of dealing with petty criminals. In 1996, when the laws of criminal procedure were reformed, sheltered investigation was abolished.

10. See Sun Siya, "The Ruling for 'Death Penalty Guarantee' Case, Li Huailiang Declared Not Guilty," *Jinghua Times,* April 26, 2013; Lu Yan, "Imprisoned for 12 Years on Insufficient Evidence—That's Definitely Wrong," *Zhengzhou Evening News,* May 10, 2013.

11. See Li Guangming, "A Strange Case Makes Us Reflect, Why Did the Safeguards Fail?" *Procuratorial Daily,* November 11, 2006. On August 6, 1998, a rape-murder occurred in a small village outside of Bozhou City, Anhui Province. Investigators identified local villager Zhao Xinjian as a suspect based on clothing left at the crime scene. Though investigators obtained a confession from Zhao, they lacked other forms of evidence, for which reason the procuratorate did not issue an arrest warrant, and Zhao was consequently released. The victim's mother was angered by this and made appeals in many quarters, finally going so far as to threaten to hang herself at the court. Unable to withstand the pressure, the procuratorate issued an indictment. In 2001, the court of the first instance sentenced Zhao to death, but the court of the second instance ordered a retrial. In 2004, the Bozhou Municipal Intermediate Court gave a suspended death sentence. In 2006, because the true murderer was identified via a different case, Zhao Xinjian was exonerated and released. See Chen Lei, "Multiple 'Truths' in a Murder-Rape Case," *Southern People Weekly* 29 (2006).

Chapter Seven: The Unlawfully Extended Custody with Tunnel Vision

1. See Supreme People's Procuratorate Research Center, *Unlawfully Extended Custody and Safeguarding Human Rights* (Beijing: Procuratorate Publishing House, 2004), 95.

2. See "The Long Road: Perspectives on Unlawfully Extended Custody," *Procuratorial Daily,* November 11, 2003.

3. See Supreme People's Procuratorate Research Center, *Unlawfully Extended Custody,* 72.

4. See Liu Pinxin, ed., *Criminal Wrongful Conviction,* 182–193.

5. During the Mao period (1949–1976), villagers tended to be organized into work teams or groups as a means of organizing and monitoring their agricultural work. Some of these organizations lasted into the 1990s.

6. According to the relevant provisions of the Chinese Criminal Procedure Law, arrest is an enforcement measure used to deprive suspects of a crime or defendants in a trial of their personal freedom. It is decided by the procurator's office or a court and implemented

by a public security organ. In practice, the public security organ detains the suspect of the crime and asks the procurator's office for permission to arrest later. Therefore, arrest does not actually begin with the decision to detain but with the approval of detention. The period of detention after arrest may include the whole course of the criminal proceedings.

7. The Chinese People's Procuratorate, which administers the People's Procurators Offices, is a government body responsible for investigating and prosecuting criminal cases. The Public Procurators' Law requires, in Article 6, that the People's Procurators Offices supervise the enforcement of laws, perform public prosecution on behalf of the state, and investigate criminal cases directly accepted by the People's Procuratorate as provided by law.

8. In 2007, as a means of guaranteeing the fair application and accuracy of the death penalty, the Supreme People's Court regained its power of authority over such cases. At present, all death sentences must be reviewed by the Supreme People's Court.

9. Article 33 of the 1996 Criminal Procedure Law states: "A criminal suspect in a case of public prosecution shall have the right to entrust persons as his defenders from the date on which the case is transferred for examination before prosecution." After further amendment in 2012, Article 33 now states: "A criminal suspect shall have the right to appoint a defender as of the date on which the suspect is first interrogated by the investigating authority or is subject to compulsory measures. During the investigation period, he may appoint only an attorney as his defender. A defendant has the right to appoint a defender at any time. When the investigating authority first interrogates a criminal suspect or subjects a criminal suspect to compulsory measures, the criminal suspect should be informed of the right to appoint a defender."

10. Article 34 of the 1996 Criminal Procedure Law states: "If there is the possibility that the defendant may be sentenced to death and yet he has not entrusted anyone to be his defender, the People's Court shall designate a lawyer who is obligated to provide legal aid to serve as a defender." The amended 2012 version states: "In cases where a criminal suspect or defendant who may be sentenced to life imprisonment or death has not retained a defender, the People's Court, People's Procuratorate and public security authority shall notify a legal aid agency to designate a lawyer to defend him or her."

11. Before 1984, Chinese judges had no particular uniform and wore plain clothes when court was in session. Since 1984, judges and procurators have worn uniforms. Until 2000, these uniforms had three different styles—for summer, spring and autumn, and winter—but all resembled military uniforms and embodied China's characteristic "militarization of the dictatorial organs." Since 2000, judges have worn a Western-style uniform with a black judge's robe, and procurators have worn dark blue Western-style suits. Judges and procurators both wear badges on their chests signifying the fairness and sacredness of the judiciary.

12. The Criminal Procedure Law states that first-instance cases in the Intermediate People's Courts can be heard by a panel of three, including a judge and people's assessors (similar to jurors), or by a panel of three judges. However, in a major criminal case like this, people's assessors are generally not used.

13. According to Article 54 of the Criminal Procedure Law, "deprivation of political rights" refers to the removal of the right to vote and to stand for election; the rights of freedom of speech, of the press, of assembly, of association, of procession, and of demonstration; the right to hold a position in a state organ; and the right to hold a leading position in any state-owned company, enterprise, institution, or people's organization.

14. China has a "dual administrative system," in which leadership is shared between Communist Party officials and government leaders. In any particular village, the party secretary will determine the basic policy direction, while the government leader (the village head, mayor, or similar position) will be responsible for implementing the policy.

15. The Criminal Procedure Law provides that if courts of appeal believe the facts on which a decision was based are unclear, or the evidence is insufficient, a sentence of death may be commuted or the case sent back for reinvestigation. However, in practice, very few courts of appeal commute the death sentence; generally, the method used is to reinvestigate the case.

16. A charge of "constant petitioning" means that the petitioner would not accept the answers given by the authority and so petitioned repeatedly.

Chapter Eight: The Nominal Checks among the Police, the Procuratorate, and the Court

1. This is a generalization and has some exceptions. Under Chinese law, cases of occupational crimes by public officials, such as embezzlement, bribery, and malfeasance, are investigated by the internal investigation bureaus of the procuratorates.

2. Properly speaking, "investigation, prosecution, and adjudication" should be used here instead of "the public security bureau, the people's procuratorate, and the people's court" because investigation, prosecution, and adjudication are not properly represented by the public security bureau, the people's procuratorate, and the people's court. But according to the conventional habit of expression in Chinese, "the public security bureau, the people's procuratorate, and the people's court" has often been used in this context.

3. This sequence refers to the cases that should be investigated by the public security bureau. According to the law in China, crimes of bribery, embezzlement, dereliction of duty, and infringement on human rights should be investigated by the people's procuratorate.

4. Liu Pinxin, ed., *Criminal Wrongful Conviction,* 51.

5. "Opinion of the State Committee for Public Sector Reform on Establishing Local Party and Government Organs," *Zhongbian* 4 (1993). This was later published in China as Local Government Organisation Reform Editorial Group, ed., *China Local Government Organisational Reform* (Beijing: Xinhua Publishing House, 1995), 72–74.

6. Political and legal-work committees are responsible for the implementation of the legal and police systems in their particular areas. Their responsibility is extremely broad, and they have often been characterized by their loyalty to the Communist Party line.

7. See Yi Xi, "State Compensation for the Prisoners Mistakenly Sentenced to Death," *Social Outlook* 3 (2003).

Chapter Nine: The Nominalization of Courtroom Trials

1. Fan Chongyi, ed., *The Law of Criminal Procedure* (Beijing: Publishing House of China University of Politics and Law, 1999), 346.
2. Its website is at http://www.chinacourt.org/.
3. We were unable to determine the number of defense witnesses and prosecution witnesses among the thirty-nine witnesses.
4. Article 150 of Criminal Procedure Law in China provides, "After a People's Court has examined a case in which public prosecution was initiated, it shall decide to open the court session and try the case, if the bill of prosecution contains clear facts of the crime accused and, in addition, there is a list of evidence and a list of witnesses as well as duplicates or photos of major evidence attached to it."
5. Gu Angran, "On the Remarks about the Draft of Criminal Procedure Law of People's Republic of China," *Judicial Interpretations of the Criminal Law and Criminal Procedure Law of People's Republic of China* (Beijing: China Fangzheng Press, 1998), 182.
6. Supreme People's Court, Supreme People's Procuratorate, Ministry of Public Security, Ministry of State Security, and Law Committee in People's Congress, "Provisions on Some Problems concerning the Practice of Criminal Procedure Law," *Judicial Interpretations of the Criminal Law and Criminal Procedure Law of People's Republic of China* (Beijing: China Fangzheng Press, 1998), 191.
7. See Liu Yingming and Liang Kun, "Where Is the Way to Develop the Evidence Review System in Criminal Trial," in *Forum on Evidence,* vol. 15, edited by He Jiahong (Beijing: Law Press, 2010), 289–291.
8. Chen Ruihua, *The Criminal Procedure of Chinese Mode* (Beijing: Law Press, 2010), 192–194.
9. Zuo Weimin, *The Prospect of Criminal Procedure in China* (Beijing: SDX Joint Publishing, 2010), 103.
10. A people's assessor told me that as soon as the trial finished, the judge or court clerk would have her sign a blank sheet of paper and then put it in the records of the collegial panel's deliberation, on the grounds that it would reduce the trouble of getting her signature later. She added that she was never told the results of the judgment unless she took it upon herself to ask.
11. See Yan Li, "The Nominalization of the Collegial Panel's Deliberation in the Primary Court and the Recovery of It," June 28, 2004, cdfy.chinacourt.org.
12. See Hu Jiating, "The 800 Days of the Man Who Was Sentenced to Death," *Lawyers and Legal System* 4 (2003).
13. See Zhang Yue and Qi Shuxin, "The Policeman Named Zhang Jinbo Unfairly Imprisoned for Rape for Ten Years," *China Youth Daily,* February 9, 2007.
14. See He Jiahong and Zhang Weiping, eds., *Foreign Evidentiary Laws: Selected Translations,* vol. 2 (Beijing: Publishing House of People's Court, 2000), 745–766.

15. The content of this discussion on administrative decision making is from *Baidupedia*, http://baike.baidu.com.
16. See Liu Pinxin, ed., *Criminal Wrongful Conviction*, 43.

Chapter Ten: The Reduction of Punishment in a Case of Doubt

1. Article 49 of the 2012 Criminal Procedure Law states, "The onus of proof that a defendant is guilty falls on the public procurator in a public prosecution case."
2. See Liu Jinyou, ed., *Evidence Law* (Beijing: Publishing House of China University of Politics and Law, 2001), 327–333.
3. The first saying is thought to have been used by some leaders of the Kuomintang in the war against the Communist Party of China in the late 1920s and early 1930s. The Western precept is known as Blackstone's formulation. See Hazel B. Kerper, *Introduction to the Criminal Justice System* (St. Paul: West Publishing, 1979), 205.
4. Shen Deyong, "How Should We Guard Against Wrongful Conviction?" *People's Court Daily*, May 6, 2013.
5. On April 29, 2010, the Standing Committee of the National People's Congress approved an amendment of the National Compensation Law. The amended law increased the compensation for mental suffering and took effect from December 1, 2010. Article 35 of this law provides: "Under the circumstances laid out in Article 3 and Article 17, in the case of mental injury, the state shall, to the extent of the infringement, eliminate the effects of the infringement for the injured party, resume his or her reputation, make an apology and pay appropriate compensation money if the infringement causes serious consequences."
6. Quoted U.S. dollar equivalents are based on an average historical exchange rate of 0.12 for 2005.
7. Bigamy is an offense according to criminal law in China. However, some people in the countryside do not take the law very seriously. Sometimes people do not go through the formalities of marriage and instead have a so-called marriage in fact.
8. This story of She Xianglin is based on reports in newspapers, periodicals, and the Internet. Direct quotations are sourced from the transcripts of the case files. Some sources cannot be identified for reasons of confidentiality. In this text, She Xianglin is a real name but Zhang Aiqing is a pseudonym; pseudonyms have also been used for other people involved in the case. See Guo Xinyang, *Critical Evaluations*, 401–441. See also the entry for "She Xianglin" in *Baidupedia*, http://baike.baidu.com.

Chapter Eleven: The Exclusionary Rules against Illegally Obtained Evidence

1. See Li Lijing, "Clear Doubts in the Wrongful Conviction of Zhao Zuohai: Multiple Mistakes across All Branches of Law Enforcement," Xinhuanet, May 10, 2010, www

.xinhuanet.com; see also the entry for "Zhao Zuohai" in *Baidupedia,* http://baike.baidu
.com.

2. Article 7 of the Provisions on Issues concerning the Exclusion of Illegally Obtained
   Evidence provides that "explanatory letters submitted by the public prosecutor
   which have been affixed with the official seal but without the signature or seal of the
   interrogators shall not be used as evidence to prove the legality of the evidence collection process."

3. The survey was done by Peng Xiao, a doctoral student at the Renmin University of China
   Law School, from September to November 2012.

4. The Supreme People's Court is currently drafting a new provision on the exclusionary
   rules against illegally obtained evidence. This author is invited as an adviser for the drafting. Hopefully, the provision would be promulgated in the near future.

5. The warnings regarding constitutional rights to remain silent and to the presence of a
   lawyer were mandated in the United States Supreme Court's decision in *Miranda v.
   Arizona,* 384 U.S. 436 (1966).

6. See Fred Inbau, John Reid, and Joseph Buckley, *Criminal Interrogation and Confessions,*
   3rd ed. (Baltimore: Williams & Wilkins, 1986), 274.

Chapter Twelve: From Investigation Centeredness to Trial Centeredness

1. He Jiahong and Zhang Weiping, eds., *Foreign Evidentiary Laws,* 462.

2. See Zhang Liqing, *Theory and Application of the Criminal Procedure Law* (Taipei: Wunan
   Press, 2004), 703.

3. Article 187 of the 2012 Criminal Procedure Law provides, "If prosecutor, litigant or
   defender, representative of litigant has a dispute about the witness testimony, and the
   testimony has great influence on the judgment in the case, and if the people's court
   believes there to be a need for the witness to appear in court, the witness shall testify
   in court."

4. The author made these suggestions in an expert advisory meeting held by the Supreme
   People's Court on April 26, 2013; in a TV lecture for the Phoenix Century Classroom
   on September 8, 2013; and in an article published in a journal of the Supreme People's
   Court: see He Jiahong, "Procedural Reform and Precaution against Wrongful Convictions," *Journal of Law Application* 9 (2013): 7–10.

Chapter Thirteen: Reform of the People's Juror System

1. During May 11 and 12, 2011, I participated in the International Symposium on Jury System held by the Supreme People's Court in the city of Suzhou, in Jiangsu Province, and
   made a speech on the subject. Concerned leaders in the Supreme People's Court,
   Wuzhong District People's Court, and Liuyang Intermediate People's Court made intro-
   ductory speeches on the development of the system of people's jurors. For example, the
   people's jurors in Wuzhong District increased from ten in 2005 to eighty in 2011. The

simple cases have been handled using the $1 + 2$ model, namely, a collegial panel consisting of one judge and two people's jurors; and the difficult cases have been handled using the $2 + 1$ model—a collegial panel consisting of two judges and one people's juror. Ninety-eight percent of the common procedure cases have been heard with the appearance of the people's jurors, 98.3 percent of which passed unanimously without appeal.

2. He Jiahong, ed., *Which Direction Shall the Chinese People's Juror System Go?* (Beijing: Publishing House of China University of Politics and Law, 2006).

3. The reform of the jury system in the 1990s in France established that felony cases should be heard by three judges and nine-member juries. Judicial reform in the 1990s in Japan established the system that major criminal cases should be heard by one judge and six "citizen jurors."

4. See He Jiahong, "My Opinion for the Reform of the Juror System," *People's Court Daily*, October 21, 2013.

5. Bo Xilai was removed as Chongqing party secretary on March 15, 2012. He was also removed from his position in the politburo on April 10. What's more, he was dismissed from the party and suspected of crimes on September 28. He was also recalled as a National People's Congress delegate on October 26. On August 22, 2013, the trial of Bo Xilai was held at the Intermediate People's Court of Jinan City, Shandong Province. One month later, Bo was found guilty of three charges: bribe taking, embezzlement, and abuse of power. He was sentenced to life in prison by the court. On October 25, Bo's appeal was rejected by the High People's Court of Shandong Province, and the ruling was declared final.

6. During the period of 1990 to 1993, I was studying at the Northwestern University School of Law in the United States, where I was awarded a doctorate of juridical science (SJD). In addition to studying the American legal system, I also learned the lawyering system there, and was influenced by the culture of lawyers. I was impressed by the role of American defense lawyers in criminal trials and came to believe that lawyers should play a more important role in promoting social progress under the rule of law in China. Therefore, I created a lawyer, Hong Jun, as the protagonist in my four crime novels, which I wrote later. The first one, *Hanging Devils: Hong Jun Investigates,* has been published in English by Penguin.

7. Li Zhuang was released from prison and went back to Beijing on June 11, 2011. He appealed to the Supreme People's Court, requesting to revoke the original sentence of Chongqing's First Intermediate People's Court and to announce his acquittal. At the time of writing this book, his appeal is pending.

Chapter Fourteen: Reform of the Criminal Retrial System

1. See Liu Pinxin, ed., *Criminal Wrongful Conviction,* 364–367.

2. See "A Young Man Executed in a Case of Rape and Murder; Ten Years Later the True Culprit Confesses and Seeks Redemption," Xinhuanet, February 14, 2007, www.xinhuanet.com.

3. See He Jiahong and He Ran, "Empirical Studies of Wrongful Convictions in Mainland China," *University of Cincinnati Law Review* 80, no. 4 (2012): 1281.

4. See Zhao Ling, "A Culprit with a Conscience and a Court Without: Nie Shubin's Wrongful Conviction," *Southern Weekend,* November 2, 2007.

5. See Zhao Ling, "Uncertain Prospects for Overturning the Nie Shubin Case," *Southern Weekend,* November 11, 2009.

6. See Zhou Xifeng, "Wang Shujin, Madman," *Xiaoxiang Morning News,* March 7, 2005.

7. See Lei Hongtao, *Legal Weekly,* June 26, 2013.

8. See Li Xianfeng, "Final Verdict: Wang Shujin is not the True Perpetrator in the Nie Shubin Case," *Jinghua Times,* September 28, 2013. At the time of writing, Wang Shujin's death sentence was being reviewed by the Supreme People's Court.

9. See "Court's Transparency in Trial Welcomed," *China Daily,* April 30, 2015.

Chapter Fifteen: Changing the Mind-Set for Criminal Justice

1. According to the dominant political theory in the People's Republic of China from the 1950s to the 1970s, contradictions in human societies can be put into two categories: the contradictions between ourselves and enemies, and the contradictions between ourselves or among the people. During that period of time, especially during the Cultural Revolution, criminals were considered enemies of the people, belonging to the category of the contradictions between ourselves and enemies.

2. See He Jiahong, "On the Value Orientation of Criminal Justice and Evidence System," *Study on Crimes* 1 (2001).

3. See He Jiahong, "On the Value Orientation of the System of Right to Silence and Criminal Justice," *Journal of the National Procuratorial College* 4 (2000).

4. See He Jiahong, "On Judicial Justice," *China Legal Science* 2 (2002).

Bibliography

Chen Ruihua. *A Chinese Model of Criminal Procedure.* Beijing: Law Press, 2010.

Chen Weidong, ed. *The Study of Countermeasures for Issues of Fact in Criminal Procedure.* Beijing: China Legal Publishing House, 2002.

Fan Chongyi, ed. *The Law of Criminal Procedure.* Beijing: Publishing House of China University of Politics and Law, 1999.

Guo Xinyang. *Critical Evaluations of Wrongful Convictions.* Beijing: China People's Public Security University Publishing House, 2011.

He Jiahong, ed. *Which Direction Shall the Chinese People's Juror System Go?* Beijing: Publishing House of China University of Politics and Law, 2006.

He Jiahong and Zhang Weiping, eds. *Foreign Evidentiary Laws: Selected Translations,* 2 vols. Beijing: Publishing House of People's Court, 2000.

Hochstedler Steury, Ellen, and Nancy Frank. *Criminal Court Process.* Translated by Chen Weidong and Xu Meijun. Beijing: China Renmin University Press, 2002.

Inbau, Fred, John Reid, and Joseph Buckley. *Criminal Interrogation and Confessions,* 3rd ed. Baltimore: Williams & Wilkins, 1986.

Kerper, Hazel B. *Introduction to the Criminal Justice System.* St. Paul: West Publishing, 1979.

Kong Qingyun, ed. *The Theory and Practice of Lawyering.* Beijing: China People's Public Security University Publishing House, 1987.

Lin Shantian. *Criminal Procedure Law.* Taipei: Wunan Press, 2004.

Liu Jinyou, ed. *Evidence Law.* Beijing: Publishing House of China University of Politics and Law, 2001.

Liu Pinxin, ed. *Criminal Wrongful Conviction: Factors and Strategies.* Beijing: China Legal Publishing House, 2009.

McConville, Mike, and Geoffrey Wilson. *English Criminal Justice Process.* Translated by Yao Yongji. Beijing: Law Press, 2003.

Supreme People's Procuratorate Research Center. *Unlawfully Extended Custody and Safeguarding Human Rights.* Beijing: Procuratorate Publishing House, 2004.

Waltz, Jon R. *Introduction to Criminal Evidence.* 3rd ed. Chicago: Nelson-Hall, 1991.

Yang Fengkun, ed. *Collected Cases of Justice Rectified.* Original text by Song Ci of the Southern Song Dynasty (1127–1279). Beijing: Masses Publishing House, 1980.

Zhang Liqing. *Theory and Application of the Criminal Procedure Law.* Taipei: Wunan Publishing House, 2004.

Zhou Ying, ed. *Criminal Investigation.* Beijing: Law Publishing House, 1982.

Zuo Weimin. *The Prospect of Criminal Procedure in China.* Beijing: SDX Joint Publishing, 2010.

INDEX

Index

forced confession by torture or threat (cont.)
investigations and convictions of, 142; laws
on evidence of, 25, 44, 46–47, 151–157,
224n.2; of Li Jiuming, 44, 45; occurrence
of, 46–47; of She Xianglin, 90–91, 92,
99–102, 114–115; studies on, 47–48;
techniques used in, 43–44, 156; of Teng
Xingshan, 26–28; tight deadlines and, 14;
trial-centered model and, 166–167; of
witness, 155–156. *See also* confession of the
accused; interrogations
Forensic Evidence Appraisal Centre, 30, 33
forensic science. *See* scientific evidence
France, 165, 170, 171, 225n.3
"from evidence to confession" model, 25–26
Fuzhou City, Mayang County, 17–22

gangs, criminal, xv, 91, 96, 97, 174, 214n.6
Gao Yao, 202
Gao Zhi, 151
Germany, 167, 170, 188
god indicating evidence, 201–202
god sheep, 202
Gong Gangmo, 174
Gou Haifeng, 53, 137, 216n.2
graphology, 204
Green Wood Uprising, 84
Guan Chuansheng, 1–3, 53
guanxi, 208–209
guilt, presumption of, 133–134
Gu Jianjun, 32, 58
Guo Xincai, 212n.5

handwriting analysis, 31, 35, 70
Hanging Devils (He), xxii, 225n.6
Han Hua, 85, 91, 141
hearsay evidence, 129, 167
Heihe Daily, xiv
He Jiahong: childhood of, xiii–xiv; on criminal
procedure reforms, xi, 121, 137, 162–163,
166–169, 199; on death penalty, 217n.7;
education of, 170, 225n.6; on evidence
system reforms, 196; on juror system
reforms, 170–174, 224n.1; mock jury trial by,
174, 176–182; presentations by, 224n.1;
published works by, xiv–xv, xxii, xx–xxi, 171;

Ren and, xv–xvii; on retrial system reforms,
183–190; work of, xv–xvi, xvii
He Liang, 85, 89, 90, 91, 142
Hmong community, 17–18
holy evidence, 201–202
homicide. *See* murder cases
hooliganism, 213n.4
household registration system, 71, 213n.5
Hubei Province, 218n.4
Hugejiletu case, xxv, 184–186, 189
human contradictions theory, 226n.1
human rights: conflicting interests on, 194–197,
226n.1; deprivation of political rights, 58,
68, 94, 106, 221n.13; judiciary process on,
165; legal rights of the accused, 56, 164,
195–197; right to silence, 157–161, 224n.5
human-tissue analysis, 29, 31, 40, 53, 216n.2

illegally obtained evidence, 47, 151–157, 161,
224n.2, 224n.4. *See also* evidence; forced
confession by torture or threat
impeaching evidence, 122–123, 167
Inbau, Fred, 158
incarceration. *See* custody of criminal suspects
indictment process, 110–111, 121, 222n.4
indirect proof of wrongful conviction, 187–188
individualization technique, 32–33
innocence, presumption of, 133–134
Innocence Movement, xi
intentional homicide regulations, 56
International Symposium on Jury System,
171, 224n.1
interrogations: of Du, 36; historical methods
of, 203; of She, 90–91, 92, 99–102; of
Teng, 26–27; of Yu, 41. *See also* forced
confession by torture or threat
Introduction to Criminal Evidence (Waltz), 36
investigation-centeredness models, 110–113,
163–167, 221n.2
investigations: 1995–2008 survey on, 10;
finding *vs.* proving evidence in, 200–201;
game of, 15–16; laws on, 164–165, 215n.11;
of occupational crimes, 221n.1; role of
public security bureau in, 110; sheltered
for, 91–92, 218n.7, 219n.9; single-factor
demands and, 14–15. *See also* evidence

232

ABOUT THE AUTHOR

AUTHOR AFFILIATION: HE Jiahong is professor of law and director of the Center for Common Law and the Institute of Evidence at Renmin University of China, in Beijing. He has published dozens of law books and five crime novels in Chinese, including *Hanging Devils* and *Black Holes,* which have been translated into several languages. He is a senior adviser to the Supreme People's Court and the Supreme People's Procuratorate. He has also lectured at many leading universities in the United States, Europe, Japan, and Australia.